Making a
New American
Constitution

Making a

New American

Constitution

George William Van Cleve

Foreword by Sanford V. Levinson

MAROON BELLS PRESS
Denver

George William Van Cleve is Dean's Visiting Scholar, Georgetown University Law Center and former Research Professor in Law and History, Seattle University School of Law. PhD, University of Virginia; JD, Harvard Law School. His most recent book is *We Have Not a Government: The Articles of Confederation and the Road to the Constitution.*

"Waiting for the Barbarians" (excerpt) from *C.P. Cavafy: Collected Poems*, Revised Edition translated by Edmund Keeley and Philip Sherrard, ed. by George Savidis. Translation copyright 1975, 1992 by Edmund Keeley and Philip Sherrard. Reprinted by Permission of Princeton University Press.

Cover photograph of first page of the 1787 Constitution of the United States source: National Archives and Records Administration.

Cover design by Michelle Ganeles, Wide Sky Studio.

ISBN-13: 978-1-7355489-0-6 (paperback)
ISBN-13: 978-1-7355489-1-3 (e-book)

For my wife and family

and for our fellow citizens:

together we hold the fate of our Republic in our hands

Waiting for the Barbarians

What are we waiting for, assembled in the forum?

The barbarians are due here today.

Why isn't anything happening in the senate?
Why do the senators sit there without legislating?

Because the barbarians are coming today.
What laws can the senators make now?
Once the barbarians are here, they'll do the legislating.

Why did our emperor get up so early,
and why is he sitting at the city's main gate
on his throne, in state, wearing the crown?

Because the barbarians are coming today
and the emperor is waiting to receive their leader....

Why this sudden restlessness, this confusion?
(How serious people's faces have become.)
Why are the streets and squares emptying so rapidly,
everyone going home so lost in thought?

Because night has fallen and the barbarians have not come.
And some who have just returned from the border say
there are no barbarians any longer.

And now, what's going to happen to us without barbarians?
They were, those people, a kind of solution.

C.P. Cavafy, *Collected Poems*

Contents

Foreword

AN ACT OF HIGH CITIZENSHIP AT A TROUBLED TIME

Sanford V. Levinson

*W. St. John Garwood and W. St. John Garwood, Jr. Centennial Chair,
University of Texas School of Law & Professor of Government,
University of Texas*

It is a special pleasure and honor to write this "foreword" to George Van Cleve's *Making a New American Constitution*. He generously credits my own writings as a partial inspiration, but there is an all-important difference between my work and his. It is true that my books *Our Undemocratic Constitution* (2006) and *Framed: America's 51 Constitutions and the Crisis of Governance* (2012), not to mention a book that my wife and I co-authored basically for a teenage audience, *Fault Lines in the Constitution: The Framers, Their Fights, and the Flaws that Affect Us Today* (2d ed. 2019), offer quite vigorous critiques of the United States Constitution. I very much advocate a new constitutional convention to engage in what Publius (Hamilton) in *Federalist* 1 called "reflection and choice" about how we are to be governed. It is not irrelevant that he was beginning his critique of an existing American government that, in *Federalist* 15, he would describe as "imbecilic" and, therefore, defending the work product of the Philadelphia Convention that could accurately be described as going well beyond its legal authorization in order to respond to what almost all of the delegates agreed were the "exigencies"—a favorite word of the time—that demanded a radical response if the country was to be saved. (Perhaps I should mention in this context that *Fault Lines* concludes with a debate between my wife and myself about the desirability of a new constitutional convention, which I strongly endorse and she finds far more frightening than enticing.)

So, obviously, I welcome Van Cleve's important contributions to the enterprise of constitutional critique. I fundamentally agree with his "state of the Union" chapter that comes after his introduction. Our situation is dire indeed. A recent book by two distinguished political scientists, Suzanne Mettler and Robert C. Lieberman, sets out what they call *Four Threats: The Recurring Crisis of American Democracy.* They consist of economic inequality; political polarization; a form of "identity politics" in which some differentiate between "real Americans" and mere residents within the United States; and, finally, presidential overreach. All are present today, which may be unique. And there is good reason to be worried.

What Van Cleve does and I most certainly do not, though, is to have the intellectual courage—some might even describe it as "audacity," a much-needed trait at these times—to make specific suggestions as to how we ought to amend the Constitution in order to make it suitable for the 21ˢᵗ century. Indeed, perhaps the most truly audacious chapter comes toward the end, when he confronts directly the barriers that face anyone who actually does want a new constitutional convention. The Constitution "authorizes" a convention, in Article V, but is thereafter entirely silent on how such a convention might be conducted. My wife's thoughtful opposition to a convention is based primarily far less on the fear that it would be "run away" (as did the Philadelphians), than on the far more likely premise that before day one of a new convention we would be at each other's throats because the Constitution provides no guidance on, for example, how delegates would be chosen or what the voting rules might be. Van Cleve recognizes that a convention will require that citizens actually think about such problems. He is not simply waving a magic wand and saying, "let's have a convention"; instead, he explains how one really might come about even if, or perhaps one might even say, especially if, it is likely to be opposed by political "leaders" committed to preserving the status quo.

For better or, quite possibly, for worse, I am the kind of academic who is more than willing to point out problems, but then fails to offer any solutions beyond such low-hanging fruit as abolishing the Electoral College. What delights me about the prospect of a constitutional convention is bringing together dedicated Americans for up to two years in which they would have the opportunity to discuss and debate with one another about every possible issue linked to what is now called "constitutional design." I myself do not know how I would ultimately come out on various issues that would be sure to be debated, including, for example, whether to retain the presidentialist system instead of adopting a more parliamentary system or, if choosing the former, to give the president a longer single term (say, six years), but allow for the possibility of a vote of no-confidence or even a national recall election after three years. But wishing for a convention and the ensuing discussion will not make it so. Action is required, and Van Cleve offers a stirring call to the kind of active citizenship that is required of all of us.

In my book *Framed,* I distinguish quite sharply between what I call "the Constitution of Settlement" and the "Constitution of Conversation." The latter is what academic lawyers especially obsess on, because that is the part of the Constitution that is endlessly litigated and about which lawyers (and the citizenry at large) can reasonably disagree with one another as to meaning (or what we like to call "interpretation"). The best example, perhaps, is the Fourteenth Amendment, filled with what Justice Robert Jackson called "majestic generalities" that we will always be arguing about, like the "true" meaning of "equal protection of the laws." Those provisions are, obviously, important, but I have come to believe that even more important, as a practical matter, are the "hard-wired" provisions of the Constitution, all of them dealing with political structures, that academic lawyers rarely even talk about precisely because they are *not* the subject of litigation. There is really no controversy, for example, as to how many votes each state has in the United States Senate. The answer is two; that's just what the Constitution says, just as it clearly says that a president serves for four-years, unless impeached or displaced by the operation of the 25th Amendment. Unlike many foreign countries, there is no provision for votes of "no-confidence" in a president; unlike California and Wisconsin, we cannot, as ordinary citizens, trigger "recall" elections of chief executives. Many other examples could be given of provisions that call not for "interpretation," but, instead, for long overdue discussions of their wisdom. This is what Van Cleve gives us so well.

Van Cleve addresses *all* aspects of constitutionalism, including, crucially, structural features of the Constitution. One of the things we should realize, for example, is that it is fruitless to place enhanced powers in Congress, say, to address economic problems, including health care, if the formal political system is so filled with veto points that the passage of legislation becomes nearly impossible. Some readers might remember from their civics courses a blackboard presentation on "how a bill becomes a law." The more apt question may be why "most bills never stand a chance of actually becoming law." The tilt toward stasis, sometimes described as "gridlock," certainly helps to account for the fact that a stunning majority of Americans, regardless of political party, express almost no confidence in Congress to resolve what they believe to be the pressing challenges facing America and believe, in addition, that the country is "headed in the wrong direction."

It is irrelevant whether I agree or disagree with Van Cleve on every one of his proposals. And, just as important, an actual convention would force us to engage in a kind of rank ordering of the proposals in terms of their importance to us, about which we could disagree even if we agreed on their desirability. As at Philadelphia, one would inevitably find it necessary to engage in compromises, to trade away things one finds less important, even if desirable, in return for votes supporting what one believes, at least at the time, to be more important. What is crucial about this book is that it invites such thoughtful deliberation; it is a welcome oasis in what often seems to be an intellectual desert, especially insofar as many books bewailing our present situation, including the aforementioned *Four Threats,* basically ignore the Constitution's role in deepening, rather than providing a potential cure for, our present crisis.

Van Cleve is almost literally up-to-the-minute in his ability to refer to Covid-19, especially inasmuch as the pandemic has served as the equivalent of a national MRI that has exposed for all to see the inner workings of a polity that is riven, one hopes not fatally, by a variety of severe socio-political (and economic) illnesses that Van Cleve diagnoses in great depth. Yale Law School Professor Jack Balkin has described the contemporary U.S. as a second Gilded Age. That period was succeeded by what we refer to generally as the Progressive Era, where both Republicans like Teddy Roosevelt and Democrats like Woodrow Wilson presented themselves as reformers; their reform agendas included criticisms of the Constitution itself. The period between 1913-1920 saw the addition of four important amendments to the Constitution. Political leaders were not afraid to suggest that the Constitution needed updating, and they acted on those convictions. Van Cleve demonstrates the need to do likewise today, forging out paths by which we might do so.

Making a New American Constitution is not only a book of genuine scholarship reflecting years of study going back to the Founding period, about which Van Cleve has written important books; it is, at least as importantly, an act of high citizenship. He offers us his own genuinely profound "reflections" and calls on us, as his fellow citizens, to debate the particular "choices" he advocates and, if we are dissatisfied, to engage in the most profound kind of "democratic" or "republican" (note the uncapitalized letters) action. That is thoughtful debate, culminating in decisions, in which everyone is motivated by what Madison in *Federalist* 10 described as a desire to achieve "the public good." Now, more than ever, a "Publian spirit" of devotion to the public good instead of only one's own more selfish "factional" interests is necessary if we are to leave a functioning and admirable United States of America as a legacy to our children and grandchildren. So I hope this book gets the wide readership it deserves and, more importantly, provokes the widespread public discussion that our situation demands. It may, alas, not be truly hyperbolic to suggest that our lives as Americans may be quite literally, and not only metaphorically, at stake.

Preface

This is a book about constitutional reform. First as a practicing lawyer, and then after becoming an early American historian, I have been thinking about the Constitution's virtues and its flaws for more than forty years. Events over the past two decades, however, have greatly increased my concerns about the Constitution's seriously adverse effects on the quality of American government and hence on our nation's future. About two years ago, I realized that I needed to write this book, in part due to my discovery that political conflicts similar to today's in important respects had led to the Constitution's adoption. I decided that I wanted to share my concerns with as many people as possible, in the hope that Americans could be persuaded that it was now urgent for us to make significant constitutional reforms.

This book follows in the footsteps of two excellent books on constitutional reform that I recommend to everyone concerned about the state of our Union. The prominent legal scholar Sanford Levinson wrote *Our Undemocratic Constitution*. Professor Levinson's insightful book is a detailed look at why major features of the Constitution fail to meet the standards of modern democracy, and suggests solutions he thinks should be debated at a new convention. Larry Sabato, a well-known political scientist, wrote *A More Perfect Constitution*. His thoughtful book proposes extensive constitutional reforms. He too recommends a convention to consider them.

Those books came out about fifteen years ago. American politics and economics have changed since in momentous ways discussed in this book, including growing income and wealth inequality, impending middle class collapse, and little or no real progress in achieving racial equality or criminal justice reform. These developments have made fundamental constitutional reform not just desirable but imperative.

I recognize that many fellow citizens may not be ready to support holding the popular constitutional convention I advocate until a crisis—an irreversible fork in the political road—is clearly upon us. I believe that this book will nevertheless be useful to them now, because it will help everyone to anticipate and develop the groundwork for reforms needed to meet that crisis. For reasons the book explains, it will arrive much sooner than many people believe. The book also provides insights into the myriad ways in which the Constitution distorts American politics, and should prove worthwhile to readers for that reason alone.

When James Madison was preparing for the 1787 Philadelphia constitutional convention, he worked in an upstairs library at his family home, Montpelier. It had a large, west-facing window with a magnificent view of the Blue Ridge Mountains, allowing him to gaze deeply into what he saw as America's future. It is time for us to move beyond Madison's republican vision, which was grafted onto the realities of a slaveholding society. But as you read this book, I hope that you'll imagine that you are looking out a window as expansive as Madison's, thinking anew about our nation's destiny.

George William Van Cleve
September, 2020

Introduction

The 1787 Constitution was drafted to resolve a political crisis that threatened to destroy the Union. After the Revolutionary War, the federal government was conducted under the Articles of Confederation—America's first constitution. The Confederation faced a series of powerfully divisive political issues. They included how to pay America's massive war debts; how to protect American commerce; how to manage western expansion in the face of concerted efforts by foreign empires and Native Americans to prevent it; and an armed rebellion in Massachusetts. The gridlocked Confederation failed to meet any of these challenges.[1]

By late 1786, it became apparent to many thoughtful Americans that the Confederation government was failing and that the Union might break apart as a result. In response to that crisis, acting outside the Articles' rules, states led by Virginia began to organize the Philadelphia Convention. The new constitution that the Convention recommended was designed to create a far more powerful new federal government that could succeed in addressing national problems where the Confederation had failed.

As great leaders such as Abraham Lincoln have recognized, government under the Constitution is ultimately founded on the republican egalitarianism articulated in the Declaration of Independence. The Declaration made human equality a fundamental principle. It then announced to the world the United States' republican credo: that just governments could only be based on popular consent, and that "the people" had the right to change their government "whenever" and however they chose.

The Constitution served the United States well during its early years by creating a republican government powerful enough to rule a continent for a small agricultural society urgently seeking to expand westward. But it did not create a government that fully embodied republican egalitarianism, especially as we understand that idea today. Among its central provisions were pragmatic compromises preserving the vested interests of wealthy aristocrats from different regions, such as those protecting slavery. Its slavery protections could only be eliminated by our bloody Civil War, in which an estimated 750,000 men died.

Today we face another political crisis as grave as that which faced the country in the 1780s. America's population is now one hundred times larger. We are a multicultural, racially diverse, heavily urbanized, and ever more technology-dependent society. And we are now in danger of being governed permanently by a wealthy oligarchy. In an era of economic stagnation, steadily deteriorating socioeconomic conditions facing millions of poor and middle-class Americans are almost certain to result in a political crisis within a generation. Our middle class is headed toward collapse, and our democracy cannot survive its demise. Today's very large divisions between rich and poor will widen, creating intractable clashes that fatally weaken or even shatter our union, perhaps violently, or give rise to autocratic rule.

To avoid such a catastrophe, it will be essential for us to make extensive political, social, and economic reforms based on constitutional changes that will enable all Americans to view their government as truly fair and firmly committed to creating equal life opportunities and justice for everyone, not just for one elite class or dominant race. These reforms and the laws they authorize Congress to adopt will together create a new social contract.

But today the Constitution is broken beyond repair. It is a serious threat to Lincoln's vision of government "of the people by the people for the people." Its numerous remarkably undemocratic features have been sharply criticized by earlier writers. This book takes a deeper look at such defects and the harms they cause.

Most importantly, however, it has now become clear that the Constitution has an even graver overarching flaw. It is preventing us from making the reforms needed to address the collapse of the middle class and to renew our rapidly decaying social bonds through a new social contract. The Constitution is therefore a massive obstruction to national unity and, as a result, to our country's survival. This book explains why that has happened, and what we will need to do to remedy that fatal flaw and create a resilient modern democracy. Following is an overview.

WHY AMERICA NEEDS A NEW CONSTITUTION

The United States suffers from chronic political gridlock. Our government is failing to resolve pressing social and economic problems; in some cases, it is virtually ignoring them. In 2018, four out of five Americans were either dissatisfied with or angry about their government. As the late Paul Volcker, former Chairman of the Federal Reserve, said, "we're in a hell of a mess in every direction." He asked, "how can you run a democracy when nobody believes in the leadership of the country?"[2] Chapter 1 of this book discusses critical government shortcomings in meeting American society's needs, especially in preventing the decline of the middle class and ensuring equal opportunity for all.

The United States is rapidly becoming a permanent plutocracy—that is, a democracy in name only. In 2018, Volcker identified plutocracy as "the central [political] issue...We've got an enormous number of enormously rich people that have convinced themselves that they're rich because they're smart and constructive. And they don't like government, and they don't like to pay taxes."[3] Some 70% of the nation's wealth is now owned by the top 10% of households, a sharp increase over its concentration forty years ago. The top 1% now own nearly 32% of the nation's wealth. And there is a very large racial wealth gap as well, so that many minorities, especially Blacks, are even more harshly affected by these disparities.

The growth of a wealthy oligarchy harms the rest of American society. Our middle class is collapsing, squeezed by increasing living costs and weakening social institutions. Workers have lost much of their bargaining power and face stagnant wages, poor working conditions, and inadequate retirement security. Many remaining middle-class jobs face destruction by technological change. Yet national policies protect crony capitalism and monopolies. Government under the Constitution has signally failed to protect the economic interests of average Americans.

It is not just economic fairness that is at stake. The heart of Lincoln's vision of democracy—Americans' political equality—is in danger as well. An observation attributed to Supreme Court Justice Louis D. Brandeis puts today's dilemma well: *We can have democracy in this country or we can have wealth concentrated in the hands of a few, but we cannot have both.* Government has been captured by the wealthy; it often responds to their political desires, not the needs and views of average citizens.

America's social fabric has been stretched to the breaking point as government has failed to meet the needs of the poor and middle class, both young and old. Economic mobility for the young has declined significantly over the past several decades. Health care is unaffordable for many Americans, and its costs are still rising. Much of our elderly population lacks retirement security. Nearly one-third of younger members of the "baby boom" generation have no retirement savings. Our overwhelmed public education system utterly fails both poor and many middle-class children. Millions of children live in poverty. Some five hundred thousand Americans are homeless; millions of others are segregated in violent, resource-poor inner cities. Many Americans do not believe that law enforcement is either fair or effective, and as the deaths of George Floyd and other Black Americans show, they are often right to think of it as brutal and racially-biased. Many imprisoned Americans face enormous obstacles to productive re-entry into society. Is it surprising that many Americans no longer have faith in our government?

The 2020 SARS-CoV-2 pandemic has cast an even harsher light on both the remarkable weakness of America's social safety net and the serious harms caused by wealth inequality, particularly to minorities. More than 182,000 Americans have lost their lives to COVID-19 as of August, 31, 2020. Serious illnesses and deaths from COVID-19 have been disproportionately higher among minority group members, in many cases because of their longstanding lack of access to necessary medical care. Black Americans, for example, have been hospitalized for COVID-19 at a rate nearly five times as high as white Americans, and have died at a rate more than double that of whites. While wealthy Americans were able to flee the pandemic or insulate themselves from it, many middle-class and poor Americans have been forced to choose between working and risking illness or protecting themselves at the cost of their livelihoods. Black and Hispanic workers have experienced pandemic-related unemployment at rates more than fifty percent higher than white workers. Studies suggest that the failure to reopen schools due to COVID-19 and instead conducting remote learning will harm poorer children, particularly minorities, significantly more than wealthy children. While a typical student may suffer about 7 months of learning loss from participating in remote learning in 2020, Black students may regress more than 10 months, and poor students may lose more than a year. Nearly twice as high a percentage of Black and Hispanic students lack access to either a computer or Internet at home compared to white students, so providing remote instruction imposes much larger hardships on minority students. Government under the Constitution will be unable to make the necessary reforms to cure these dangerous safety net failures and major inequities by creating a new social contract for reasons discussed in this book.[4]

The United States is also increasingly robbing future generations to avoid political conflict. By early 2020, before the pandemic began, we faced a steadily growing $23 trillion national debt. The Social Security and Medicare Trust Funds are estimated to run out by about 2035. More than 40 million students have often strangling education debts. State and local governments have trillions of dollars of other unfunded liabilities. These growing burdens will hasten the collapse of America's middle class.

THE CONSTITUTION GIVES UNFAIR POLITICAL ADVANTAGES TO THE WEALTHY

We have reached a political dead end under the Constitution. Economic growth alone cannot cure our problems. Instead, today's badly impaired government legitimacy and deteriorating socioeconomic conditions can only be successfully combated by creating a new social contract, including a stronger safety net. Yet America's wealthy oligarchy has an enormous stake in protecting its wealth and power by preventing such changes. Chapter 2 shows that our flawed Constitution is central to today's gridlock. It favors the wealthy in contests over the fairness of strengthening the social safety net, taxation, and limiting wealth concentration.

Political polarization, money in politics, racism, and other factors play a role in worsening gridlock. At a deeper level, though, many of America's political conflicts—though by no means all—instead boil down to disputes over economic fairness, especially the desirability and fairness of taxation. A well-known example was the twenty year struggle over whether the Constitution should permit Congress to impose a progressive income tax. But in recent years, there has been a long-term political realignment that seriously hampers making reforms to increase economic fairness, and the Constitution greatly worsens its effects.

Neither major political party today is a fully ideologically coherent coalition, so any shorthand description of a party's philosophy will at best describe a "center of gravity." Due to the political influence of the wealthy, both parties also generally support policies such as "corporate welfare" that benefit wealthy stockholders. But the warring conservative and liberal views dominant in the major political parties today over how best to foster economic growth nevertheless have clear tax and wealth distribution consequences. The Republican Party generally opposes increased government taxation and limits on wealth concentration. The Democratic Party frequently favors policies that would require increased taxation and result in wealth limitations. These partisan differences are not purely ideological; they reflect the clashing economic and political interests of the parties' social group constituencies.

The Democratic and Republican coalitions have developed firm, largely distinct (though on occasion somewhat overlapping) geographic bases in rural and urban America. That long-term partisan realignment is a perfect recipe for chronic gridlock—effectively maintaining the status quo. The Constitution reinforces that deadlock because it sharply tilts our national political playing field against progressive taxation and limits on oligarchic wealth.

The Constitution's pervasive small-state bias (discussed below) artificially strengthens the anti-taxation coalition, which is heavily Republican, in both electoral and legislative conflicts. It correspondingly weakens forces supporting increased economic fairness, which lean strongly Democratic. Recent Supreme Court decisions have reinforced the Constitution's bias in favor of oligarchic wealth. Constitutional rulings such as that in *Buckley v. Valeo* and its progeny including *Citizens United v. FEC* have unleashed a flood of billions of dollars of campaign funding by the wealthy that flows to both major parties, often secretly. Moreover, the middle class already pays regressive wealth taxes (i.e., property taxes) every year on much of its households' entire wealth. But it is quite possible that the Supreme Court will hold that similar taxes on the capital property (e.g., stocks and bonds) held primarily by the wealthy, such as the wealth tax proposed by Senator Elizabeth Warren, are constitutionally prohibited.

The Constitution's flawed separation of powers and its anti-democratic distribution of political power also contribute heavily to government's failures. These issues are discussed in chapters 3 and 4. These chapters are not intended to provide a comprehensive catalog of the Constitution's shortcomings such as those found, for example, in earlier writings by Sanford Levinson and Larry Sabato (discussed in the Preface). Instead they have two purposes: to examine the nature and causes of certain deep flaws more closely, and to illustrate the major deformities in politics and government that result from them.

THE CONSTITUTION'S SEPARATION OF POWERS NO LONGER WORKS

The Constitution's three main government institutions were designed to be separate power centers pitted against each other to prevent abuses of power. But the system of checks and balances at the Constitution's heart has broken down. Chapter 3 shows that that is because those institutions now often either work very differently than originally intended, or don't work well at all.

The American presidency has become "imperial." The president's powers frequently resemble those possessed by a king. The Constitution (as now interpreted) gives presidents enormous discretionary powers over war and foreign affairs. They deploy troops in many cases with little or no advance input from Congress, rendering its essential power to declare war meaningless.

The president's neo-imperial powers are not limited to war and foreign affairs by any means. The president has extensive discretionary authority over the massive federal bureaucracy, which regulates much of America's economy and social relations, including climate change, labor and health policy decisions. The president also controls a constantly expanding, increasingly intrusive, and yet often ineffective post-9/11 law enforcement and national security establishment. Recent presidents have claimed broad executive powers, often seeking to govern without Congressional consent through executive order. But the Constitution makes removal of incompetent or abusive presidents exceptionally difficult.

While the presidency has grown stronger, Congress has become dysfunctional, so that it frequently cannot check presidential abuses of power. Congress is gridlocked by divisions between the major party coalitions with the result that pressing problems cannot be remedied. Moreover, Congress no longer functions as a real legislative decision-making body, thanks in part to gridlock, the creation of a massive administrative state, and the existence of many "safe," i.e., non-competitive, congressional seats. Because their offices are so secure and comfortably paid, most members of Congress would be unwilling to retire unless promised somewhere between $1 and $5 million (depending on their position). Congress has abdicated much of its policy control to administrative agencies controlled by the president, or to the courts, by making remarkably vague delegations of authority to those agencies in countless statutes over nearly a century.

In the absence of clear congressional directions, the Supreme Court—an unrepresentative elite institution—has stepped into the vacuum and now by default makes many basic decisions on American government and social policy. In 2012, for example, it made a final, effectively unchallengeable decision about whether the United States could constitutionally adopt a national health insurance system. The

Court's emergence as the holder of vast unaccountable authority is compelling evidence of the bankruptcy of republican government.

The Founders' checks and balances have been destroyed. We are slowly abandoning the reality of republican government and instead becoming a de facto elective monarchy dominated by a wealthy oligarchy. The United States now increasingly resembles Great Britain's aristocratic monarchy at the time of the American Revolution. That would mean that the Revolution had been a failure in the eyes of most of the Founders.

THE CONSTITUTION HAS FAILED AS A FOUNDATION FOR REPRESENTATIVE DEMOCRACY

The Constitution has also failed as a foundation for American democracy. It created a representative government, but it was one intended to give the wealthy elite strong influence. Today's ideas about what makes a representative democracy legitimate are markedly different. And even the Founders never intended the Constitution's remarkable distortions of the popular will.

Chapter 4 illustrates this by analyzing some, but by no means all, of the Constitution's main flaws as an instrument of modern democracy. For example, in 1787, Virginia, the largest state in population, had about nine times as many free people as Delaware, the smallest state. Despite that, all states were given two equal Senate votes by the Constitution. Today the largest state, California, has more than sixty-five times as many people as the smallest state, Wyoming. Yet California and Wyoming each still have two Senate votes. Such constitutionally dictated political "equality" between extraordinarily unequal states is anti-republican.

Moreover, the disproportionate Senate influence of small states clearly distorts national decision-making in systematically damaging ways. Brett Kavanaugh would not be a Supreme Court justice today except for the exaggerated voting strength of small states in the Senate, for example. Chapter 4 shows that changing Senate voting strength to reflect population would result in policies far better designed to meet the needs of large states and especially those of major urban areas. Foreign policy, education, climate change, energy, and consumer protection policies, among others, all would be substantially changed.

There are many other structural distortions of democracy found in the Constitution. For example, the Electoral College enables popular minorities to elect the President. Since 2000 alone, two presidents have been elected despite losing the popular vote. Another example: the Constitution gives Supreme Court justices life terms. With today's increased life expectancies, justices can now routinely serve for thirty or forty years, markedly expanding both their power and presidential control over the Court.

The Constitution's structural biases and exceptionally rigid amendment process also strengthen gridlock and protect the status quo by making reaching national consensus on fundamental issues, and then carrying out desired policies, far more difficult than it should be. That is a perfect recipe for national drift. It means that any issue (e.g., immigration policy) which it is not politically imperative to resolve will not be resolved. True, sometimes drift does little harm; but as the rise of totalitarian regimes including Hitler and the Nazi party in the 1930s shows, national drift can also lead to disaster. In today's volatile world, the United States cannot afford to drift.

All of the Constitution's critical defects could be considered and remedied at a new general constitutional convention. Unless we hold such a convention, none of the Constitution's flaws will be cured, because piecemeal reforms are virtually impossible. And a convention is the only forum where a constitutional "grand bargain" (that is, an agreement that simultaneously resolves a broad range of contentious issues) can be reached.

THE UNITED STATES NEEDS A NEW CONSTITUTIONAL CONVENTION

Many people on both the political left and right say they just want one constitutional change that they're confident "will really fix things." Chapter 5 considers the prospects for such piecemeal (or "freestanding") amendment-by-amendment reform. The Constitution is one of the most difficult to amend in the world. Its stringent requirements and America's long-term political divisions together form an insurmountable obstacle to virtually all piecemeal reforms.

The Electoral College will be abolished by amendment "when pigs fly." An alternative approach for direct presidential election, the National Popular Vote Initiative ("NPVI"), will not succeed. Failure also unquestionably awaits efforts to overturn Supreme Court campaign finance decisions such as *Citizens United*, to adopt a balanced budget amendment, or to change the Second Amendment. While the Equal Rights Amendment might prove a very rare exception, if adopted it is likely to be mired in litigation for decades.

Some prominent constitutional scholars claim that the need for constitutional amendments can be avoided by the Supreme Court's "informal amendment" of the Constitution through interpretive approaches such as "living originalism," or through "court packing" schemes. But as Sanford Levinson has argued, such interpretive approaches cannot overcome the large distortions caused by the Constitution's structural provisions such as equal state Senate voting. Nor can they possibly restore Congress' viability. Leading political scientists also believe that relying on such interpretive approaches will ultimately deprive constitutional institutions of any authority. For these reasons, "informal amendment" will inevitably lead to the end of republican government. Congress will continue to decline, and the presidency will become more imperial. Court packing would be very likely to destroy the Court's legitimacy. While one can certainly defend interpreting the Constitution as a living document in cases that require elaborating established constitutional principles, that cannot ultimately sustain representative democracy. In order to effect lasting change while preserving democracy, the Constitution must be amended through a representative process instead.

All signs point to the conclusion that the Constitution cannot be amended on a piecemeal basis with respect to any divisive issue. Nor will Congress call a convention under Article V. Fortunately, we can hold a popular convention outside the rigid requirements of the Constitution's Article V amendment process, as chapter 6 explains.

WE NEED TO HOLD A POPULAR CONVENTION

Leading Founders such as James Wilson and Edmund Pendleton told state conventions during the Constitution's ratification that its adoption could not abolish the right of the people to hold a convention to reform it whenever they chose. Both the Declaration of Independence and the history of the 1787 Philadelphia Convention show that the Founders believed what they said. The Founders wholly disregarded the amendment procedures of our first constitution, the Articles of Confederation.

Similarly, the Constitution's Article V procedures can be disregarded by a popular convention. But political, as opposed to legal, safeguards will need to be in place. A popular convention must be seen as politically legitimate to succeed; that will require it to adopt procedures such as supermajority ratification of its work. There is no compelling reason to follow Article V's rules voluntarily. Article V confers entirely unwarranted veto power over conventions and ratification contests on small states. Yet small states are often not functional equals of larger states, or even financially viable.

THE "DANGERS" POSED BY A CONSTITUTIONAL CONVENTION ARE GREATLY EXAGGERATED

There is a common anxiety expressed by people—whether on the left or the right politically—about holding a constitutional convention. They fear a "runaway" convention, which they claim would inevitably be dangerous. Wouldn't a convention, they say, be likely to expand or cripple the Bill of Rights; further protect gunowners or outlaw guns; outlaw abortion or make it unlimited; destroy states' rights; or take some other step they view as outrageous? They insist that a convention will open a political Pandora's box. Chapter 6 puts to rest those fears.

Of course, even a convention called to consider only one issue, such as a balanced budget amendment, in theory might "run away" and instead propose a broad range of changes. But only one fact actually matters in considering the supposed "dangers" of any convention. It has no power to make anything more than a proposal—which has no binding force whatsoever unless and until it is ratified.

The delegates to the 1787 Philadelphia Convention did not propose certain major constitutional changes—such as uniform minimum voting qualifications—that many of them supported because they thought that the Constitution might well not be ratified if such proposals were included. Similarly today, requiring approval of a new convention's proposals by a voter supermajority will effectively limit the range of acceptable proposals. A convention will not become a Pandora's box. Chapter 6 shows that there is little reason to fear special interest domination of a convention's work. A properly structured convention will not be captured by special interests, unduly limited by "politics as usual," or be dominated by raging passions.

HOLDING A POPULAR CONVENTION: ISSUES AND REFORMS

Chapter 7 discusses the organization, funding, and conduct of a popular convention, particularly the critical issues to be addressed in the convention "call." A well-crafted call prepared by a carefully recruited national organizing committee can launch a strong popular movement in support of the convention's work. It will encourage the essential participation of non-elected leaders and citizens in the convention process, including service as delegates, and provide the basis for raising convention funds. The call should propose convention timing and arrangements. It should present a possible reform agenda for debate during delegate elections, but impose no limits on the convention's agenda. It should set terms for delegate elections and for delegate allocation. The convention will be unable even to consider many essential reforms unless delegates are allocated to states not equally but instead proportionally based on population.

Chapter 7 shows that it should be possible to raise the funds needed for the convention's work by contributions from small donors around the country. It also discusses how convention organizers can anticipate and respond to efforts that will almost certainly be made to block the convention, including lawsuits, congressional intervention and state boycotts. Finally, Chapter 7 discusses significant convention procedures, and how a convention can protect itself against special interest manipulation.

Chapter 8 presents a suggested reform agenda for a popular convention. Its proposals could lay the foundation for a new social contract; create a new, stronger and more flexible federalism; and strengthen the inadequate New Deal social safety net. Together, agreements on these issues could form the basis of a convention grand bargain that could gain broad support.

The new constitution should strengthen America's decaying social bonds. It should build new foundations for equal opportunity for all Americans by creating rights to adequate primary and secondary education, childcare, environmental protection, and healthcare. It should strengthen the social safety net, by requiring that the homeless, children in foster care, the elderly and disabled, and other vulnerable groups receive adequate care. The constitution should mandate that governments provide adequate funding to fulfill these rights, and the convention should consider whether that should include reparations for slavery.[5]

The new constitution should restore public control of private wealth and power. It should mandate that Congress must either establish a system of public interest economic and social regulation of massive technology companies such as Facebook, Google, and Apple, or order them to be broken up. It should limit inherited wealth. The convention should decide whether limits should also be placed on certain types of wealth acquisition. It should give Congress clear authority to tax wealth.

The new constitution should also make sorely needed political and institutional reforms. Political reforms should include direct election of the President and proportional Senate voting strength for states. They should also include changes to restore Congress' ability to legislate, including ending campaign financing by the wealthy; prohibiting gerrymandering; voting reform; and possible elimination of the two-party duopoly in politics. Reforms are also needed to make serving in Congress more attractive to a broad range of citizens, including increased competition for seats; term limits; redrawing congressional districts to cross state lines, and electing some congresspeople at-large.

As to institutional reforms, the convention should reconsider the separation of powers and limit presidential and Supreme Court authority. Separation of powers changes (if that concept is retained) might include strengthening Congress by allowing or requiring presidents to choose members of Congress as cabinet officers. The grounds for impeachment and removal of a president from office should be broadened to include incompetence or malfeasance, or systematic refusal to enforce any valid law. Presidents should be removable for committing troops without the advance consent of Congress, except in specified cases. Presidential powers over law enforcement and executive agencies need significant clarification. Reforms should also include limits on the power of the Supreme Court. These could include term limits for Justices and limiting the court's jurisdiction to exclude certain kinds of cases, or empowering the Senate to overturn certain types of Court decisions.

The constitution should establish a new federalism based on careful reassessment of federal and state responsibilities. The convention should carefully consider whether in light of the strong national interest in high-quality public education, it should continue to be primarily a state and local responsibility. It should also consider whether it is in the national interest to guarantee equal educational opportunity to all of America's children.

The ideal of equal justice for all classes and races must not only be reaffirmed but fully realized. America cannot survive continued racial bias in law enforcement. The convention should consider how to restructure law enforcement powers, including police and other government officials' liability for use of force, responsibilities, and funding at all levels of government accordingly. And the convention should establish uniform national voting rights for convicted individuals who have served their sentences.

The convention should consider whether a balanced budget amendment would be desirable. But it would also be very worthwhile to review the federalism-related fiscal structure of the United States. The convention might, for example, propose fiscal reforms to assist states in meeting their revenue needs to the extent they perform "national interest" functions such as drug or gun law enforcement or public education.

Finally, a new constitution should provide a workable amendment process. Possible changes would include allowing states containing a large enough percentage of the population (say, two-thirds) to initiate a future convention. Ratification of constitutional amendments should generally occur based on a supermajority popular vote (again, perhaps two-thirds).

CONCLUSION

America needs a new constitution if our republic is to survive the long-term political stalemate, middle class collapse, and racial inequities and divisions we are experiencing. The 1787 Constitution's structure and Supreme Court interpretations of it have given powerful protection to our wealthy oligarchy. The separation of powers has broken down. Our government now increasingly resembles an aristocratic elective monarchy. The Constitution prevents us from breaking today's gridlock. Its institutions are remarkably ineffective in enabling government to address many critical issues that affect communities across America. Its rigid amendment process makes significant constitutional changes a virtual impossibility. It is a major obstacle to creation of an essential new social contract.

We can reassert control of politics by holding a popular constitutional convention to make a new constitution suited to our country's needs. Only a convention will have the ability to reach a grand bargain proposing a series of constitutional changes, and virtually all essential reforms will not occur otherwise.

We must not let unthinking veneration for the Constitution or partisan efforts to exploit fears of the unknown deter us from collectively shaping our nation's future. Republics can die slow deaths, just as the Roman republic did as it became an empire ruled by military force. It is up to us to avoid Rome's fate.

PART I

Why America Needs a New Constitution

1

Our Union is Failing

Each year, the President of the United States reports to Congress on the state of the union. In the television era, these State of the Union addresses have become lengthy, spectacle-crammed speeches in which presidents seek to persuade viewers of their policies' wisdom and to cajole or threaten Congress into adopting them. But let's suppose instead that a president—in a final address before leaving office—decided to give an honest, dispassionate, nonpartisan assessment of the true state of our union. What would he or she say in such a report? I'm convinced that it would go something like this:

"Members of Congress and my fellow citizens. For more than two centuries, both Americans and immigrants who have come here have believed in and struggled to realize our country's promise as a land of freedom, equality, and vast opportunity. But today I must report to you that we face a political crisis—our American dream is dying. We could continue to believe that we are exceptional, blindly confident that we could never suffer such a fate. But you know as well as I do that the handwriting is on the wall: our government has lost the trust and confidence of most of its citizens. A few years ago, a remarkable 40 percent of registered voters said they had lost faith in democracy.[6] Recent polls show that for the first time on record, a majority of Americans are dissatisfied with democracy.[7] An estimated 80 percent of Americans are angry with or dissatisfied with the federal government.[8] Public trust in government is now lower than twenty percent.[9] That is an exceptionally bad omen, for the people's trust in our government is the true source of our nation's strength; we cannot survive without it.

Unfortunately, there is good reason for the widespread feeling that the "system is broken": the American middle class is collapsing, and republican government cannot survive its collapse.[10] Yet our government is chronically gridlocked. It cannot make changes to meet the country's many seriously pressing needs. Our political rigidity is a mortal threat to our long-term survival. To overcome this grave danger, we must face facts. We must describe our difficulties honestly and seek their true causes without fear or favor. Tonight, I will describe to you the major hazards our country faces to begin an essential discussion of what we can do about them. I will give you chapter and verse about our crisis, but let me start by summarizing it for you this way:

America's economy and political system today are increasingly dominated by a small group of extremely wealthy individuals—what is traditionally called an oligarchy. That is very bad news for our republic. Our middle class is the political heart of our democracy, and it is slowly decaying due to the rise of this oligarchy. Its members are struggling more every day economically. The main social institutions that have nurtured its children, such as public education, are increasingly overwhelmed. Americans are now often living in separate worlds segregated by race and wealth, not sharing a commonwealth. Social cohesion is steadily declining. Our social safety net is failing to protect either today's elderly or future generations. And the middle class faces breakdown unless government policies change. Our society may well end up with a very small class of "haves," and a very large class of "have nots," a sure formula for incessant political and civil strife that will inevitably end democratic government. In short, our union is failing, and our government has allowed it to fail.

With that summary, let me review for you major aspects of America's seriously threatening economic and social conditions today.

ECONOMIC INEQUALITY

Members of Congress, I will begin by talking about economic inequality because it is politically poisonous to our republic. Like an acid, economic inequality steadily corrodes the foundations of democracy and the vitality of indispensable common institutions such as public education. The wealthy can use their wealth to avoid participation in public institutions and concerns. They can often avoid sharing the burdens of common life. If you own a plane with a pilot, you don't need to care about, or to do anything about, bad public airline travel. If you live in a mansion in a gated suburban community, you don't need to care about, or to do anything about, violence against the poor in highly segregated urban areas.

Worst of all, large-scale wealth inequality will ultimately endanger democracy itself. It steadily weakens the middle class even as it robs the poor of hope for their future. If it becomes too great, inequality condemns struggling citizens to despair, making many of them willing, even eager, to escape or subvert the existing social order through crime or sedition. Their actions may cause a predictable backlash, increasing support for the creation of an authoritarian state governed by force that will end our democracy.

The unpleasant but unavoidable reality is that Americans are much more unequal economically today than they were forty years ago, when Ronald Reagan became president. For nearly fifty years after the Great Depression and the new American social contract created by the New Deal, the level of wealth concentration fell. Since about 1980, the reverse has been true, and wealth has become increasingly concentrated.[11] It has increased at the expense of middle class and poorer Americans, who are also often heavily in debt, sometimes for life.[12]

According to the Federal Reserve, some 70% of the nation's wealth is now owned by the top 10% of households. The share of the nation's wealth held by the lower 90% of households has fallen by about one-fourth during the past thirty-plus years. Income inequality in the United States has also increased over that period.[13] The lion's share of the benefits of recent economic growth has been captured by the country's wealthiest families.[14] This evidence strongly supports the conclusion that much of the lower- and middle-class economic progress following the adoption of New Deal policies and post World War II-era growth has been reversed over the past four decades.

We might be less concerned about increased wealth inequality if it were a transient phenomenon, or if we expected that different families would become wealthy over time. But today's increased wealth concentration is persistent. Intergenerational social mobility in the United States is now fairly limited compared to many other developed countries, especially in certain regions of the United States such as the Southeast.[15]

According to a recent Brookings Institution analysis:

> stagnant incomes and falling wages have meant that fewer
> Americans are growing up to be better off than their parents.
> Upward absolute intergenerational mobility was once the
> almost-universal experience among America's youth. No
> longer. Among those born in 1940, about 90 percent of
> children grew up to experience higher incomes than their
> parents...This proportion was only 50 percent among those
> born in the 1980s.[16]

Economic immobility is greatest among American families with the lowest and highest income levels. Extremes of severe poverty and substantial wealth are more likely to persist over time, while people are less likely to move into, and more likely to fall out of, the middle class.[17] Such decreased mobility will especially harm minority Americans and their children.

Thus the United States has become a wealthy oligarchy that is likely to last unless something is done to address the problems of inequality and economic unfairness. Americans will very probably disagree about why the rich have grown far richer over the past several decades. Supporters of "free" markets will argue that these changes result primarily from the "natural" operation of capitalism. They will point to causes such as increased international competition and other changes in the economy, including the rise of Apple, Google, and other global technology companies. They will contend that the economic rewards of growth have properly gone to people who helped bring about the new global and technological economy, so government either can or should do nothing about rising inequality and economic fairness.

But in today's global economy, the free market account of economic change is seriously incomplete for several reasons. First, recent studies by leading political scientists have shown that in reality, federal government policies such as tax laws that decreased the average effective rate of taxation of the very wealthy; favorable taxation of hedge funds; permitting unrealistic accounting for corporate stock options; and loosened banking regulation, rather than market forces, have played a major role in shifting the distribution of income and wealth in favor of the rich.[18] The free market account also ignores the fact that since at least the early twentieth century, national government power has played an essential role in fostering and protecting American companies and other aspects of economic growth in the developing global economy (e.g., military power protecting corporate property abroad; global protection of free trade and intellectual property rights). Today, nearly all American companies would be highly unlikely to be able to operate effectively in the global economy without the many protections provided to them largely without cost by the exercise of national military and "soft" power in our international relations. Companies also receive "corporate welfare" through direct and indirect subsidies in the federal budget, estimated at $100 billion per year in 2012.[19]

The arguments used to defend the sharply increasing concentration of wealth also fail to account for American government's major role during more than a century in protecting competition against monopolies under the antitrust laws and in regulating new technologies such as electric utilities and telephone companies so that they benefited citizens at reasonable cost. Government has frequently failed to provide such competition and consumer protections in recent years. Today, for example, American consumers frequently pay far higher prices for increasingly essential technologies such as internet service than citizens in many other countries do. A 2015 study by the Center for Public Integrity found that U.S. internet prices in various cities were 3 ½ times higher than in comparable French cities, and that consumers had a far smaller choice of service providers.[20] And a conservatively estimated one-fifth of all "America's billionaires made their money in industries in which government capture or market failure is commonplace."[21]

Beginning with the nineteenth century rise of populism, during the Progressive era, and emphatically again in the New Deal, our citizens rejected as un-American the idea that an economy that works well only for the wealthy and reduces everyone else to poverty or wage slavery is acceptable. Over more than half a century, victorious popular struggles against economic elites led to the creation of powerful new government tools to protect the public interest, including progressive income taxation, antitrust, and utility regulatory laws. These powers and other democratic reforms were created either by constitutional amendments such as the Sixteenth Amendment or because of unmistakable signs that additional amendments would be adopted if courts and Congress did not change unfairly restrictive constitutional interpretations and policies. Through popular action and constitutional reform, America's government could now be given added powers needed successfully to combat growing inequality and prevent monopoly exploitation of our citizens.

The fundamental question for Americans today is instead a broader one—whether our overall political system created by the Constitution is responsive and resilient enough to make critically needed and widely supported political reforms to restore and maintain economic fairness before society becomes fatally inflamed by social and political violence. History shows us plainly how the future of the United States could look if nothing is done. The French and Russian revolutions both occurred because those countries' governments were frozen against changing policies that adamantly protected the economic and political privileges of their wealthy aristocracies. Of course, we can continue to imagine that "it can't happen here." But history also tells us that when it comes to political violence and authoritarianism, in the long run there are no exceptional countries.

GROWING POLITICAL INEQUALITY

Members of Congress, a second major threat to our republic comes from the increased domination of politics by the wealthy. As Supreme Court Justice Louis D. Brandeis observed, highly concentrated wealth and democracy are incompatible. The inevitable result of great economic inequality will be a democracy in name only. It should not surprise us then that there is actually strong evidence that today America already is an oligarchy run by the wealthy rather than a representative democracy. The wealthy control politics despite the deceptive appearances created by American leaders' democratic rhetoric and our theoretically democratic institutions.

Prominent political scientists have recently shown that there is often a large gap between majority public opinion about what national policies are desirable, and the opinions of the wealthy about their preferred policies. These studies—of more than seventeen hundred government policy decisions over several decades—have shown further that government often tends to follow the policy views of the wealthy, not those of the general public, especially when the wealthy oppose a change in the status quo.[22] Leading political scientist Martin Gilens found based on this research that the disproportionate influence of the wealthy has had important distorting effects on a range of government policies. He concluded: "government policy would differ if it more equally reflected the policy preferences of all Americans. For example, in the economic domain we would expect a more progressive tax system, stricter corporate regulation, and a higher minimum wage."[23]

Another recent study of public policy formation concluded that its data strongly suggested that the United States was actually controlled by the wealthy and by influential businesses, endangering representative democracy. Its authors said: "...our analyses suggest that majorities of the American public actually have little influence over the policies our government adopts....We believe that, if policymaking is dominated by powerful business organizations and a small number of affluent Americans, then America's claims to being a democratic society are seriously threatened."[24] A thoughtful writer concluded that one important implication of these studies was that "on many issues, the rich exercise an effective veto. If they are against something, it is unlikely to happen."[25]

The domination of politics by the wealthy means that government policy is controlled by an economic elite with a strong shared interest in preserving its members' wealth against policies to advance economic fairness. It is a profound mistake in thinking about politics today to conclude that oligarchic dominance results only from the liberal or conservative ideology of particular members of that elite (e.g., the Koch brothers). It is both temptingly easy and popular to villainize the ideologies or lifestyles of particular wealthy people. But it is far more important to recognize the powerful influence exerted by the wealthy as a self-interested political class, nearly all of whose members share at least one major common objective—their wealth's preservation and growth.

The fact that the American majority does not actually rule our country won't surprise many citizens, and it goes a very long way toward explaining their lack of trust in government. Most commonly, people believe that the domination of politics by the wealthy is traceable to the fact that they are major donors to political campaigns. They often conclude that we could solve the problem of wealth in politics just by changing the Constitution to prevent campaign financing by the wealthy. That type of amendment will be impossible to achieve by itself under the current Constitution.[26] But even if we could change the Constitution to achieve that goal, the influence of wealth cannot actually be removed from politics merely by eliminating campaign financing by the rich. Many parts of the Constitution will need to be reformed to achieve that goal, because the dominance of American politics by the wealthy and the failures of Congress actually have far deeper roots than the mere financing of campaigns.

As the United States became the dominant world power after World War II, Washington, D.C. became an imperial capital. The District of Columbia and its suburbs are now among the nation's richest areas. Ten of the nation's fifteen wealthiest counties were in the Washington D.C. metropolitan area as of late 2014. That was not because Washington, D.C. is a major manufacturing or financial center or home to global technology companies. Instead, it was largely the result of the sprawling government-based economy created using taxpayer money by politicians and by their future employers— lobbyists, consultants, and other "Beltway bandits."

As a wealthy imperial capital, Washington has become a place many politicians never want to leave after arriving from the rest of America, because life there is extremely good to them. They have large paid staffs, high salaries and excellent health and pension benefits. Even better, they are unlikely to be defeated once they are elected—they have what are effectively lifetime appointments. As of 2013, a study found, "since World War II, on average 93.3 percent of all incumbent representatives and 81.5 percent of all incumbent senators running for reelection have been returned for office."[27] Life in our wealthy imperial capital can also be very financially rewarding, especially compared to opportunities in officials' home districts.

Many members of Congress either arrive in Washington as wealthy individuals, become wealthy while in office, or become wealthy in Washington after leaving office. As of 2014, more than half of all members of Congress were millionaires.[28] As of 2015, the median net worth of Senators was $3.2 million, or about 30 times the median net worth of American households. The median net worth of members of the House of Representatives was $900,000, or about nine to ten times median household net worth.[29] And members of Congress are uniquely well-positioned to increase their wealth through government service.

There is an enormous amount of money to be made from government and politics in Washington by well-placed individuals. Many are former government officeholders who have found ways to capitalize on their time in office to become rich without going to jail. They have often done so by doing the bidding of the wealthy while in office; when they leave office, they can be counted on to continue those efforts. These time-serving bureaucratic officials and former members of Congress are not at all inclined to "rock the boat," because seeking political change the wealthy dislike is often an irreversible detour off the road to future politically-generated wealth.

From these circumstances and others I haven't time to discuss tonight, it is clear that the control of politics by the wealthy will continue unless there are fundamental changes in the political independence of elected officials, in the way they understand and carry out their responsibilities, and in how effectively they can be held accountable. But our current non-competitive political system— created under and protected by the Constitution—virtually guarantees that today's incumbent officeholders can keep their well-paid sinecures (and very large pensions) for as long as they like. Our constitutional system itself needs to change significantly in order to restore effective republican government. But that cannot happen if the middle class collapses. I will now turn to that critical subject.

THE MIDDLE CLASS IS COLLAPSING

Members of Congress, America's transformation into a wealthy oligarchy means that the badly weakened middle class faces continued decline that will lead to its collapse in the decades just ahead. There are three reasons that will lead to its virtual disappearance if national policies are unchanged. First, the middle-class' shares of national wealth and income are declining. Second, the central social institutions that support it are being overwhelmed by socioeconomic forces its members cannot control. And third, current government policies are very likely to result in far higher taxes on already burdened middle-class households within a decade or so.

The size of the middle class has declined from 60 percent of the population to 50 percent over the past forty years or so, according to some analysts.[30] Most importantly, its share of national income and wealth has decreased significantly over the past several decades. The share of national income received by the middle class was 43% in 2014, down substantially from 62% in 1970.[31] During that period, life has also steadily become more difficult both economically and socially for middle-class families.

Middle-class households now face a considerably higher cost of living than previously. In her recent book *Squeezed: Why Our Families Can't Afford America*, Alissa Quart concludes that "middle-class life is now 30% more expensive than it was 20 years ago." She cites the rising costs of housing, education, health care and child care in particular.[32] Her study finds that "in some cases the cost of daily life over the last 20 years has doubled."[33] As discretionary income has shrunk, the quality of American middle-class life has declined. Moreover, as the life stories in *Squeezed* show, many people are now struggling just to stay in the middle class at all in the face of economic and technological change. Other families are maintaining their middle-class standard of living only by taking on debt which will burden them and their children for their entire lives. That includes more than one and one-half trillion dollars of student loan debt, an enormous mortgage on an entire generation's futures.

Even more troubling, however, is that core social institutions supporting middle-class life that are designed to advance the futures of both poor and middle-class children are fracturing as well. What is more, America's New Deal-era social safety net itself is now in danger of failing both existing poor and middle-class retirees and future generations. Following are some examples of major institutions being pulled apart by social and economic strains. In many cases, poor and middle-class children suffer by far the worst consequences. I will begin with major labor market changes that have deeply affected middle-class life.

Women participate in the outside-the-home labor force today to a much greater extent than they did fifty to seventy-five years ago. In 1950, about one-third of women worked outside. By 2014, roughly 73 million women, or 57%, did. A recent Brookings Institution report concluded that this change actually staved off what would otherwise have been a major economic decline for the middle class. It said:

> Though modest, the improvement in middle-class family incomes over the past several decades is entirely thanks to women's added work hours and earnings...Were it not for women's economic contributions, middle-income families would have experienced stark declines in income over the 1979 to 2013 period. The Council of Economic Advisers reported that 'Essentially all of the income gains that middle-class American families have experienced since 1970 are due to the rise in women's earnings.'[34]

This profound labor market alteration has also had important consequences for children and families.

As women have moved into the outside labor force, governments have done relatively little to assist families in providing childcare. A significant part of family earnings must therefore be spent on it. A 2012 study concluded that "the annual cost of child care for an infant in a child care center is higher than a year's tuition at the average four-year public college in most states."[35] A more recent study shows that the average cost of two-children childcare in the United States after tax subsidies as a percentage of typical mid-level family income is about 50% higher than the European-country average, and amounts to more than 20 percent of income.[36]

Other important changes in patterns of family life have also had significant and often adverse consequences for children's social mobility. Many more American children today are growing up in single-parent families than was true fifty years ago. In 1960, 9% of children lived in single-parent families. Fifty years later, the percentage had roughly tripled. By 2017, solo parents cared for eighteen million children, or about one-fourth of all children.[37]

These changing family patterns have profoundly important and often very negative socioeconomic consequences for millions of children. In 2016, an estimated 35 percent of children in female-headed families lived in poverty, compared to 17% in male-headed families and only 6.6 percent of children in two-parent families.[38] These altered family life patterns have put major added stresses on various social institutions intended to nurture children, particularly the public education system.

PUBLIC EDUCATION IS FAILING

Members of Congress, for a century and a half, America's public education system has been a central institution preparing American children from diverse cultures and socioeconomic backgrounds for common public life and enhancing their futures. Estimated annual expenditures on public primary and secondary education nationwide are roughly $650 billion which, as you know, is about the same size as the U.S. defense budget.[39] But despite this large public investment, overall student performance is mediocre, and the education system is under increasing pressure to meet social needs greatly beyond its capacities. One important result is that the system is fracturing; increasingly, parents are avoiding public education when they choose how to educate their children.

For some time now, American public education has not been producing students who are internationally competitive in core competencies essential in a technological world with global competition.

A 2017 Pew Research study reported that:

> One of the biggest cross-national tests is the Programme for
> International Student Assessment (PISA), which every three
> years measures reading ability, math and science literacy and
> other key skills among 15-year-olds in dozens of developed
> and developing countries. The most recent PISA results, from
> 2015, placed the U.S. an unimpressive 38th out of 71
> countries in math and 24th in science. Among the 35
> members of the Organization for Economic Cooperation and
> Development...the U.S. ranked 30th in math and 19th in
> science.[40]

The cost of public education increased by a factor of 4.7 between
1980 and 2013—far above the general rate of inflation.[41] But over the
past forty years there has been little or no improvement in student
performance.[42] A 2016 study concluded that "for the nation's 17-year-
olds, there have been no gains in literacy since the National
Assessment of Educational Progress began in 1971. Performance is
somewhat better on math, but there has still been no progress since
1990. The long-term stagnation cannot be attributed to racial or ethnic
differences in the U.S. population. Literacy scores for white students
peaked in 1975; in math, scores peaked in the early 1990s."[43] The weak
performance of United States students on measures of literacy and
numeracy compared to those in many other countries is especially
troubling because on a per student basis the United States spends more
for education than almost any other country.[44]

Moreover, today the public education system is expected to meet a
growing range of social needs stemming from conditions outside
schools over which educators have little or no control. Meeting these
needs effectively requires very large amounts of financial and technical
resources because they are inherently resource-intensive problems.
For example, public schools now feed impoverished children. In fiscal
year 2018, about thirty percent of all students enrolled in public
education—fifteen million children—received free or low-cost school
breakfasts. More than half of all students—thirty million children—

received free or low-cost school lunches. These programs cost roughly $18 billion annually.[45]

Schools also are increasingly expected to meet specialized education needs, but their financial resources for doing so lag far behind the levels actually needed to meet those needs effectively. Public schools educate millions of children of families from numerous non-English speaking countries of origin, as well as millions of students in special education programs. Recently, nearly 10 percent of all public school students nationwide were English Language Learners (ELLs), and in some states the percentage is considerably higher.[4647] The schools' great difficulties in effectively addressing this situation are apparent from the fact that as of 2017, only about 65 percent of ELL students graduated from high school, in contrast to 82 percent of remaining students nationwide.

Schools are being overwhelmed by growing demand for ELL services. In the past fifteen years, the percentage of public school children who are English language learners (ELLs) has increased by nearly 20 percent. About five million schoolchildren each year are now ELLs.[48] Yet within the past few years, 32 states reported shortages of ELL-qualified teachers. Clearly, many schools are not presently capable of meeting the educational needs of many ELL students. To do so effectively would require billions of dollars of additional funding that they do not have.[49]

A similarly large gap between demand for specialized services and schools' resources exists in the case of special education programs. As of 2015-16, roughly 6 million children were in special education programs, about the same number as in 2005. But the number of special education teachers declined by about 17 percent between 2005 and 2012.[50] At the same time, costs for such programs have been increasing. In the 2005-2006 academic year, California schools alone reported special education expenditures of roughly $8.5 billion. By 2015-16 that had grown to about $13.2 billion—a 55 percent increase.[51]

Nor is funding provided by higher levels of government adequate to cover special education costs. As of 2013-14, federal and state governments provided an additional $30 billion in revenues to fund special education, or about $4,700 per student.[52] However, some estimates suggest that the cost of educating special education students is actually more than double the cost of educating other students. If so, federal and state funding levels would be many billions of dollars lower than needed to cover schools' actual added costs.

The increasingly diverse school population's needs are placing extraordinary strains on public school systems' resources. But the education system's financial resources are sharply constrained by the nation's historic commitment to localism in education and funding mechanisms that have significant limitations, particularly the property tax. Property taxes cannot meet schools' needs due to powerful political pressures to restrain their levels. Widespread public resistance to property tax increases should not surprise us, because such taxes are regressive annual wealth taxes that bear particularly heavily on the elderly and middle-class families with stagnant incomes. The use of property taxes as a primary school revenue source also creates large inequities within and between states in levels of education funding.

Current education policies have created a greatly overburdened education system that is trying to do progressively more with stagnant or even reduced resources. Yet even in the face of steadily increased social demands, inefficiency, and egregious competitive failure by the public education system, the United States continues to treat education as largely the province of local leaders. But because government has been unable to find ways to shore up public education in the face of major social and economic changes, state and local public officials have increasingly been willing to allow families to abandon the traditional public system.

More than ten million children—at least 15 percent, and perhaps as much as 20 percent, of the entire elementary and secondary school-aged population—are now being educated outside the traditional public education system. An estimated three million children were enrolled in charter schools in the 2017-2018 school year.[53] Governments have also permitted the abandonment of the public education system by millions of American parents who believe that they can provide a better education by home-schooling their children. According to the National Center for Education Statistics, an estimated 1.6 million children were homeschooled as of 2016.[54] Finally, another 5.9 million children attend private schools.

The obvious desire of many middle-class parents to abandon the public education system is ample testimony to its failure to cope with the strains it is experiencing. As prominent expert Nick Hanauer recently wrote, public education is really only successful in certain areas of the country where there is added social capital available to support it. He wrote:

> ...The nation still has many high-achieving public-school districts. Nearly all of them are united by a thriving community of economically secure middle-class families with sufficient political power to demand great schools, the time and resources to participate in those schools, and the tax money to amply fund them. In short, great public schools are the product of a thriving middle class, not the other way around. Pay people enough to afford dignified middle-class lives, and high-quality public schools will follow. But allow economic inequality to grow, and educational inequality will inevitably grow with it.[55]

America's declining middle class increasingly cannot provide the social capital needed to support public education; nor can local governments fill that gap. As a result, many middle-class children are now being offered an education that cannot fulfill the strong national interest in preparing them for the realities of global competition and the lives they will experience. Many will fail to attain a middle-class quality of life, and will instead experience decreased social mobility and a lower standard of living, as a result of the school system's failures. And the public education system suffers from still another important obstacle to its success stemming from America's continued racial and rising income segregation.

RACIAL AND INCOME SEGREGATION

Members of Congress, another important measure of America's social cohesion is the degree of our racial and wealth integration. But more than fifty years after the civil rights revolution began, the United States is still a highly racially segregated society, and income segregation has actually increased over the past several decades. Americans today often live in different social worlds that have little contact with each other. Based on 2010 Census data, a Brown University study found that although most urban whites now live in less segregated neighborhoods than in 1980, their neighborhoods were still highly segregated when compared to minority neighborhoods. It reported that:

> Stark contrasts are readily apparent between the typical experiences of whites versus that of each minority group….[T]he typical white lives in a neighborhood that is 75% white, 8% black, 11% Hispanic, and 5% Asian. This represents a notable change since 1980, when the average whites' neighborhood was 88% white, but…the experience of minorities is very different. For example, the typical black lives in a neighborhood that is 45% black, 35% white, 15% Hispanic, and 4% Asian. The typical Hispanic lives in a neighborhood that is 46% Hispanic, 35% white, 11% black and 7% Asian….[56]

In 2014, writer Ta-Nehisi Coates described one highly segregated urban neighborhood, North Lawndale in Chicago. It was 92 percent Black, compared to a citywide average of about 30 percent. Its infant mortality rate was twice the national average. Forty-three percent of North Lawndale residents lived below the poverty line, twice the Chicago average. Nearly three times as many residents received food stamps as in the rest of Chicago. Coates added that a different Black Chicago neighborhood with one of the highest incarceration rates had a rate more than 40 times as high as the white neighborhood with the highest rate. He concluded: "North Lawndale is an extreme portrait of the trends that ail black Chicago. Such is the magnitude of these ailments that it can be said that blacks and whites do not inhabit the same city."[57]

In 2019, North Lawndale had a per capita rate of violent crime almost 50 times higher than one of Chicago's safest neighborhoods, Forest Glen.[58] The neighborhood experienced more than 280 shootings and more than 30 homicides in 2016 alone.[59] If these statistics seem too abstract, there is a good way to begin to understand the wrenching pain and damaged lives they often represent: watch director Spike Lee's movie, *Chi-Raq*. It shows in realistic, gripping detail that living in a highly segregated urban area like the south side of Chicago is very much like involuntarily spending life in a war zone from which there is no escape. Lee's depiction is confirmed by nonfiction accounts. A 15 year-old North Lawndale teenager profiled in 2017 by Dahleen Glanton of the Chicago *Tribune* insisted that he carried a gun "only for protection." He told Glanton: "'You've got to protect yourself because you never know if someone is going to be shooting at you or hit you with a car or something.'" He added: "'Sometimes people just think you have money, and it can cost you your life.'" In a 15-month period, there were 23 shootings and three homicides in the six-block area where the teenager lived.

Glanton reported: "Clifford Nellis, executive director of the Lawndale Christian Legal Center, estimates that more than 90 percent of the young people his agency comes in contact with are carrying guns for self-defense. 'These kids have a real risk of being shot, and they tend to have guns because that's the reality they live in,' said Nellis."[60] Data on Chicago shooting locations vividly illustrates the pervasive gun violence in highly segregated poor neighborhoods like North Lawndale that utterly destroys lives, including those of innocent children.[61] These are intolerable conditions in which no American should have to live, and in which hope for the future often dies out. They make a mockery of the idea that Americans live in an equal opportunity society.

More than sixty years after the Supreme Court's decision in *Brown v. Board of Education* declaring segregated schools unconstitutional, many public schools are still racially segregated as well. For example, in New York City in 2010, a report showed that in nineteen out of thirty-two school districts, 10 percent or less of the students were white. Based on that report, one study concluded that "the majority of Caucasian parents had opted out of the system altogether."[62]

According to another study by the UCLA Civil Rights Project, school segregation nationwide has actually increased over the past thirty years. It found that "by 2016, 18.2% of public schools were between 90-100% nonwhite, compared to 5.7 % of schools in 1988, the year the U.S. reached peak school integration levels."[63] Alana Semuels of *Time* recently reported that "in the Twin Cities [Minneapolis-St. Paul], the number of schools in which more than 90% of students are people of color increased from 21 in 1998 to 102 in 2018."[64]

Semuels concludes that segregation has especially affected Black Americans. Some scholars believe that pervasive housing and school segregation have significantly contributed to the lack of Black economic mobility. Myron Orfield, a Minnesota law professor who has studied increased segregation in the Twin Cities, told Semuels: "If you live in a segregated neighborhood, every single bad thing in the world happens to you: you don't get a loan for housing, and the schools lead to jail. If you go to an integrated neighborhood, none of these things happen."[65]

Very large racial wealth gaps have also persisted over decades. There are continuing large differences between the median wealth of middle-income white families and that of middle-income Hispanic and Black families, which increased after the 2007 recession. The gaps between white families and Black families are particularly large and persistent. According to a 2020 *Washington Post* analysis of Black families' income and wealth:

> In 1968, a typical middle-class black household had $6,674 in wealth compared with $70,786 for the typical middle-class white household...In 2016, the typical middle-class black household had $13,024 in wealth versus $149,703 for the median white household, an even larger gap in percentage terms. 'The historical data reveal that no progress has been made in reducing income and wealth inequalities between black and white households over the past 70 years,' wrote economists Moritz Kuhn, Moritz Schularick and Ulrike I. Steins in their analysis of U.S. incomes and wealth since World War II.[66]

These data suggest that the United States has made comparatively little progress in achieving racial equity over the past fifty years. This conclusion is reinforced by the fact that a far higher percentage of whites own homes than Black families do; this gap has remained essentially the same over the past twenty-five years.[67] Ta-Nehisi Coates wrote that in 2014 more than a third of Blacks had zero or negative wealth, while only 15 percent of whites did. This meant, he said, that "effectively, the black family in America is working without a safety net. When financial calamity strikes—a medical emergency, divorce, job loss—the fall is precipitous." Coates noted that Black families also "remain handicapped by their restricted choice of neighborhood." And these income and wealth statistics do not take into account the debilitating social and economic results of mass incarceration that disproportionately affect millions of Black Americans, or their voting disenfranchisement in many jurisdictions even after they serve full sentences for offenses.[68]

Moreover, studies show that neighborhood income segregation grew considerably between 1970 and 2009. Much of that growth was due to the increasing segregation of the rich from all other families.[69] Members of the wealthy oligarchy are becoming steadily more unequal to other citizens, not just in wealth and income but in their increasingly limited participation in common social life, including its burdens and responsibilities. The wealthy are increasingly using their wealth to insulate themselves from the deteriorating social and economic conditions that are now a daily part of the lives of many middle-class and poor Americans. That includes soul-destroying levels of violence in many major cities, exceptionally poor education, and extremely limited job opportunities. As long as the wealthy are able to insulate themselves, they have little or no incentive to support needed improvements in social conditions for other Americans.

EMERGING TECHNOLOGIES AND DECLINING SOCIAL COHESION

Today America's overall social cohesion appears to be declining in other important respects as well. In recent years, largely unregulated technology companies such as Facebook have become the foundations of enormous wealth and influence.[70] Although these technologies are increasingly becoming an essential part of everyday life, consumers often lack adequate protection against the anticompetitive behavior of the companies that control them, and their technologies are frequently unavailable to poor and rural Americans at reasonable cost. Moreover, we have learned that pervasive technologies the companies tightly control such as social media can actually become major sources of political manipulation and disinformation, and can inflame and worsen social divisions rather than improving the abysmal quality of political dialogue. They also create the potential for both enormous privacy violations through omnipresent surveillance and for the imposition of censorship that will protect and aid the powerful. In any event, social media and other digital technologies cannot adequately substitute for common social institutions that have historically strengthened democracy such as public education; nor can they begin to replace the shared social experience of real-world integrated communities. Declining social cohesion harms all of us and threatens republican government.

Moreover, at the same time that supportive social institutions are decaying, both the poor and the middle class face other serious threats: the destruction of their retirement security and sharply climbing tax burdens.

OUR RETIREMENT SYSTEM IS FAILING

Members of Congress, a central feature of the New Deal social contract was the promise of a secure, decent retirement after a lifetime of work. But retirement is increasingly a time of constant economic insecurity or even an impossible dream for many people. Despite requiring workers to pay taxes for decades, the Social Security and Medicare systems today fail to provide average workers with a retirement that includes basic life necessities and a decent degree of comfort. And these systems themselves are now in serious danger of financial collapse. Yet over the past several decades, corporate policies acquiesced in by American leaders have destroyed an important part of the retirement resources for workers.

In 2019, the average Social Security payment was slightly less than $1,500/month. Average single workers receive income from Social Security about 40 percent (or $400/month) above the current federal poverty level.[71] An estimated 44 percent of single seniors, and 21 percent of married couples, currently rely on Social Security for more than 90 percent of their retirement income.[72] In many cases, workers receiving average Social Security payments will be impoverished if not bankrupted even by recurrent ordinary medical expenses, because Medicare does not adequately protect them.

A recent Stanford Center on Longevity report found that "in 2013, average out-of-pocket health care spending by Medicare beneficiaries was 41 percent of average per capita Social Security income."[73] As a result, millions of retirees who rely on Social Security and Medicare alone and have no significant assets will almost certainly be forced to live at or below poverty level if they experience any major health expenses. As if this were not bad enough, the Social Security Trust Fund and main Medicare Trust Fund (Hospital Insurance) are now projected to run out of funds to pay even these limited benefits in fifteen years (Social Security) or six years or less (Medicare).[74] If Congress cuts program benefits as a result, many more elderly Americans would be forced to live in poverty even though they are nominally covered by both Social Security and Medicare.

Because Social Security provides limited benefits to most workers, employer pensions have historically been crucial to their ability to live decently during retirement, particularly in higher-cost living areas such as major cities. But even while middle-class wage levels have stagnated, American workers have become far less likely to receive substantial, reliable pensions from employers. Only about half of workers even have access to a work-based retirement plan of any kind.[75] Far less well-known is that even workers who receive retirement benefits now often receive pensions that are far less generous than those similarly situated workers received only a generation ago.

Historically, many employers provided workers with "defined benefit" pensions. Workers were usually paid a specified percentage of their salary (based on length of service) for life during retirement. Many fewer workers today receive such pensions. As of 2010, only 18 percent of workers (about 30 percent of households) had defined benefit plans. Today, such protective plans are often available only to government employees and unionized private-sector workers. As one study showed, "...Pension coverage is much higher [than average] in the public sector (78 percent) and among unionized workers (67 percent) in the private sector. In contrast, only 13 percent of non-union private-sector workers are covered."[76]

Thanks to Congress' acquiescence, most employers now instead provide only "defined contribution" retirement plans. Most of the contributions made to such plans and the performance of the retirement funds in which they are invested are normally workers' full responsibility. Employees who are unable to afford to save, make poor investment choices, or encounter a stock market downturn or collapse will end up with little or no retirement income beyond Social Security. The lion's share of the financial risk and burden of paying for retirement has been shifted to workers. The earlier American pension system has largely been destroyed at the behest of companies who wanted to escape paying its costs. Such companies are often controlled by wealthy stockholders who have no need for any retirement income system and are therefore largely indifferent to the current system's failure to protect many workers.

Many workers have been unable to replace disappearing employer pensions with their own retirement funding. In 2018, the Stanford Center on Longevity found that all groups of workers, but younger workers especially, were saving inadequate amounts to replace even 70% of their working income levels after retirement. And nearly one-third of the baby boom generation (average age, 58) have no retirement savings at all, and will be forced to rely on Social Security alone.[77] The report concluded that "...the vast majority of American workers of any age will be unable to replicate and maintain their standard of living if they retire fully from working at age 65. This may be a crisis for those households that are unprepared for a significant drop in family income or aren't prepared to work beyond age 65."[78]

As can be seen, our entire retirement system is now in imminent danger of collapse, but little or nothing is being done by Congress to rebuild and improve either Social Security or Medicare to protect retirees, let alone younger generations. When Congress is forced to act on this problem, it will very probably further damage poor and middle-class workers by increasing workers' payroll taxes or extending retirement ages. Moreover, there is good reason to think that the middle class will shortly face other new federal tax burdens as well.

THE MIDDLE CLASS FACES HEAVIER TAXES

Members of Congress, I predict that middle tax burdens will almost certainly increase significantly within about a decade unless government policies change. In 2019, Congress debated whether to permit total national debt to rise above $22 trillion. In 2020, Congress has agreed to deficit-spend more than $3 trillion for coronavirus stimulus relief. The national debt has grown over the past thirty years—and especially over the past twenty years—as the government has run a deficit during most years in that period. In essence, the United States has lacked the political will to match its tax collections to citizens' desires to benefit from spending. Though economists disagree about whether either deficits or the national debt should concern us, that is a debate for another day. Instead, what concerns me here tonight is that continued deficit-financing of government will hurt the middle class most, by eventually requiring its members to pay higher taxes just at the time when they can least afford it. Here is the background for my conclusion.

In early 2019, the nonpartisan Congressional Budget Office (CBO) projected that by 2029 very large additional increases in federal debt would result from current national spending and tax policies. The amount of federal debt held by the public (only part of the total) will nearly double, to about $26 trillion. Even disguised in the staid language of bureaucratic reports, CBO's discussion conveyed its alarm. It said that as a result: "The likelihood of a fiscal crisis in the United States would increase. Specifically, the risk would rise of investors' being unwilling to finance the government's borrowing unless they were compensated with very high interest rates...Interest rates on federal debt would rise suddenly and sharply...." CBO concluded, in other words, that by the end of this decade the United States could hit a major financial wall with devastating consequences.

In CBO's view, increased debt is likely to require annual United States net interest payments to increase dramatically. By 2029, it expects that interest payments on the national debt will more than double, reaching a level of $928 billion/year. (By way of comparison, that is about the same amount that the federal government now collects from *all* payroll taxes paid under the Social Security system).[79] Under current policies, the middle class will be expected to pay a large share of these costs through substantially increased taxes.

THE BURDEN OF INCREASED TAXES WILL NOT BE SHARED FAIRLY BY THE WEALTHY

Some people may believe that the burden of these higher taxes will be shared fairly by everyone through our supposedly "progressive" income tax system. But in reality, the existing federal and state tax system is nowhere near as progressive as is often claimed, for two reasons. First, our overall tax system is much less progressive than the federal income tax. Most observers think that federal income taxes have some degree of progressivity, despite recent claims that that is inaccurate.[80] But the total tax burden Americans face is actually a combination of large regressive state and local taxes and federal payroll taxes, which hit the lower and middle classes hardest, together with federal income taxes. Examples of regressive taxes that are major sources of government revenue include sales taxes and property taxes. Property taxes have very aptly been described as "America's regressive middle-class wealth tax," since much of middle-class wealth consists of the value of people's homes.[81]

Institute on Taxation and Economic Policy ("ITEP") data illustrate the overall burden of taxes and income. They show that state and local taxes are regressive, requiring lower income and middle-income taxpayers to pay a higher percentage of their income than higher income taxpayers pay. For example, in 2019 taxpayers in the lowest 20% income bracket paid an average of 12.7% in state and local taxes, while taxpayers in the top 1% paid less than 10%. The result is that the overall tax system is less progressive than the federal system is commonly thought to be, and its progressivity was decreased by 2018 tax law changes.[82]

But even more importantly, because the federal tax system is heavily based on taxing income, it allows enormous amounts of property owned by the wealthy either to escape taxation for very long periods or forever, or to have it taxed at lower rates than wage income. For example, in 2010, Warren Buffett, Chairman of Berkshire

Hathaway, Inc., reported taxable income of less than 1 percent of the $7 billion increase in the value of his stock that year. But he paid no taxes on the $7 billion capital gain, because it was an "unrealized" gain. A recent study estimates that such unrealized capital gains—which are not taxed at all under current law—make up 34 percent of the assets of the wealthiest 1 percent of households, which held $6.6 million in unrealized capital gains apiece, on average, in 2013. The comparable figures for households in the bottom 90 percent are just 6.1 percent of assets and $9,000 in unrealized gains, respectively.[83]

In short, the wealthy do not pay income taxes on a large fraction of their assets. In contrast, middle class homeowners must pay property taxes on their major source of wealth— the entire unrealized capital gain in their homes—every year. Claims often made about the supposed progressivity of our national tax system are therefore incomplete at best, and at worst highly misleading.

Middle-class taxpayers already pay 23% or more of their annual income in total taxes. Requiring them to pay higher taxes to finance increased federal debt costs will add a significant additional economic burden. Using CBO's estimates, middle-class taxpayers would be forced to bear a $150 billion—or 30 percent—a year increase in their federal income tax burden.[84] These added taxes will further damage the middle class, and that will happen just at the wrong time, when the middle class will also be asked to pay new taxes to shore up the failing retirement system.

The retirement system's impending failure will lead to demands for some combination of cuts in benefits, later retirement ages, or increased payroll taxes. If middle-class taxpayers are required to pay increased payroll taxes, the increased debt and retirement-related taxes would together amount to a major increase in overall middle-class tax burdens. The middle class's shrinking share of wealth and income will be reduced further, hastening its economic collapse.[85] Institutions such as public education will also unquestionably be harmed as a result.

The collapse of the middle class will more heavily stratify society into two main classes: the wealthy oligarchy and the growing ranks of the poor. That will inevitably end our republic. It will be replaced by authoritarian rule if the country survives.

CONCLUSION

Members of Congress, I leave you with these closing thoughts, which I very much hope you will take to heart. Our democracy is in danger because we are now being governed by a wealthy oligarchy and the middle class is headed toward collapse as a result. Based on existing and readily foreseeable changes in social and economic conditions, we can expect a very dismal future for many members of the middle class and their children as they struggle to maintain a middle-class standard of living and quality of life. Middle-class incomes are stagnant; its members' share of national wealth is declining; and the institutions that support it such as public education and retirement security are overwhelmed or in some cases wholly inadequate. As the middle class collapses, the futures of the poor and minorities, especially Blacks, will inevitably worsen as well. Because the middle class is the political heart of democracy, its collapse will ultimately destroy democracy itself.

Neither major political party today has anything resembling a realistic set of proposals to avoid these disastrous outcomes. Our nation's republican future is bleak unless we act decisively to reform government itself. Thank you for your kind attention, and good night."

****

Dear reader: I hope that the president's State of the Union address has given you a clear sense of the political crisis we face. It will not be solvable through "politics as usual." As chapters 2 through 4 show, that is because the Constitution and Supreme Court interpretations of it are important sources of that crisis.

2

The Constitution Unfairly Protects America's Wealthy Oligarchy

Today a wealthy oligarchy possesses an excessive share of national wealth and power, which threatens to destroy our representative democracy. Both the Constitution's structure and the Supreme Court's interpretations of it play important roles in unfairly protecting that oligarchy. The Constitution gives a significant political advantage to opponents of economic fairness by artificially increasing the power of small states predominantly represented by Republicans. Supreme Court decisions constitutionally barring government regulation of political spending by the wealthy have greatly strengthened their influence. And there is a distinct likelihood that the Court will decide that the Constitution prevents Congress from limiting America's largest fortunes through various tax measures that would increase economic fairness.

Debates over whether the federal government should use its authority to control concentrated wealth and power and to seek economic fairness for its citizens are not new ones for Americans. In our recent history, the Constitution played an important role in such debates from the last part of the nineteenth century onward, and was again centrally important in similar controversies during the New Deal. It is still directly involved today in disputes over issues such as national healthcare, which is ultimately a very large-scale conflict over economic fairness.

During such controversies, the Constitution has often been a powerful barrier to reforms that many citizens strongly believed would increase economic fairness. For example, the Supreme Court decided in 1895 that the Constitution prohibited Congress from enacting a progressive income tax.[86] Americans then fought vigorously for nearly twenty years over whether Congress should have that power, whose main purpose was to make the tax system fairer by making the wealthy bear more of the costs of community.[87] Finally in 1913, the Sixteenth Amendment authorized progressive income taxation. As New Deal policies recognized, progressive taxes also limited excessive wealth concentration and could redistribute resources to needier citizens. It is less well known, however, that acute concerns over economic fairness also existed in America's earlier history. Government's ability to prevent oligarchy and to promote economic fairness were important public concerns in the 1780s and during the drafting of the Constitution.[88]

THE FOUNDERS, WEALTH, AND THE CONSTITUTION

The 1787 Constitution was designed to protect unequal wealth-holding, not to level the rich and the poor. For example, Founders such as Alexander Hamilton praised institutions such as the federal judiciary in part because they thought they would serve as bulwarks against popular attempts to adopt "unjust and partial laws" that were "serious oppressions of the minor party in the community" ("minor party" often then referred to the wealthy).[89]

But Hamilton himself clearly recognized that a wealthy oligarchy would also inevitably be equally oppressive. As he told the Philadelphia Convention, "Give all power to the many, they will oppress the few. Give all power to the few, they will oppress the many. Both therefore ought to have power that each may defend itself agst. the other."[90] Hamilton was not alone. A distinguished historian concluded that "the Fathers were especially fearful that the poor would plunder the rich, but most of them would probably have admitted that the rich, unrestrained, would also plunder the poor." As Gouverneur Morris told the Convention, "Wealth tends to corrupt the mind and to nourish its love of power, and to stimulate it to oppression. History proves this to be the spirit of the opulent."[91] In part to prevent such conflicts, Hamilton and other Founders sought to promote a dynamic, expanding society that provided maximum economic opportunity consistent with the protection of legitimate wealth. For similar reasons, many of them were strongly opposed to large hereditary wealth accumulation and its corrupting influence on republican government.

Leading American revolutionaries such as Thomas Jefferson and John Adams were adamantly opposed to the idea that a hereditary aristocracy like the British aristocracy would ever be permitted to exist in America. Great Britain's aristocracy combined massive inherited private wealth with its complete control of government through its dominance in Parliament. For centuries, Great Britain had been governed primarily to increase aristocratic power and wealth. Many Founders were familiar with the economic thought of Adam Smith, who had strongly challenged the British aristocracy's self-interested governance. Smith had argued in his classic 1776 work *The Wealth of Nations* that the British aristocracy's imperialist, anti-competitive policies enriched them, but did so by sacrificing the economic interests of average Britons.[92]

American leaders also saw any hereditary aristocracy as a prime source of political corruption that would inevitably destroy republican government by encouraging luxury and other vices and preventing government based on merit. The Founders therefore strenuously sought to avoid the possibility that a new aristocracy like the British aristocracy would be created in the United States. As a highly visible symbol of their deep concern, the Constitution expressly provides that "No Title of Nobility shall be granted by the United States." But they saw the potential for creation of a dangerous new aristocracy as far broader than that. After the Revolutionary War, astute leaders were well aware that proposed new American central government institutions such as a standing army or a national bank could be manipulated not only to protect but to create private wealth, just as had happened in Britain.

Many leading Founders such as Elbridge Gerry therefore viewed any union of private wealth and government power as a fount of corruption that would inevitably lead to the creation of an American aristocracy, destroying republicanism. They strenuously sought to keep them separate in making government policy after the Revolution and in drafting the Constitution.[93] They would have seen today's growing oligarchy of the wealthy as a threatening new aristocracy that should be repressed by federal government power. Ironically, however, the Constitution they wrote now protects that oligarchy against control by the popular will in fundamental ways. Here is a description of the Constitution's original wealth protections, followed by an examination of how and why they protect oligarchy in the United States today.

The 1787 Constitution (and the Bill of Rights) protected the existing distribution of wealth in America using both legal and political means. The Constitution contained various legal protections for private property. For example, its "Contracts Clause" protected creditors against widespread efforts during hard times in the 1780s by debtors to reduce or escape their debts.[94]

But many Founders did not think that the Constitution's legal wealth protections were strong enough, especially to protect unpopular (or unevenly distributed) kinds of wealth such as slave holdings. Major constitutional political protections were therefore created, often reflecting fears that one group (or region) of the country might unfairly use federal powers to deprive another region or group of its property.

THE CONSTITUTION'S POLITICAL WEALTH PROTECTIONS

Of particular importance, the Constitution contained a stringent political limitation on federal taxation powers, prohibiting certain taxes referred to as "Capitation, or other direct" taxes unless they were imposed by apportionment among the states "in Proportion to the Census." This "direct tax" apportionment requirement was the basis on which the Supreme Court invalidated the progressive income tax in 1895, as mentioned earlier. That provision is still the source of controversy about the extent of Congress' wealth taxation powers today, as we will see later.

The Constitution's structure also created other substantial political wealth protections. It protected wealth indirectly by preserving or formalizing major aspects of the pre-existing distribution of political power. That substantially limited the federal government's practical ability to alter the distribution of wealth even where it would otherwise have been constitutionally permissible. The following paragraphs describe these additional constitutional wealth protections.

Under America's first Constitution—the Articles of Confederation—each of the original thirteen states had one equal vote in a government run by a one-house Congress (there was no separate executive or judiciary). Equal state voting was required despite the fact that it was well understood that some states were far larger and wealthier than others. Some major Founders had never accepted the idea that the states should be equals. When the Articles were first debated, for example, John Adams of Massachusetts told the Continental Congress that "the individuality of a colony is a mere sound," i.e., a nonsensical idea.[95] Adams argued that it was profoundly misguided and dangerous politically to treat states as equals as long as they were greatly unequal in wealth and population.[96]

By the time of the 1787 Philadelphia Convention, a number of leading delegates either publicly or privately shared Adams's views, particularly about state equality.[97] Many delegates saw the states as too powerful. Influential delegates such as James Madison believed that various states had seriously abused their powers. The delegates concluded nearly unanimously that the United States could never have a workable national government as long as states reserved to themselves powers such as taxation critically needed by the Union. But to reach agreement on the decision-making structure of a new government with such broad authority, it was first necessary to redistribute political power.[98]

The Constitution therefore had as its indispensable foundation a significant redistribution of political power between the states. It based states' relative voting strengths in the House of Representatives and the Electoral College heavily on their populations. (In the era's predominantly agricultural economy, states' populations correlated very strongly to their wealth). Many of the most important new federal powers granted by the Constitution including taxation could be exercised by majority vote, not by a supermajority as the Articles had required. Unfortunately, at the 1787 Philadelphia Convention, obtaining essential federal powers became politically possible only after very substantial concessions were made to protect powerful vested economic and political interests.

The 1787 Constitution therefore did not create a fully level playing field for conducting representative government. Instead, necessity forced two major compromises. The Convention gave two Senate votes to each state, thus giving greatly disproportionate power to small states. The Senate's structure disregarded entirely the great disparities in states' population and wealth. (At the time, for example, Virginia's free population was roughly nine times the size of Delaware's). That meant that the six smallest of the original thirteen states, which at the time together had about 20 percent of the total free population, received 46 percent of the total Senate votes.

In a second major compromise, the Philadelphia Convention agreed to give the five major slave states exaggerated political power through the "Three-Fifths Clause." That provision artificially increased the slave states' populations in allocating House of Representatives seats and Electoral College voting strength. As of 1820, slave states received a premium of about eighteen seats in the House, or 8 percent of its total seats, due to the Three-Fifths Clause.[99] That premium substantially influenced national policies in their favor by protecting both their agricultural export economies and their persistent efforts to expand slavery westward. This constitutionally-created sectional political advantage was eliminated when the Fourteenth Amendment to the Constitution was adopted "only at the point of a gun" as a direct result of Northern victory in the Civil War.[100]

THE CONSTITUTION'S SMALL STATE BIAS PREDOMINANTLY AIDS REPUBLICANS, PROTECTING WEALTH INEQUALITY

The small states' Senate voting premium still exists, however. But due to socioeconomic changes, its size and impact have actually grown. The twenty-eight smallest states that together have about 20 percent of America's total population now have 56 percent of the total Senate votes. Meanwhile, the ten largest states, which have more than half of the entire population of the United States, have 20 percent of Senate votes. The Senate is now the small states' political bastion. Their Senate voting premium significantly distorts national policies on many critical issues, as does their voting premium in the Electoral College (these distortions are discussed in detail in chapter 4).

Moreover, today the Constitution's small state biases also effectively give a systematic advantage in national elections and governing to the Republican Party and to corporate business interests, both of which are generally opposed to increased economic fairness and to limiting wealth concentration. Over recent decades, the major political parties have each become dominant in different geographic areas of the country. The Democratic party has become dominant in large, urban states; the Republican party has become dominant in much of rural America, including many of the smallest states.

Although many of the Constitution's relevant provisions have not changed since 1787, the nature of American society has changed dramatically since then. Today, more than 80 percent of Americans live in urban areas; in 1787, about 95 percent lived in rural areas. Most small states are today far less urbanized than the national average, while most large states have become heavily urban. The ten largest states are far more heavily urbanized than the ten smallest states (81 percent average vs. 61 percent). Moreover, rural and heavily urban states' socioeconomic conditions have diverged significantly as well. These changes have in turn led to shifts in the geographic dominance of the major parties.

As the noted economist Paul Krugman and others have recently pointed out, today there are systematic differences between the economic performance of various states and regions.[101] Since about 1980, per capita incomes and educational levels in various regions have diverged significantly from each other. That followed about a half-century from 1929 to 1979 in which they had been converging.[102] For example, in 1980, per capita personal income in Mississippi had risen over several decades until it was about 70 percent of that in Massachusetts; now it is about 55 percent. Today some small states cannot even realistically be described as viable economic units (as discussed in chapter 6).

Some parts of America are now much wealthier and more economically diverse than others, and those areas are increasingly represented by Democrats. In 2018, congressional districts represented by Democrats had about fifteen percent higher median household incomes, and about 50 percent higher average Gross Domestic Product, than congressional districts represented by Republicans.[103] Democratic districts are as a whole significantly wealthier than Republican areas.

The markedly increased economic divergence between regions and states has had important political consequences. Krugman concludes that it contributes to partisan divisions. As he puts this, "there are obviously other forces at work, but our toxic political environment is clearly not helped by the fact that one party [Democrats] effectively represents the winners from regional divergence, while the other [Republicans] represents the losers."[104] That conclusion dovetails remarkably well with the findings of political scientists that increasing political polarization over the past several decades has been strongly correlated with the growth of economic inequality. At the same time as economic inequality has increased, Republicans in Congress, many of whom represent more rural and often poorer areas, have frequently become considerably more conservative compared to their party predecessors.[105]

Today, the predominantly Republican representatives of rural areas and small states are much more likely to oppose increasing economic fairness through taxation or expansion of social welfare programs than are representatives of urban areas. Disputes over economic fairness are likely to persist because they are driven by interest. Representatives of rural areas oppose increased economic fairness and limiting wealth concentration not just on ideological grounds, or due to racism, as some argue, but because their constituents often oppose such policies and it is very much in their political interest to follow their voters' views, as the following discussion suggests.

Today, many small states' economies are dominated by federal military installations, global natural resource companies, or equally large agribusinesses. Many small state residents are not independent farmers or small business owners; instead, they are employees of their states' dominant companies or government. They often think that the most important political issue they face is keeping their jobs, since really well-paying jobs are relatively scarce in small states. This means that they are likely to support policies they see as being in the interests of businesses operating in their states, which almost always include opposing increased state and local taxation. For various reasons, many small state voters also believe that on issues involving taxation and government spending their political interests conflict with those of residents of large urban areas.

And in some cases, small and large state interests are unquestionably in conflict. For example, small states do not generally need or want extremely expensive infrastructure developments such as major water and sewer systems or ten of billions of dollars for mass transit. They do not need to support large police forces—New York City has twenty times as many officers as Wichita (almost three times as many officers per capita). Their residents are often opposed to paying increased taxes for massive infrastructure and extensive government services in other states, particularly without any corresponding benefits for themselves. Politicians who represent small rural states are often likely to oppose policies that increase economic fairness because it is in their political interest to mirror their voters' views on such issues.

In addition, the racial and ethnic compositions of large and small states are very different, as are the relative sizes of their immigrant populations. As one analyst pointed out in 2018, "many of the smaller states remain more white and native-born than the nation overall. Wyoming, the smallest state, for instance, ranks 46th in the share of immigrants in its population and 43rd in the share of its under-18 population that is nonwhite."[106] As of 2012, the proportion of non-Hispanic whites in the ten smallest states was roughly one-third higher than the national average. The immigrant populations in states such as California and Texas are an order of magnitude larger than such populations in states such as Montana and North Dakota. The significantly differing geographic and economic circumstances of large and small states have profoundly important political consequences, because their citizens face starkly different challenges in creating and sustaining healthy social and economic communities.

But the two major political parties have not changed their ideologies in ways that can bridge these differences. In reality, on most important issues today they represent different core constituencies. (Though there is some overlap in their constituencies, the degree of overlap has significantly lessened over the past fifty years.) With respect to motivating voters' support and winning elections, the parties' differing constituencies can usefully be divided in the following ways: predominantly urban vs. heavily rural and, most importantly, favoring vs. opposing policies that increase economic fairness.[107] Just as Democrats have difficulty appealing to non-urban voters, Republicans have trouble appealing to urban voters. Neither circumstance should surprise us: these different groups of voters have dramatically different wealth levels and starkly different views about economic fairness.

As wealth has become more concentrated and the middle class has stagnated, America's political parties have become heterogeneous coalitions that exist today primarily to capture various government benefits tailored for their constituents. In the current political environment, where available benefits are limited because growth is scant and the national debt is large, such capture is usually a "zero-sum" game. In such a game, benefits to one party's constituents will be obtained only at the cost of benefits for the other party's constituents. This harsh reality means that struggles over economic fairness and taxation—often framed as arguments about something else—have become sharply partisan.

As they struggle politically over economic fairness, the major parties do not have a level playing field. Today, the Constitution's rules tilt the political playing field in favor of small states and therefore typically in favor of the Republican party.[108] The Constitution's bias favoring small states gives the Republican party a series of advantages: extra votes in the Senate; extra seats in the House (even without counting seats gained through gerrymandering); and a significant chance to win the presidency in close elections despite losing the popular vote. That political slant frequently allows Republicans either to govern or, almost equally importantly, to block change, even when their views are in the minority.

The ultimate reason for the Constitution's systematic favoritism toward Republicans is that the small state political bias created by the Constitution has grown more significant as American society has become far more heavily concentrated in urban areas. As a 2018 article in the *Economist* explained:

...Changes in where Americans live and contradictions in their constitution...have opened gaps between what the voters choose and the representation they get in every arm of the federal government. In recent decades these disparities have consistently favored the Republicans...In the past three House elections, Republicans' share of House seats has been 4-5 percentage points greater than their share of the two-party vote. In 2012 they won a comfortable 54% of the chamber despite receiving fewer votes than their Democratic opponents; in 2014 they converted a 51% two-party-vote share into 55% of the seats.[109]

The same problem of political under-representation due to voter concentration exists in the Senate. The *Economist* analysis found that in 2018: "...Adding together all the votes from the most recent election of each senator, Republicans got only 46% of them, and they hold 51 of the seats. According to research by David Wasserman of the Cook Political Report...even if Democrats won the national vote by six percentage points over a six-year cycle, they would probably still be a minority in both houses [of Congress]."[110]

The primary reason for the disparities between party voting strength and actual representation resulting from elections is that the parties now typically represent geographic areas with sharply different population densities. As of 2018: "...Places where people live close together vote Democratic, places where they live farther apart vote Republican. Today the 13 most densely populated states have 121 Democratic House members and 73 Republican ones; the remainder have 163 Republicans and 72 Democrats."[111]

In the thirteen most densely populated states in 2018, nearly two out of every three members of the House was a Democrat—a very large majority compared to national averages. In the remaining thirty-seven states, including all of the smallest states in the country, more than two out of every three members of the House was a Republican—an even more lopsided majority in the opposite direction. It is not an overstatement to describe the Democratic party in the House today as predominantly an urban coalition party, while the Republican party is predominantly a rural coalition party.

A similarly large partisan disparity exists in the Senate representation for large and small states. As of 2018, according to one analysis, "Republicans now hold 35 Senate seats and Democrats just 25 across the 30 smallest states. Democrats in turn hold 24, and Republicans just 16, Senate seats in the 20 largest states. Put another way, about half of the Democratic senators represent the 20 largest states, while over two-thirds of the Republicans represent the 30 smallest states."[112] In sum, the skewed Senate partisan geography is quite similar to that in the House of Representatives.

The parties' coalitions are now heavily weighted toward representing different geographic areas of the country, these data show. This simple fact has very large political consequences due to the Constitution's structural rules. To choose just one example, the nomination of then-Judge Brett Kavanaugh to the Supreme Court would unquestionably have been defeated if Senate representation were not constitutionally based on two equal votes per state. That conclusion follows directly from the 2018 party breakdown of large and small state representation in the Senate and the fact that the 51-49 Senate vote to confirm Justice Kavanaugh divided almost exclusively along party lines. Small states' disproportionate and heavily Republican Senate voting power was essential to Kavanaugh's confirmation.

The Electoral College system the Constitution mandates for presidential elections (discussed in chapter 4) also confers a large political advantage on small states and their voters. The ten smallest states contain about 3 percent of the total U.S. population, but their voters cast about 6 percent of total electoral votes, or about 4 electoral votes per 1 million residents. The ten largest states hold more than 50 percent of U.S. population, but their voters cast about 45 percent of all electoral votes, or less than one-half as many electoral votes per million residents as the smallest states.[113] This power disparity is a major reason that small states have traditionally resisted any change in the Electoral College system.[114]

Small state voters' Electoral College power also tends to favor Republican candidates in presidential elections. Data developed by political scientist Jonathan Rodden of Stanford University shows that voters in sparsely populated rural areas are very likely to favor

Republican presidential candidates, while voters in denser urban areas are far more likely to favor Democratic presidential candidates.[115]

And in some cases, small states' Electoral College power can be decisive. As is well known, the Electoral College system was responsible for the elections of both George W. Bush in 2000 and Donald Trump in 2016. Both men lost the popular vote, but were elected nevertheless because they received majorities in the Electoral College. Both Bush and Trump won nearly 70 percent of the electoral votes in the twenty-eight smallest states. Those states have only 20 percent of the nation's population, but cast 27 percent of all electoral votes in each of those elections. If Bush had not received his disproportionately high small-state Electoral College margin (i.e., a percentage there much higher than his overall Electoral College percentage), he would have lost the 2000 election. And he would still have lost even if he had indisputably won the Florida popular vote and therefore received all of Florida's electoral votes without having to be awarded them by the Supreme Court, as actually happened in 2000.

The Supreme Court's 5-4 decision in *Bush v. Gore* in 2000 awarding the Florida votes to Bush was technically responsible for his victory.[116] But as this pattern of small state Electoral College voting shows, in the most fundamental sense, those states' heavily Republican voting strength was ultimately responsible for Bush's victory. And there is a different way to appreciate the enormous power conferred on small states by the Constitution in presidential elections. As Justice Stephen Breyer pointed out in his dissent in *Bush v. Gore*, the Constitution and federal law actually required that the 2000 election should have been decided by Congress, not by the Supreme Court, with the two houses deciding how to count the disputed Florida votes.[117]

Yet if the 2000 election had ultimately been held in the House of Representatives, as might well have then occurred, Bush would still have won. His victory would have been due entirely to yet another remarkable small state bias built into the Constitution's rules for contested presidential elections. In such "contingent" elections, each state casts only a single vote.[118] Bush would have won with the votes of twenty-six Republican-controlled states representing less than forty-five percent of the total U.S. population. In fact, if all twenty-eight of today's smallest states had voted for Bush, he would still have been elected President, even if House members from states including eighty percent of the American population had all voted against him. The Constitution's anti-democratic provisions governing such elections were last changed in 1804.

Taken together, the results from recent House of Representatives, Senate, and Presidential elections show that because the Republican party is now a party predominantly representing smaller, often rural states, the Constitution's ingrained favoritism for small states now provides a significant advantage to that party. Since Republican officeholders almost uniformly oppose increased taxation and limiting wealth concentration, electoral advantages for the Republican party conferred by the Constitution are important barriers to economic fairness. This point bears repeating: the Constitution today has a built-in political bias favoring oligarchic wealth because its artificial strengthening of small states now gives systematic political advantages disproportionately to Republican opponents of economic fairness and their allies.

But the Republican political advantage in national elections is by no means the only way in which the Constitution is biased in favor of the holders of concentrated wealth. The Constitution as currently interpreted by the Supreme Court also poses several other major obstacles to limiting oligarchic wealth and power. Next, we will consider the constitutional protection it gives the wealthy for their steadily increasing and powerful interventions in the political process.

SUPREME COURT RULINGS HAVE GREATLY EXPANDED THE INFLUENCE OF THE WEALTHY IN POLITICS

Participation by the wealthy in election financing has increased significantly over the more than forty years since the Supreme Court's 1976 decision in *Buckley v. Valeo*.[119] In that decision, the Supreme Court struck down federal limits on independent election expenditures; on candidates' own campaign expenditures; and ceilings on campaign expenditures, as violations of the First Amendment guarantee of free speech.[120] In *Buckley*, the Court sanctioned unlimited spending by wealthy candidates and unbridled political activism by wealthy individuals to advance their agendas.[121] It could fairly be said that the involvement of several billionaires in the 2016 and 2020 presidential elections as candidates or activists is one of *Buckley*'s inevitable results. But these well-known examples are just the tip of the iceberg of wealth in politics today.

In 1980, contributors in the top .01 percent in household income accounted for 15 percent of the money going into federal campaigns. As of 2012, the top 0.01 percent of households' share of campaign contributions had nearly tripled, growing to more than 40 percent.[122] That year, the two largest individual federal election donors, Sheldon and Miriam Adelson, donated more than $93 million by themselves. The Adelsons are usually large Republican-cause donors. However, wealthy individuals such as Democratic presidential candidates Tom Steyer and Michael Bloomberg who generally support liberal causes also have given very large amounts of money (directly or indirectly) to politicians or become candidates themselves. Other large contributions are made secretly by making them through "dark money" PACs that are organized in order to enable such secret contributions. One "dark money" PAC alone, the Sixteen Thirty Fund, contributed $140 million to liberal causes and (indirectly, at least in theory) Democratic candidates in the 2018 election cycle. The largest single anonymous contribution to that Fund exceeded $50 million.[123]

Wealthy donors expect various benefits from their contributions. They are similar in their intended effects to the millions of dollars in "speaking fees" paid to former presidents and senior cabinet officials from both major parties by companies such as Goldman Sachs that amount to a legal, widespread form of political access- and influence-buying. However, though contributions by the wealthy may advance a variety of sometimes conflicting ideological goals, as a group the rich have one important thing in common: they rarely give money to any politician who favors programs or policies that would require significant limits on concentrated wealth holding or its increased taxation.

A leading campaign finance study concluded that large amounts of campaign contributions go to both parties from the wealthy. It also concluded that contributions to Democrats were an important factor in making it far less likely that even Democratic officeholders would support limiting oligarchic wealth. The study found that:

> While Republicans had a slight advantage in fundraising from the top 0.01 percent during the 1980s, this trend had reversed by the mid-1990s, with Democrats raising more than Republicans from the top 0.01 percent in six out of eight election cycles between 1994 and 2008. Only in the last two election cycles did Republicans regain the advantage in fundraising from the top 0.01 percent. *While it is difficult to gauge the effect of the Democrat's reliance on contributions from the wealthy, it does likely preclude a strong focus on redistributive policies.*[124]

Former Washington Post editor Robert G. Kaiser reached much the same conclusion in his study of Congress. Congress had previously had radical members who wanted to control the "privileges of the rich," he said, but by 2009 "such firebrands were all but extinct." He concluded that "the moderation shown now even by liberal Democrats surely was influenced by the political money game."[125] A former very senior Democratic leader of the House of Representatives told Kaiser that the imperative need to raise campaign contributions "'does affect legislation' by convincing members to avoid angering moneyed interests."[126] Not surprisingly, 75 percent of Americans believe that "campaign contributions buy results in Congress."[127]

Moreover, election contributions by wealthy individuals are only part of the overall story of campaign financing by the wealthy. The Supreme Court has now interpreted the Constitution to significantly expand their ability to contribute both directly and indirectly to election activities. In 2010, the Court decided in *Citizens United, Inc. v. FEC* that federal restrictions on electioneering communications and advocacy by corporations and unions were unconstitutional.[128] In 2014, in *McCutcheon v. FEC*, the Court then struck down as unconstitutional limits on aggregate campaign contributions that had been established by the Federal Election Commission pursuant to federal law.[129]

The federal law challenged in *Citizens United* provided that corporations and unions could not engage in independent political expenditures favoring or opposing the election of identifiable candidates. These restrictions were Congress' effort to keep certain kinds of organized group money with potentially corrupting influence out of politics. (Similar restrictions on corporate and union expenditures also existed under roughly twenty states' laws). But in a 5-4 decision, these federal and state restrictions on independent expenditures were struck down in *Citizens United* as violations of the First Amendment speech rights of both profit and nonprofit corporations and unions.[130] In effect, in *Citizens United* the Court broadened *Buckley v. Valeo*'s holding to include expenditures by (often large) associations of individuals.

The Supreme Court majority in *Citizens United* squarely rejected an "abuse of economic power" rationale for limiting corporate speech. Some earlier Supreme Court decisions had held that corporate speech restrictions could be justified because they would prevent corporations from obtaining "'an unfair advantage in the political marketplace'" by using "'resources amassed in the economic marketplace.'"[131] They had refused to sanction organized interest groups' use of their wealth to influence elections as a form of free speech largely immune from government regulation. The *Citizens United* majority argued, however, that earlier precedents established that First Amendment protections did not depend "on the speaker's 'financial ability to engage in public discussion.'" They insisted that it was also irrelevant under the First Amendment that corporate funds might be used to advocate ideas for which there was little public support.[132]

The *Citizens United* decision has been controversial from the outset. President Barack Obama took the highly unusual step of directly attacking it in his 2010 State of the Union address to Congress.[133] Leaders such as former presidential candidates John Kerry and Senator Bernie Sanders have proposed that the Constitution be amended to reverse the decision. Nearly all, if not all, Democratic U.S. Senators now support a constitutional amendment to reverse it.[134] The political consequences of *Citizens United* and later related decisions such as *McCutcheon* seem clear, no matter which view of the First Amendment one supports here.[135]

The Supreme Court's campaign finance decisions have unquestionably permitted increased influence of wealthy individuals in financing political campaigns, both directly and through their control of corporate expenditures. In fact, as a result politicians are now awash in a flood of political money, much of it contributed by wealthy individuals or corporations they control. In the 2016 election cycle, corporations made a total of $3.4 billion in donations to federal campaigns. By comparison, labor unions contributed $213 million.[136] A recent report by the nonprofit organization Public Citizen shows that about $3 billion has been raised by "Super PACs" since 2010.[137] Super PACs can raise unlimited amounts of money to campaign for or against office-seekers (in theory, without co-ordination with campaigns), but have to disclose their donors' identities and list expenditures.

Since 2014, pro-Republican and pro-Democrat Super PACs have "been roughly on par with one another" in fundraising.[138] The wealthy have played a major role in the growth of Super PACs. Nearly half of all funds contributed by wealthy individuals to Super PACs were donated by twenty-five very wealthy individuals. These twenty-five individuals and their spouses contributed $1.4 billion to these organizations since 2010; that is an average of more than $50 million per household over four federal elections. The top 100 individuals and organizations gave 60 percent of the super PAC money given in 2014.[139]

Also since 2014, thanks to loosened legal restrictions, wealthy individuals have had another option for making very large campaign contributions. They can made through what are nominally joint fundraising efforts on behalf of several campaigns. The joint fundraising device has the effect of evading contribution limits. In 2020, wealthy individuals are now legally able to contribute more than $500,000 per year each to the Trump and Biden presidential reelection campaigns. As the *Washington Post* reported, such arrangements were "made possible through pivotal legal changes in 2014...While a person can give a maximum of $5,600 to Trump's campaign committee, a donor can legally give 103 times more in support of Trump's reelection through the new joint fundraising arrangement." This expanded joint fundraising device has been employed at the presidential level at least since 2016, when donors were legally able to give more than $350,000 per donor to Hillary Clinton's campaign.[140]

As mentioned previously, under current law, wealthy political donors can conceal their identities from public disclosure by donating money to so-called "dark money" nonprofit groups. A September 2018 report estimated that the top fifteen "dark money" groups, typically funded primarily by wealthy individuals and interests whose identity is kept secret, have raised and spent at least $600 million since *Citizens United* was decided. A recent report suggests that amount has risen to nearly $1 billion by early 2020. Both liberal and conservative groups operate dark money funds.[141]

Increased political spending by the wealthy has serious adverse effects that extend well beyond political campaigns. One thoughtful constitutional scholar, Lawrence Lessig, concluded that the powerful influence of money in politics led to the loosened banking regulation that was a primary cause of the 2008 financial crisis. He said: "the way we fund campaigns has rendered certain crucial sectors of the economy sensible-regulation-free zones…Exhibit 1: the financial sector."[142] Another leading study found that "the lifting of restrictions on outside spending led to a substantial increase in independent political advertising, which almost quadrupled (in absolute terms and as a percentage of total spending) between 2008 and 2016." By 2016, outside spending had reached about $1.6 billion, and represented approximately 25 percent of total federal election costs.[143] These statistics vividly illustrate the enormous increase in political activity by the wealthy in less than a decade after *Citizens United*.[144] Decisions about the corporate political spending that is increasingly influencing post-*Citizens United* elections are disproportionately under the control of wealthy corporate managers and major shareholders, not ordinary citizens.

Buckley and its progeny including *Citizens United* were triumphs of legal form over political reality, as the spending and elections data presented above show. The Supreme Court majority's view rests on an abstract principle: that free speech and money are equivalent in determining whether independent campaign expenditures by organized groups and aggregate spending limits can constitutionally be limited. But that view ignores the reality that in the United States today, a small group of extremely wealthy individuals has vastly more money available to spend on politics than the rest of America's citizens. It also disregards the fact that an equally small—and in many cases overlapping—group of people, most of them also wealthy, manage or have large shareholdings in major corporations that also have far more money to spend on politics than the rest of America's citizens or its labor unions.

In *Citizens United*, the Supreme Court drew an arbitrary—and, in any event, legally and politically unenforceable—distinction between direct corporate and union campaign contributions, which may constitutionally be limited, and indirect "independent" campaign activity or support, which cannot be barred. The wealthy are unquestionably the largest beneficiaries of this massive Supreme Court-sanctioned explosion of political finance, and they and their financially-recruited allies in both parties generally oppose limiting wealth concentration.

Because the campaign finance decisions including *Citizens United* are grounded on the Constitution, only a constitutional amendment can reverse them (leaving aside "court packing," discussed in chapter 5). But a constitutional amendment such as one reversing *Citizens United* will not be adopted unless it is part of a complete rewriting of the Constitution, as we'll see in chapter 5. And there is yet another very important bias protecting oligarchic wealth in the Constitution. There is a distinct chance that the Supreme Court's current majority will interpret it to bar Congress' efforts to control excessive wealth through measures such as a wealth tax or taxation of unrealized capital gains.

THE CONSTITUTION IS BIASED AGAINST WEALTH TAXATION

The Constitution granted the federal government broad tax powers. But as mentioned earlier, it contained a fundamental political limitation on those powers: it prohibited "Capitation, or other direct" taxes unless they were imposed by apportionment among the states "in Proportion to the Census."[145] As discussed earlier, this strict limitation appears to have been an effort to protect individual regions—and probably distinctive types of wealth such as slave wealth as well—against efforts by any other region (or several regions in alliance) to use federal tax powers to shift an unfair share of the burden of taxation onto that region or its source of wealth.

As mentioned previously, the constitution's direct tax apportionment requirement led a sharply divided Supreme Court to decide in *Pollock v. Farmers' Loan and Trust Co.* (1895) that the first post-Civil War federal progressive income tax was unconstitutional (unless apportioned).[146] The *Pollock* majority viewed it as a form of direct tax. The Court's ruling effectively limited Congress' tax power to imposing taxes such as import tariffs, which are often regressive because they typically burden lower income taxpayers more heavily than wealthier taxpayers. The ruling defeated the primary purpose of the progressive income tax, which had been created to avoid continued heavy federal government reliance on such regressive taxes. The *Pollock* dissenters complained bitterly that the majority was relying on a novel legal view of the meaning of "direct" taxation that had no precedent in earlier Court decisions. An impassioned Justice Henry Billings Brown wrote bitterly: "The decision involves nothing less than the surrender of the taxing power to the moneyed class."[147]

Pollock gave rise to a lengthy political struggle led by Populists and later by Progressives that centered on claims that regressive existing taxes were unfair to the poor and middle class.[148] As a result of their efforts, the Constitution was amended nearly twenty years later to authorize progressive income taxation by adding the Sixteenth Amendment. However, the Amendment's language did not completely eliminate the Constitution's requirement that direct taxes be laid only based on apportionment, but instead carved out an exception from that requirement with respect to taxes on income.[149] Nevertheless, passage of the Sixteenth Amendment permitted wealth redistribution through progressive income taxation. That might lead some to argue that the Constitution is now, legally at least, neutral on the issue of limiting oligarchic wealth, but that is plainly mistaken.

As discussed in chapter 1, in the United States today middle-class wealth holding is primarily in the form of real property (usually people's homes). Middle-class wealth is nearly always annually subject to state or local property taxes, which are a regressive form of wealth tax. State and local governments collected more than $500 billion in property taxes in 2016. Property taxes were their largest single source of revenue.[150]

Upper-class wealth holding, on the other hand, is heavily concentrated in the form of capital holdings, particularly stocks and bonds (as discussed in chapter 1). The market value of those capital assets is not currently subject to federal lifetime income or wealth taxes of any kind. Only when capital gains in such property are "realized" upon a sale by their owner is such property subject to federal income taxation under current law. But in most years, only a small fraction of capital gains are realized, because the wealthy do not ordinarily need the income from capital asset sales.

During the period 2010-2014, for example, the major American stock markets gained about $12 trillion in value, but only about 20% of those gains—totaling about $2.5 trillion—were apparently realized. On average, less than $80 billion in capital gains taxes were paid each year on those gains, or about one-sixth the total taxes being paid by middle-class property owners on their real estate wealth annually. Hundreds of billions of dollars in unrealized capital gains permanently escape taxation every year even after the stock and bond property owner's death due to their favorable tax treatment.[151]

The lion's share of capital gains that are actually realized accrue to wealthy individuals. In 2018, for example, 69% of all capital gains went to taxpayers in the top 1% income bracket.[152] The average effective tax rate on capital gains during 2010-2014 was about 15%.[153] All in all, under our current tax system, the wealthy can avoid paying income or wealth taxes on a large part of the gains in the value of their capital holdings completely in many cases, and pay relatively small taxes when they do pay them at all.[154] Middle-class property owners have no comparable ability to avoid or minimize wealth taxes on their homes.

Yet Congress might lack the power to do anything to rectify the strikingly unequal taxation of wealth by different classes of taxpayers. The Constitution's restrictions on federal tax powers may protect the nation's wealthiest individuals against new taxation designed to increase economic fairness and limit concentrated oligarchic wealth. Potentially important methods of taxation to increase fairness, such as taxes on unrealized capital gains or wealth taxes, might well be found by the current Supreme Court majority to be unconstitutional direct taxes, unless they were apportioned between the states on the basis of population. But that would create a constitutional catch-22. If Congress were forced to apportion wealth or unrealized capital gains taxes among the states, that would utterly defeat their purpose, which is precisely to levy them only on the wealthy and not on other taxpayers. Just as happened when *Pollock* struck down the income tax, requiring apportionment of wealth taxes or unrealized capital gains taxes would as a practical matter prevent Congress from imposing them in the first place, because it could not impose them on only the wealthiest individuals.[155]

THE CONSTITUTION AND THE WARREN WEALTH TAX

For example, Democratic Massachusetts Senator Elizabeth Warren proposed a wealth tax during her 2020 presidential campaign. Under her proposal, the tax would be 2 percent a year on the total wealth of individuals with a net worth of more than $50 million, and 3 percent a year on the total wealth of individuals with a net worth of more than $1 billion. According to the discussion of Senator Warren's proposal on her campaign website, the "richest 130,000 families in America now hold nearly as much wealth as the bottom 117 million families combined."[156] The website gives an heir to a large fortune as an example of the kind of person who would be affected by the wealth tax. That should not surprise us. A minimum of 35 to 45 percent, and by some estimates as much as 55 percent or more, of all wealth in the United States is inherited wealth.[157]

As a result, the Warren wealth tax would actually tax a considerable amount of inherited (as opposed to entrepreneurially-created) wealth. That means that imposing such a tax would be very consistent with the view of many Founders that the United States should not allow large hereditary fortunes to persist and grow. It is not my purpose here, however, to enter into the debate over the merits of Senator Warren's proposal. Instead, my claim is only that the Constitution may well be interpreted to prevent Congress from ever adopting such a tax without apportionment, which would defeat its purpose. In all likelihood, the uncertainty over the proposal's constitutional fate alone would prevent Congress from ever enacting it in the first place. The

Constitution is therefore biased in favor of protecting oligarchic wealth here as well.

Many prominent constitutional law scholars argue that Senator Warren's proposed tax would be constitutional. They claim that for various reasons it is not a "direct" tax of the kind that the Constitution requires to be apportioned among the states.[158] But whether theirs is the better interpretation of the Constitution or not, its acceptance must surmount a very large obstacle: the views of the current Supreme Court. A thoughtful scholar and constitutional historian, Professor Noah Feldman, has written that the constitutionality of the Warren wealth tax proposal presents a "genuinely open question" in light of the current conservative bent of the Supreme Court.[159] Professor Feldman's conclusion that it is very uncertain whether the Court will hold such a tax to be constitutional without apportionment is in all likelihood correct.

Feldman notes that opponents of a wealth tax's constitutionality would be able to cite the opinions and legal writings of leading Founders such as James Madison and Alexander Hamilton in support of their views.[160] Both Madison and Hamilton appear to have thought that the Constitution's bar on laying direct taxes without apportionment would apply to wealth taxes such as the Warren proposal.

Hamilton, the brilliant former Secretary of the Treasury under George Washington, represented the United States in the first Supreme Court direct tax case, commonly called the "Carriage Tax Case."[161] His "brief" in that case shows that he planned to inform the Court that subjecting private wealth to a general assessment (such as a wealth tax) would be a direct tax requiring apportionment.[162] Other leading contemporaries may have agreed with Hamilton.[163] So the views of some Founders and important early Republic leaders could be read to support the contention that the Warren wealth tax would be a direct tax, which must be apportioned among the states to be constitutional. And there is some significant later history that clouds the issue further.

A few years after the adoption of the Sixteenth Amendment in 1913, Justice Oliver Wendell Holmes, Jr. famously claimed that the Sixteenth Amendment was intended to "get rid of nice questions as to what might be direct taxes."[164] But as tax scholar Erik Jensen pointed out, "Holmes provided no evidence or authority in support of that proposition."[165] Jensen argues that there is legislative history from the congressional debate over drafting the Sixteenth Amendment contrary to Holmes' position.

For example, Senator Norris Brown of Nebraska, the original Senate author of the proposed amendment that ultimately became the Sixteenth Amendment, flatly rejected the suggestion by another Senator that Brown should change his amendment to strike the "direct tax" language entirely from the Constitution.[166] For these and other reasons Professor Feldman discusses, it is distinctly possible that a wealth tax might be struck down by the current Supreme Court majority relying on an "originalist" perspective as a "direct tax" that cannot be imposed without apportionment.[167] As has often been the case in recent years, Chief Justice Roberts' views are likely to prevail, since the rest of the current Supreme Court would be likely to divide equally on such an issue. And Chief Justice Roberts' approach on similar issues has tended to be an "originalist" one.[168]

The uncertainty about the outcome of the Supreme Court's ultimate decision on a wealth tax's constitutionality alone might well prove politically fatal to the tax's passage by Congress in the first place. Tax opponents would quite plausibly point out the high probability of enormous political and legal resistance to the implementation of the tax if it were adopted, including years of litigation. Almost inevitably, they would point out, such resistance would include massive political retaliation by extremely wealthy individuals with virtually unlimited financial and legal resources against any member of Congress who had supported a wealth tax. Practical and self-interested political considerations such as these would undoubtedly discourage at least some members of Congress (and realistically, perhaps a significant number) from ever voting for its adoption in the first place.

Even if Congress did adopt a wealth tax, evasion and other forms of resistance to it would be greatly aided by constitutional doubts. The result would be years, perhaps even decades, of litigation that would be ended only by a Supreme Court ruling—or possibly only by a series of Supreme Court rulings. New national policies such as expanded healthcare access whose implementation depended on anticipated wealth tax revenues would be politically stillborn. Major national policy reforms cannot realistically be advocated and developed based on revenues that may never be forthcoming or that may be obtained only a decade in the future.

In sum, the Constitution's biases protecting oligarchic wealth, including small states' disproportionate influence, together with the political influence of the wealthy, might prevent Congress from ever adopting a wealth tax—even one desired by a clear majority of the American people. If Congress did enact a wealth tax, the Supreme Court's decision on the tax's constitutionality would be controlling even if it divided 5-4 against the constitutionality of the tax, as certainly might happen. Only a constitutional amendment could overcome the Court's decision. But as chapter 5 shows, it will not be possible to amend the Constitution to empower Congress to impose a wealth tax unless other parts of the Constitution are rewritten as well.[169] That raises a deeper question about the scope of the Supreme Court's constitutional authority.

Why is it desirable that the Supreme Court be the ultimate arbiter of whether a majority of the American people can authorize their government to adopt policies increasing economic fairness or to bar the excessive influence of wealth in politics, especially when the Court's theoretical authority for doing so is a few brief, ambiguous phrases in a 230-plus year-old document? This is essentially the same type of constitutional issue raised by our current political willingness to concede to the Supreme Court the authority to make a final decision on constitutional grounds about whether Congress could authorize a national health insurance program, the Affordable Care Act (a problem discussed further in chapter 3).

When the Affordable Care Act was adopted, a majority of the public, Congress, and the President supported it. It was similar to social care programs that most other major western democracies have had in place for more than fifty years. Ultimately, it called for increased economic fairness, and it was intended to strengthen America's social safety net. Why should the Constitution enable nine unelected appointees accountable to no one to make such fundamental choices about national policies increasing economic fairness? Who benefits from this constitutional design today other than America's wealthy oligarchs?

CONCLUSION

The Founders strongly desired to prevent the creation of a wealthy new aristocracy that might seize control of American government and destroy republicanism. But as we have seen, the Constitution today is biased against government efforts to increase economic fairness that could limit the power of America's growing wealthy oligarchy. It creates a small-state political advantage that strongly favors (primarily Republican) opponents of increased fairness, tilting the playing field in their favor. Supreme Court decisions such as *Citizens United* reinforce this bias by protecting efforts by the wealthy to expand their influence on campaigns and governance by both parties. The Constitution itself might well be read by the Supreme Court to bar certain forms of wealth limitation and increased fairness such as wealth taxes, including taxes on unrealized capital gains. The Constitution and the Supreme Court's interpretations of it unfairly protect oligarchic wealth. Why should the Supreme Court have the final say on what are ultimately political value choices about major national policies?

3

The Separation of Powers
No Longer Works

At the 1787 Philadelphia Convention, delegate James Wilson argued that governments could fail in one of two ways. He told the convention: "bad governments are of two sorts. 1. that which does too little. 2. that which does too much: that which fails thro' weakness; and that which destroys thro' oppression."[170] The Founders took Wilson's claim to heart. They tried to design a government powerful enough to meet the pressing challenges America faced, but that would also be unable to abuse its powers. The Constitution's separation of powers was an integral part of that plan. It gave relatively independent bases of power to the government's different branches, and divided authority to make and enforce laws among them.

It would have amazed James Wilson to learn that operating under its separation of powers, our government could now be too weak to make urgently needed political reforms and yet could simultaneously abuse its powers. Two centuries later, an imperial presidency now faces a supine, gridlocked Congress and a Supreme Court that has arrogated to itself authority gained only through the political branches' defaults. The Constitution's separation of powers has failed us, and we now have the worst of both worlds.

Some observers might argue that the Constitution's separation of powers was inherently flawed because it rejected a system of parliamentary government, such as that found in Great Britain.[171] Supporters of separated powers, on the other hand, might contend that it is unworkable today because the powers of various institutions have changed in ways that the Founders did not intend or anticipate. In the new constitutional convention this book advocates, the respective merits of parliamentary and separation of powers systems should be reconsidered in the light of several centuries of experience.[172]

However, this chapter has a much more modest goal: to examine the flaws in our existing system and the reasons for them.[173] I ask whether, in light of the Founders' underlying purposes in establishing the separation of powers and today's changed circumstances, it is desirable that major institutions continue to have the powers that they have actually exercised in recent decades. I also consider whether we should be satisfied with the existing relationships between government's different branches.

The Constitution's separation of powers emerged from a complex, multifaceted debate at the Philadelphia Convention.[174] An important part of its discussions concerned efforts to make the government sufficiently energetic, particularly by creating a strong executive. But the separation of powers ultimately agreed upon also balanced the government branches' powers against each other, for two main reasons: (1) protection against tyranny. Separation of powers was intended to divide government's lawmaking and enforcement powers in order to prevent it from becoming overcentralized, or tyrannical; and (2) to prevent aggrandizement of power by any one branch. Separation of powers was intended to prevent any branch from abusing its designated powers by empowering the other branches to check the exercise of their competitors' powers.[175]

As the Philadelphia delegates recognized, we cannot assess how the separation of powers functions in a political vacuum. As James Madison explained, to make the separation of powers work "ambition must be made to counteract ambition. The interest of the man must be connected with the constitutional rights of the place."[176] Whatever powers government branches have on paper, they can remain properly balanced only when leaders of different branches seek equally to uphold the distinctive powers of their institutions. For example, if Congress has broad constitutional powers of investigation, but never uses them or uses them only for partisan advantage, its leaders are not protecting their institution. The institutional competition needed will occur only when the proper incentives exist for each institution's occupants. We need therefore to understand the incentives that motivate those who today control the government's different branches. Following are examples of the questions raised by this approach about the Constitution's separation of powers.

Why is it desirable for a president to have authority to send troops into a distant country such as North Korea, and ask Congress for approval only after they invade? Why should members of Congress be able to serve for an unlimited number of terms, particularly if they are elected from districts or states in which there is no political competition? Why is it desirable for Senators to be eligible to run for president after one six-year term in the Senate (or an even shorter time), if that damages the Senate as an institution? Why should Supreme Court justices be able to serve for more than twenty-five years? Why should the Supreme Court have the power to decide presidential elections, or to decide whether the United States can have a national healthcare insurance system?

THE IMPERIAL PRESIDENCY

The 1787 Convention created an executive considerably more powerful than most other government executives, such as states' governors, then were. The president was given command of United States military forces, and the power to veto legislation unless two-thirds of both houses of Congress overrode his decision. He or she could nominate virtually all major federal officials and judges (subject to Senate confirmation). And she could be removed from office only by a supermajority impeachment vote. The new presidency was far more powerful than many Founders wanted it to be. Some Philadelphia delegates were so concerned about potential abuse of executive power that they wanted the president to be removable by a majority of state legislatures, or to serve at the pleasure of Congress.[177]

The relative powers of the presidency and other branches of government have not shifted over time as a result of the Founders' choices, however; instead they have evolved because of political developments.[178] Franklin Delano Roosevelt was a vastly more powerful president than James Madison. Roosevelt's extraordinarily broad powers were delegated to him by Congress as a result of public fears and perceived necessity during the Great Depression and World War II. But Congress also set limits to Roosevelt's powers when its majority thought that he sought to expand them excessively.

For example, Congress overwhelmingly rejected Roosevelt's 1937 Supreme Court packing plan, despite its arguable constitutionality, supermajority Democratic control of both House and Senate, and Roosevelt's very large 1936 re-election popular vote margin. As that history suggests, understanding the branches' changed relations depends on appreciating how political circumstances have influenced them, not on arguments about the Founders' supposed original intent about their powers.

During much of the country's expansion, presidents who sought increased powers often received popular—and frequently elite—support. Jefferson, Jackson, and Lincoln—three of America's strongest presidents—defied perceived constitutional restraints on their offices to meet what they saw as America's political needs. Their decisions often were popularly ratified (in retrospect, sometimes unfortunately so). In the twentieth century, Woodrow Wilson and later the progressives who served under Franklin Delano Roosevelt sought permanently to strengthen the presidency, especially in the period during and after the New Deal, to advance what they viewed as enlightened modern government. They believed that government should be administered by disinterested experts who would discern and protect the "public interest" against the corrupting influence of "special" interests. They thought that expert administration would best be protected by a strong president who would represent the national interest, not the parochial interests supported by individual .

For a half-century after the New Deal, public opinion supported a strong presidency, especially in national security affairs, and a large expansion of administrative government. Many effects of this post-New Deal conferral of responsibility on the executive branch have been positive. Today, among many other things, it administers an essential system of social welfare, including retirement, health and education funding; regulates public health and air travel safety; and manages massive federal public lands, including magnificent national parks and wildernesses.

But over the past fifty years, even strong presidency advocates have begun to fear that the presidency was becoming imperial. These fears became quite widespread during the presidencies of Lyndon Baines Johnson and Richard M. Nixon, particularly in the seminal work of historian Arthur M. Schlesinger, Jr.[179] Both presidents were attacked for their "imperial" conduct of the war in Vietnam and related military actions such as the secret invasion of Cambodia. Nixon was also discovered to have repeatedly abused the powers of the presidency and to have acted criminally during the Watergate scandal.[180] Though Congress passed a series of laws after Watergate intended to control presidential power, many observers believe those laws have proven ineffectual.[181]

For example, Congress passed the 1973 War Powers Act, which was intended to limit abuse of the president's "Commander in Chief" power, but effectively left to the president broad discretion to use military force in the first instance.[182] Congress failed to strengthen the Act even after a blue-ribbon commission led by former Secretaries of State James Baker and Warren Christopher (who represented both major parties) concluded that it did not work and recommended changes in 2008.[183] Allowing presidents to continue to engage in imperial military adventures—the result of the Constitution's vagueness combined with Congressional weakness—raises important questions about both the viability of the separation of powers and national security.

The Constitution establishes an explicit separation between Congress' power "to declare War" and the president's power as Commander in Chief of the armed forces and militia. The purpose behind this fundamental aspect of the separation of powers is clear. Making war unquestionably places at great risk all the resources of the nation and its people. The Founders intended that before the United States committed itself to engaging in war against another country, Congress must approve that commitment. The Founders did not think that any president—no matter how capable—should be able to unilaterally enter or force the United States into a war. Instead, under the Constitution, war by the United States would be regarded as legitimate only when it was an exercise of majority will made through separately elected congressional representatives.

But in practice, the line between declaring war and making war has not always been clear. Since the early days of the Republic there have been bitter struggles between presidents aggressively pushing the country toward war and Congress. For example, in 1846 President James K. Polk sought a pretext to start a war with Mexico, which he favored. Then-Congressman Abraham Lincoln unsuccessfully opposed Polk's actions as a monarchical abuse of power. However, in the eighteenth and nineteenth centuries, most wars potentially involving the United States had a very slow fuse, since it took months for ships to cross the oceans separating the United States from the rest of the world. And the United States had a remarkably small permanent military compared to today's. If additional troops were required to fight a war of any real size, Congress would have needed to raise them, sharply limiting a president's power to act unilaterally. The president's role as Commander in Chief was accordingly a far smaller part of the office's responsibilities for most of that period, and usually much more directly subject to Congressional intervention and supervision.

Since World War II, however, many observers believe that Congress has largely abdicated its responsibility to prevent unilateral presidential military actions.[184] Instead, presidents have frequently conducted military policy based on claims of constitutional authority or broad, vague delegations of power from Congress that permit them to act with a relatively free hand for a considerable period of time before Congress intervenes. During the summer of 2019, for example, both houses of Congress voted to block United States arms sales to Saudi Arabia and the United Arab Emirates. In July, President Donald Trump vetoed three congressional resolutions that prohibited arms sales to them. The Trump administration also declared an emergency to circumvent Congress and accelerate arms sales to various countries—including Saudi Arabia and the United Arab Emirates.[185]

In short, President Trump is following a military policy in the Middle East that is at odds with the views of a majority of Congress. And he has a far larger military, and much more deadly weapons, to use in pursuing that policy. Since World War II, the size of United States permanent military forces has grown dramatically, to more than one million men and women on active duty. And the advent of missile-based nuclear weapons means that utterly devastating, largely irreversible destruction across the entire planet could occur in a span of hours because a president ordered it, without even consulting Congress.

Meanwhile, the Supreme Court has refused to intervene in disputes between the president and Congress over foreign affairs and military actions on virtually every occasion, claiming that those are "political questions." But Congress itself has limited power to control presidential adventures abroad. Under the Constitution, removal by impeachment requires a supermajority vote, and congressional funding cutoffs can be vetoed or even ignored by a president. Still, Congress has done little or nothing to restrain presidential power in this arena. In national security matters, the presidency has become imperial.

Some observers would argue that at much the same time, the "military-industrial complex" President Dwight David Eisenhower strenuously warned the country against has become a major influence on national policy. Since 1990, the United States has consistently accounted for between one-third and forty percent of all world military spending. The United States' defense budget has increased roughly 50 percent during that period, to 600 billion dollars per year or more in 2011 dollars.[186] Over the past thirty years in particular, the United States has, despite its democracy-spreading rhetoric, become a nation defined heavily by its exercise of military power across the planet. It now bears a stronger resemblance to the Roman empire than to the peaceful commercial republic most of the Founders hoped that they were creating.

Over the past twenty years, the United States has spent more than $5 trillion on wars in Iraq and Afghanistan and has intervened militarily in numerous other parts of the world, such as the Syrian civil war. These recent war expenditures are as large as the estimated direct cost of the entire Civil War, if they are not in fact greater.[187] The United States' massive permanent military establishment would have utterly dismayed many of the Founders, and would have been bitterly opposed by early presidents such as Thomas Jefferson.

The course of United States military affairs over the past several decades raises important questions about the future of republican government. Does the United States have a constitutional process for choosing presidents or congresspeople that reliably puts individuals into office who are qualified to control the actions of a globe-spanning military establishment and to formulate a coherent foreign policy? Do federal elected leaders also have the necessary political incentives to exercise such control given the economic and political influence of the military-industrial complex?[188]

Over the past twenty-eight years, the United States has had only one president, George W. Bush, who had performed any actual military service. Bush served in the Texas Air National Guard for a short time. At present, less than 20 percent of members of Congress have any military experience, down from about 70 percent of Congress with such experience in the years after World War II. Common sense alone suggests that neither Congress nor recent presidents have had sufficient military knowledge and background to exercise effective long-term control over the immense American military establishment. And other facts reinforce that concern.

Among other things, the leaders of the armed forces today have far more permanence in their positions and control of military resources than do most federal elected officials. As of 2019, the generals and admirals who are members of the Joint Chiefs of Staff have an average of more than thirty-five years of military service. Their collective knowledge of the operations and capabilities of the United States armed forces far exceeds that of the country's civilian leadership. And given the complex, worldwide, and enormously secretive organization of the Department of Defense, these military leaders' ability to control the actual deployment of military resources also far outstrips that of the country's civilian leaders.

Broad presidential powers over military action and limited civilian control over the military together mean that the separation of powers has seriously failed in a way that would have greatly concerned many Founders. They would want us to ask: Has the United States actually followed a coherent foreign policy in the past twenty years during our extensive military adventures, one carefully debated and approved by Congress? What does the nation actually have to show for its vast expenditures of life and money in wars and quasi-wars over the past several decades? Are we engaged in dangerous "imperial overstretch," as some noted scholars have argued?[189] The Founders would have agreed that Congress had failed in its constitutional policy formation responsibilities, and would have wanted to know why. Political scientists believe that Congress has abdicated its responsibility because its members want to avoid blame for America's military and foreign policies. The reasons for that are discussed in the next section.[190]

Presidential government has also expanded markedly since the New Deal through numerous laws and policies as to which Congress made little or no effort to provide clear standards before delegating its authority.[191] Of course, Congress has often made broad delegations to the executive branch during national emergencies. But in recent years, even in peacetime Congress has frequently made delegations of authority under standards so broad that they leave enormous discretion to executive branch officials.

Over the past several decades, statutes have permitted federal agencies to regulate in the "public interest." They have enabled agencies to set "fair and equitable prices" and "just and reasonable" rates. And they have authorized agencies to set whatever air quality standards are "requisite to protect the public health."[192] These exceptionally broad delegations of authority often permit agencies to impose millions, and in some cases, tens of millions of dollars worth of costs on citizens and regulated industries using standards that executive officials alone have developed. These regulatory authority delegations stand in stark contrast to the remarkably precise, fine-tuned provisions of the federal tax code.

But in recent years, thoughtful observers have become increasingly persuaded that the primary basis on which Congress' delegations have been rationalized—the disinterested expert administration model of government—is flawed. Doubts have multiplied about whether there is any objective "public interest" that agencies can seek to establish, or whether instead decisions made using such a general standard are inevitably politically-driven value choices. Agencies can be and often are captured by the industries that they are supposed to regulate. And regulatory officials often have de facto life tenure, shielding them against removal for anything short of obvious criminality, which severely limits even a president's ability to control or improve agency performance.

Yet the Supreme Court has upheld virtually all of Congress' broad regulatory power delegations against claims that they violated the separation of powers because Congress cannot constitutionally delegate its legislative power.[193] At present Congress is free to make broad social policy delegations, handing off the hard choices about exactly what policy the government should ultimately adopt on various issues to administrative agencies. The broad choices Congress leaves open then become the subject of enormous lobbying efforts to shape the decision-making process, and are often followed by years of costly litigation before the government finally adopts and executes any policy at all. In the case of the 1990 Clean Air Act amendments, for example, major litigation concerning regulations issued pursuant to that law involving hundreds of millions, if not billions, of dollars in costs was still under way for ten to as much as fifteen years after Congress adopted the statute's broad language. Congress could have prevented much of that litigation by legislating more specific outcomes, but chose not to do so.

To understand why Congress has transferred much of both its national security authority and its domestic authority to the president, we need to take a closer look at the "broken branch," as it has recently been called.

CONGRESS: THE BROKEN BRANCH

We have already seen that Congress is gridlocked over major social policies that involve debates over economic fairness or wealth redistribution, such as national healthcare insurance, and that the Constitution contributes significantly to that stalemate. But Congress' paralysis extends far beyond such redistributive issues. For example, many citizens support additional federal gun control regulations. Opinion polls show that about 80-90 percent of Americans support universal background checks for gun sales. Reasonable background check requirements for such sales would undoubtedly be constitutional. Yet Congress has generally proven unwilling to act on such gun control issues.

Congress' inaction on pressing national issues and its passive acceptance of increasing power in the presidency and judiciary have led some experienced observers to call it the "broken branch."[194] Former Indiana Congressman Lee Hamilton chaired the House Committee on Foreign Affairs, served as Vice-Chair of the 9/11 Commission, and was one of the most widely respected members of

Congress of his generation. After describing negative changes in the way Congress operates including the "breakdown in the legislative process," Hamilton said that "no one today could make a coherent argument that the Congress is the co-equal branch of government the Founders intended it to be."[195]

Many observers point to increased political polarization and partisanship as causes of Congress' dysfunction.[196] Polarization and partisanship have increased in recent years, but Congress' failure to act on pressing issues has a much deeper cause. Congress has abdicated responsibility for both national security and domestic policy because its members want to shirk responsibility, and because our non-competitive two-party political system enables them to do so. Congress' escape from accountability is made even easier by our bicameral (i.e., two house) Congress. As Yuval Levin, an astute observer, recently concluded, "Congress is weak because its members want it to be weak."[197]

Some analysts blame the Republican party in particular for increased ideological extremism, excessive partisanship, or both.[198] But as Levin points out, the hard truth is that there is plenty of bipartisan blame for Congress' failures to go around.[199] Anyone who doubts that should recall that Congress has delegated broad authority to the president and the courts over decades, no matter which party was in control. Or we could consider the bipartisan way in which Congress in recent years has been willing to practice "free lunch" economics, with both parties effectively telling voters that they can have something for nothing.

Under the Constitution, Congress has exclusive control over both taxes and spending. By early 2020, Congress had allowed the debt to grow to more than $22 trillion; it had quadrupled over the past twenty years. By late 2020, the size of publicly held debt relative to our economy is expected to be larger than at the end of World War II. The triumph of "free lunchism" in both major parties has eliminated any real efforts to control the debt, and has prompted twenty-eight states to seek a balanced budget constitutional amendment (discussed in chapter 5). Whether concerns about the debt are valid or the Constitution should be amended in that respect are both irrelevant here. What matters instead is that the debt's growth is an unmistakable symptom of Congress' institutional weakness. Whenever possible, majorities in recent Congresses want to avoid responsibility for making political choices that require significant sacrifice.[200] Ultimately, claims about Congressional gridlock or failure to balance taxes and spending based on partisanship and polarization—though both undoubtedly play some role—do not get to the heart of that chronic bipartisan failure of political will.

Instead, as James Madison thought, our ultimate focus in understanding Congress' behavior as an institution should be on the ambitions of members of Congress.[201] We need to consider what political aspirations Congress' members actually have. Today there are two classes of members of Congress, viewed from that perspective. There are a relatively small number who view their positions merely as stepping-stones to higher office (either the Senate or the presidency). For presidential aspirants, which includes an increasing number of (often very junior) Senators, the more powerful the presidency becomes, the less appeal the legislative work of Congress holds. The large majority of members of Congress, however, instead see their positions as secure, comfortable, and perhaps eventually lucrative, lifetime careers.

A perceptive observer has written that if there were a Millionaires Caucus in Congress, it would control Congress because a majority of Congress would belong.[202] Many members of Congress are wealthy individuals by any standard. It should therefore not surprise us that many of them perform their service in Congress in ways calculated to maintain and increase their wealth. But in order to become wealthier through officeholding, members of Congress must keep their jobs. That means that for many of them, keeping their jobs is their first priority. There is no question that these are jobs worth keeping, and that members want to keep them.[203]

Members of Congress are paid fairly well by most Americans' standards—their pay alone puts them in about the top ten percent of all United States income recipients. They also have excellent health benefits and generous pensions. As of 2018, about three hundred members who retired under Congress' traditional pension system were receiving an average federal annuity of $75,528 per year (some may receive Social Security benefits as well). Another three hundred members who retired under a less generous newer system were receiving an average federal pension of $41,208 per year, not including Social Security benefits to which they are also entitled. These pension amounts are between two and one-half and four times as much as the average Social Security recipient received in 2019.[204] Lawrence Lessig also finds that more than 400 members of Congress have created campaign fundraising devices such as "leadership PACs" that often provide them with generous additional personal travel, meals and entertainment benefits that amount to discretionary non-taxable compensation. Leadership PACs raised more than $50 million in 2014 alone.[205]

Each of 435 House of Representatives members receives more than $1 million for office expenses alone, which typically pays for more than a dozen full-time staff in Washington and the member's district (most Senators receive more funding; in large states, much more). These staff have various responsibilities, but they are universally hired with the unmistakable expectation that they will devote themselves to making sure that their representative keeps his or her job at the next election. Much larger amounts are actually spent to support each member of Congress. A very conservative estimate of the total budget for the Congress (and ancillary agencies such as its police force) alone in FY 2020 is roughly $5 billion, or about $10 million per member. As of 2015, more than 19,000 staff supported Congress' work.[206]

As one knowledgeable observer concluded, by most Americans' standards this is a very comfortable work life. He wrote:

> Where else can someone draw a salary of $174,000; have a staff of several dozen catering to their (and their family's) every whim; enjoy special access to information and resources at the highest levels of government; forge lucrative relationships with people of immense power and influence; take taxpayer-funded jaunts to all corners of the country and the world; and command constant attention from the local and national media—all in exchange for producing little in the way of tangible outcomes?[207]

So, members of Congress have desirable jobs, and almost always want to keep them. An average of ninety percent of Congress' members have run for reelection in recent Congresses. The good news for them is that keeping their jobs is not difficult. Voters cannot place term limits on their service, thanks to a Supreme Court ruling that such limits are barred by the Constitution.[208] And most members of Congress face almost no serious competition for their jobs. Over the thirty years ending in 2009, on average more than 85 percent of all members of Congress who ran for reelection were re-elected.[209] In the last decade, there has been little change in that picture.[210]

Not surprisingly, the average tenure in office of members of Congress is now triple what it was in the nineteenth century. Studies show that most members of Congress would not voluntarily give up their positions unless they were offered between $1 and $5 million (2019 dollars) to retire, depending on the office held.[211] And many who do retire become even wealthier working as Washington lobbyists or in other businesses in the Washington area. As one knowledgeable congressman put it, "Capitol Hill is a farm league for K Street" lobbying operations.[212] According to Lawrence Lessig, "between 1998 and 2004, more than 50 percent of senators and 42 percent of House members" who retired became lobbyists. In contrast, in the 1970s, 3 percent of retiring members became lobbyists. As of June, 2011, 195 former members of Congress were registered lobbyists.[213] Government growth has made Washington one of the very most affluent regions in America, especially during recessions (see chapter 1). Most members of Congress, in short, are well-paid, time-serving careerists, not citizen-legislators.

Members of Congress are able to be careerists because the two major parties have effectively divided up the national political market between them. There is little real inter-party political competition in most states. Today, most observers agree that only about 15 percent of the 435 seats in the House of Representatives are actually competitive seats. In part, the lack of competition stems from the large costs involved in running for Congress, which thorough studies suggest are so large that they are a major barrier preventing most ordinary Americans from ever seeking office.[214] Widespread gerrymandering practiced by both parties to protect their incumbent officials against competition also plays a role. And under the constitutionally permissible "first-past-the-post" voting and single-member district systems now used to choose Congress, there is virtually no chance that a third party will receive any representation, even though about 40 percent of voters tell pollsters that they are independents who do not belong to either major party.[215]

Because members of Congress are careerists, whenever possible they will avoid taking responsibility for any issue that threatens their ability to be re-elected. That frequently requires taking steps to avoid political accountability. The lack of competition for their jobs often makes that possible, because there is no serious challenger to argue that they should be held accountable, especially for inaction. The Constitution is also helpful in aiding congressional efforts to escape accountability, by shifting apparent responsibility for events to other branches of government.

For example, if Congress permits the president to engage in foreign wars without declaring war, the Supreme Court will refuse to do anything about it. As we have seen, the Court has declared that type of issue to be a "political question." Therefore, unless Congress' members think that voters will retaliate against them for failing to control the president's actions, they have no incentive to do anything about them. As a result, they assess whether a presidential military intervention is popular or in any event is one that voters are largely indifferent about. In either case, Congress will defer to the president, and avoid a vote.[216]

Where domestic policy is concerned, members of Congress also have large incentives to avoid hard choices. Congress often fails to act on important national problems on a "bipartisan basis," because its members in both parties have been captured by special interests. For example, as the constitutional scholar Stephen Griffin points out, Congress failed to address severe problems in regulating the savings-and-loan industry in the 1980s, and the banking industry in the 1990s and 2000s, until these industries collapsed. Neither party's members of Congress made any real effort to ensure that these industries were properly regulated. Leaders from both political parties had both political and in some cases direct financial conflicts of interest that preventing them from acting. As Griffin notes, constitutional scholar

Lawrence Lessig, a campaign finance expert, concluded that the banking industry collapse was connected to large-scale campaign financing provided by that industry to members of both parties of Congress to "persuade" them to allow dangerous unregulated banking practices to increase dramatically.[217]

Similarly, Congress failed on a bipartisan basis to improve the performance of the intelligence community despite strong recommendations supporting reform because Congress would have had to redistribute power internally in order to do so. Griffin argues that Congress' failure played an important role in the 9/11 disaster. But Congress' desire to avoid accountability even when it has not been directly captured by a special interest extends far beyond these important cases.[218]

For example, suppose that Congress is considering whether to pass a law requiring air pollution controls that would affect various industries in a particular congressional district or state. It will have a choice whether to create general standards in the law, such as providing that the controls should "adequately" protect human or animal health, or whether to decide what precise levels of air pollution will be permissible.

If Congress creates general air quality standards, choosing and implementing the actual control requirements will be left up to a federal agency. The agency will be responsible for deciding how large an economic burden is imposed by its regulations on specific companies. The agency regulation will have precisely the same economic effect as if the agency were imposing a tax on those companies. The agency (and perhaps in some cases the president) will end up taking the political blame for that. If Congress had established precise pollution levels, on the other hand, it would effectively have imposed a tax of a particular size on those same industries, and members would have had to vote on the tax.

To avoid responsibility, nine times out of ten Congress will avoid establishing precise pollution control levels, claiming that such a decision should be left to experts. In reality, of course, Congress could make such decisions after hearing expert testimony, just as it does in many other cases involving expert judgment. But Congress instead delegates authority to a regulatory agency to shift away from itself as much as possible of the blame for the ultimate pollution tax, which will have to be paid either way. Congress' ability to shift and diffuse responsibility makes holding members of Congress politically accountable far more difficult. As discussed further below, this problem is made worse by the Constitution's bicameral Congress, since members of one house of Congress can and often do blame the members of the other branch for inaction.

Not surprisingly in light of Congress' enthusiasm for shirking responsibility, over the years since the New Deal began to build the modern administrative state, Congress has delegated hundreds, if not thousands, of important policy decisions to federal agencies under very general standards. Because presidents appoint the officials who control most agencies, Congressional delegations of authority to agencies generally increase the power of the president. Congress then typically promises that it will conduct oversight of resulting executive branch actions, but it is very rare that Congress devotes concerted, systematic effort to such oversight. In reality, through congressional delegation, large discretion is shifted permanently to the executive branch and the courts.

Of course, it's quite possible to argue that most of these congressionally delegated decisions are better left to agency experts. But that claim ignores the fact that many of the decisions inevitably involve subjective value tradeoffs, which are then made by unelected career officials who effectively have lifetime tenure. And it overlooks the fact that agency independence is often a recipe for long-term agency inaction when partisan appointees who serve as agency co-leaders end up in stalemates with career officials. It also disregards the fact that industries can and do capture many of the agencies that are making regulatory decisions. Sometimes regulatory capture takes place with the active assistance of presidentially-appointed senior officials, many of whom are previous industry officials. Washington, D.C. and its wealthy suburbs are home to thousands of highly paid and well-funded lobbyists. Many of them are responsible for making sure that regulators leave their industries entirely alone, or if that is not possible, make decisions favoring them. The notion that congressional policy delegation is either acceptable or desirable because decisions are then made by "disinterested" "experts" disregards these and other important political realities.

Judicial review of agency actions often does not even begin to cure such problems. The federal courts employ standards to determine the constitutionality of statutes delegating authority to agencies that are themselves vague and indefinite (e.g., is there an "intelligible principle" behind the delegation?).[219] As a result, it is frequently actually the Supreme Court majority that decides whether an agency will ultimately be allowed to follow its chosen course of action. Courts thus play a significant role in determining whether policy choices that could have been—and perhaps should have been—made by Congress ultimately become law at all. Of course, the federal courts cannot be held accountable for such decisions because the Constitution gives them life tenure, and impeachment of judges is nearly impossible.

THE PROBLEM OF BICAMERALISM

As mentioned previously, the Constitution's bicameralism adds to the difficulty of holding members of Congress accountable.[220] Bicameralism contributes to congressional inaction by diffusing responsibility so that members of Congress can easily blame someone else for the government's failure to act. For example, it clearly contributes to congressional inaction on the issue of gun control. Even if a House of Representatives majority passed clearly constitutional gun control legislation, the Constitution would make it fairly easy for Senators representing a minority of the population to block it.

Today, senators from twenty-nine states with the highest average levels of gun ownership control 58 percent of the votes in the Senate, even though their states represent only 46 percent of the nation's population.[221] Most of the senators from those states are opposed to gun control legislation. Senators from the twenty-one states with the lowest average levels of gun ownership have 42 percent of the votes in the Senate, even though they represent 54 percent of the nation's population. Many of the senators from those states support gun control. Even if every one of those states' Senators supported gun control legislation, they would not have sufficient votes to pass it in the Senate. That allows many members of the House of Representatives to escape accountability for failing to act on an issue such as gun control. They can accurately argue that they cannot compel the Senate to act even if they do. At the same time, members of both houses of Congress also know that they can engage in low-cost political theater by voting for gun control legislation which they are well aware will never be adopted by the other house, so they can please its supporters without actually causing its opponents to pay any significant price.

As we have seen, the predominantly careerist Congress has acted in the face of gridlock, much of it stemming from the Constitution, to delegate large amounts of authority to the executive branch. Congress has been willing to abdicate its policymaking responsibilities because a majority of its members can do so and yet manage to keep their comfortable, well-paid career positions without facing voter retaliation. As a result, today voters' actual ability to hold leaders accountable is primarily limited to elections for the presidency. Even that nominal accountability may be frustrated because under the Electoral College a president may be elected by a popular minority. As indicated, the Supreme Court has repeatedly helped Congress to abdicate its responsibilities. But the Court's powers have also increased due to Congress' weakness, and it is to that issue we now turn.

THE SUPREME COURT: MORE POWERFUL BY DEFAULT

The Supreme Court has gained increased power by default as the representative political system has become gridlocked and unable or unwilling to resolve issues. In many recent cases, intractable political controversies have been treated by Congress not as potential subjects for legislation but intentionally turned into fodder for court disputes. Contrary to popular and much scholarly opinion, members of Congress are often not naïve or ignorant about the existence of legislative language vagueness or ambiguity, but instead are acutely aware when they have passed ambiguous or potentially unconstitutional legislation. In doing so, they are intentionally "passing the buck" to the courts.

Some of these politico-legal disputes concern the interpretation of statutes. Here the Supreme Court's rulings are in theory not politically (as opposed to legally) final, since Congress itself could (and occasionally does) change them by amending the law. But where Supreme Court decisions rest on constitutional interpretation, they can be overturned only extremely rarely because of the prevailing view that under the Constitution the Court gets the final word, generally referred to as the idea of judicial supremacy.[222] Where public opinion is divided even roughly equally on a constitutional issue, amendments overturning court decisions will either not occur at all, or occur only decades later when political circumstances have changed markedly, as in the case of the Sixteenth Amendment (the amendment issue is examined in chapter 5).

On constitutional issues, therefore, the Court often has not just the final legal word, it has the final political word. In recent years, the Court has been able to increase its authority as a result of chronic government gridlock because it has stepped into the power vacuum created by stalemates on fundamental national issues. Two outstanding examples are the Court's arrogation of power during the 2000 election, and its decision on the constitutionality of the Affordable Care Act. Should nine unelected justices have constitutional authority to decide such issues with finality, or are they instead political problems that should be resolved by democratic means?[223]

BUSH v. GORE AND PRESIDENTIAL LEGITIMACY

The Supreme Court's 2000 decision in *Bush v. Gore* decided the 2000 presidential election in George W. Bush's favor.[224] In that 5-4 decision, the Supreme Court overruled a decision by the Florida Supreme Court which had ordered a recount of the presidential election votes there, and blocked any recount. The effect of the Court's decision was that Bush was deemed to have won the popular vote in Florida—though evidence suggests that Bush might quite possibly have lost a recount.

By awarding Florida's popular vote to Bush, the Court also awarded Bush Florida's twenty-five electoral votes, thereby providing him with the necessary Electoral College majority to win the presidency. (Of course, the existence of the Electoral College itself allowed Bush to win the presidency despite losing the nationwide popular vote to Albert Gore, Jr. by about 500,000 votes. If the Electoral College had not existed, the Florida vote dispute could not possibly have changed the national popular vote outcome, and probably would not have occurred.)

But, as Justice Stephen Breyer pointed out in a brilliant dissent in *Bush v. Gore*, instead of deciding the presidential election on its own, the Supreme Court should have followed an alternative required by the Constitution and specifically provided for by federal law. The Court should have directed that the Florida election dispute be decided by Congress. Justice Breyer wrote:

> ...The Twelfth Amendment commits to Congress the authority and responsibility to count electoral votes. A federal statute, the Electoral Count Act, enacted after the close 1876 Hayes-Tilden Presidential election, specifies that, after States have tried to resolve disputes...Congress is the body primarily authorized to resolve remaining disputes....The legislative history of the Act makes clear its intent to commit the power to resolve such disputes to Congress, rather than the courts: 'The two Houses are, by the Constitution, authorized to make the count of electoral votes. They ...must determine, from the best evidence to be had, what are legal votes . . . .'....'The power to determine rests with the two houses, and there is no other constitutional tribunal.'[225]

It is true that if the House of Representatives had ultimately decided the 2000 presidential election under the Twelfth Amendment, the outcome would also probably have been a victory for Bush.[226] But there was nevertheless a profoundly important difference between what the Supreme Court did in *Bush v. Gore* and what would have happened if the House had instead voted. In the latter case, the political process would have operated without being short-circuited by a group of unelected judges. Unlike the Supreme Court, members of Congress could have been held accountable by the voters for their decision. The Supreme Court's decision allowed all members of

Congress to escape accountability for Bush's election as a minority president.

We can see the great difference allowing the political process to work would make to the vitality of republican government by recalling the circumstances surrounding the bitterly contested presidential election of 1800. That election was decided by the House of Representatives because Thomas Jefferson and Aaron Burr had tied in the Electoral College. The House of Representatives took thirty-six ballots before electing Jefferson president. At the time, there were claims that Jefferson was ultimately elected only because he had agreed to several major policy demands made by his Federalist Party opponents. Jefferson always denied those claims. But if he had in fact made political concessions as a compromise to gain election, that would have been precisely how a democratic political process is supposed to work. Moreover, voters who were unhappy with Jefferson's election would have been in a position to hold their congressional representatives who supported him accountable. (As things turned out, of course, Jefferson proved to be a popular president who had little difficulty being re-elected in 1804).[227]

In sharp contrast, voters who were unhappy with the Supreme Court's decision in 2000 awarding the election to George W. Bush had no recourse against the justices, since impeachment would have been a political impossibility. Many Americans believed that the Court majority (all Republican appointees) had acted in a partisan manner in deciding the case in Bush's favor. As Justice Breyer and other dissenters pointed out, the Court's decision seriously damaged its own legitimacy. As Justice John Paul Stevens wrote: "Although we may never know with complete certainty the identity of the winner of this year's Presidential election, the identity of the loser is perfectly clear. It is the Nation's confidence in the judge as an impartial guardian of the rule of law."[228]

And the Court had also unintentionally weakened the legitimacy of George W. Bush's presidency. A poll taken in July, 2001 showed that almost 30 percent of voters did not regard him as the legitimate president of the United States; fifty-two percent of all Black voters believed he had stolen the election.[229] Any leader will have a harder time governing when a significant part of the public does not regard him or her as legitimate. That is especially true when a president must govern in a time of possible war that may call for the use of Commander in Chief powers, as President Bush did after the 9-11 attacks. Can we afford to elect presidents whose very occupancy of the office is deemed illegitimate by many citizens?

In *Bush v. Gore*, the Court inserted itself into a political vacuum and abandoned the republican political process, arrogating power to itself. The Constitution does not explicitly give the Supreme Court the power to decide that type of election dispute. In fact, as Justice Breyer pointed out, the Constitution is better viewed as depriving the Court of that power. Why is it desirable for the Supreme Court to have the power to make final, unchallengeable decisions about political questions such as the outcome of a presidential election?

THE COURT AND THE FATE OF NATIONAL HEALTHCARE INSURANCE

The Supreme Court's 2012 *NFIB v. Sebelius* decision on the constitutionality of the Patient Protection and Affordable Care Act ("the Affordable Care Act" or "ACA") raises similar questions about its proper constitutional role.[230]   The ACA had two especially controversial provisions that raised constitutional concerns. The so-called "individual mandate" provision of the ACA required individuals who lacked employer-provided health insurance that met "minimum standards" to purchase such insurance or to pay a monetary penalty (which grew larger over time). The Medicaid provisions of the ACA required states to expand their coverage under Medicaid to all individuals who had incomes below 133 percent of the poverty level. The law threatened states with the cutoff of all federal Medicaid funding if they refused to expand their Medicaid programs (it provided partial expansion funding as a carrot).

In *Sebelius*, an ideologically-split majority of the Supreme Court held that the "individual mandate" provision of the ACA was constitutional. A different ideologically-split majority decided that Congress could not constitutionally compel states to expand their Medicaid programs.[231] In the following discussion, we are not in any way concerned with whether either the ACA individual mandate or its Medicaid expansion were good or bad policy. Instead, the question is whether it is desirable for the Constitution to allocate final authority over Congress' power to legislate on such social policy issues to the Supreme Court.

The issue raised by the individual mandate was whether Congress had authority to enact a law requiring Americans to buy health insurance whether they wanted it or not. On that issue, the Court splintered: four justices said Congress had no such power under the Constitution's Commerce Clause; four justices said that of course it did; and Chief Justice Roberts said that Congress had power to provide a tax disincentive intended to persuade people to buy health insurance as the ACA did, but no power to compel them to do so. The Court majority upheld the ACA mandate as an exercise of Congress' tax power.

On Medicaid expansion, a majority of the Court agreed with Chief Justice Roberts that the Constitution required Congress to treat the states as independent political entities. That meant that they could not constitutionally be compelled to expand their medical coverage for the poor by a threatened cutoff of federal Medicaid funding. Congress could give the states incentives to expand their Medicaid programs, but could not compel them to do that. The Court's decision meant that in the future, whether many Americans living in poverty received adequate medical care would depend on what state they lived in, and not, as Congress had intended, simply on whether they were American citizens.[232]

The differing views of the Court's justices in *Sebelius* depended largely on their clashing views of federalism. The conservative justices saw federalism as a commission to the Supreme Court to referee between what they viewed as limited federal powers on the one hand, and the rights of states and individuals on the other.[233] That understanding of federalism has support in the text of the Constitution and in our nineteenth century history. However, it is difficult to square it with the more recent history of the various twentieth century New Deal and Great Society legislation approved as constitutional by the Court.

The Constitution was not formally amended during the New Deal except for the Twenty-First Amendment, which ended Prohibition. Still, it is reasonable to view that era's novel federal social legislation and the Supreme Court's approval of it as a watershed expansion of the federal government's powers over economic regulation and social issues such as retirement security. As one constitutional scholar put it, many observers concluded that the Supreme Court had decided as a result of the New Deal and its aftermath that Congress had "plenary and virtually unlimited" legislative power.[234]

For example, by the mid-1930s, after the experience of the Great Depression, few seem to have seriously believed that the Constitution would prevent Congress from adopting an unprecedented Social Security Act. The Supreme Court upheld the Act's taxes imposed to create the Social Security system by a vote of 7-2 in *Helvering v. Davis* (1937).[235] Justice Cardozo's majority opinion said that Congress had enacted the Act in the exercise of its wide discretion under the general welfare power. The Court held that the Act did not violate the Tenth Amendment despite objections that it infringed states' powers.

In *Sebelius,* the Court's four liberal justices advocated that post-New Deal view of Congress' broad legislative powers as to the ACA mandate. Two of them agreed that Congress had power to compel Medicaid expansion by the states.[236] The four most conservative justices insisted that the Constitution restricted Congress' powers with respect to both issues. The Court's ideological split over the reach of Congress' powers has far-reaching consequences for our future, and threatens to weaken Congress further.

If only one justice had voted differently in *Sebelius*, Congress would have been prohibited from adopting its preferred national health insurance program including the individual mandate unless the Constitution was amended. Given the intense divisions over the desirability of the ACA as policy, it is exceptionally unlikely that the Constitution could have been amended to enable the adoption of such a law. Five members of the Supreme Court therefore literally possessed the unchallengeable power to prevent the United States from having the national health care insurance system that Congress and the president had agreed to enact.

That is a remarkably large amount of authority to give a politically unaccountable body. And it is an especially large amount of power to give a court many of whose members were appointed by presidents more than a quarter of a century before *Sebelius* was decided. There were legitimate arguments pro and con about whether the ACA was good policy, but those are political concerns, best resolved in the democratic political arena. Why should we want the Supreme Court to have the final word about whether Congress had the power to pass the ACA?

Moreover, we have ceded that power to the Supreme Court even though in deciding the constitutionality of such major social legislation its justices are relying on its interpretation of provisions of the Constitution created to deal with eighteenth century conditions, such as the Commerce Clause, in order to analyze twenty-first century social problems. For example, the drafters of the Commerce Clause could not conceivably have imagined that it would ever be used to decide Congress' power to adopt the Affordable Care Act mandate. Whatever the precise scope of that Clause may be, its core is the regulation of economic relationships between states and the federal government with respect to the internal and external trade of the United States. Nowhere in the Atlantic World did a national healthcare system exist when the Constitution was written.

What is ultimately most important to appreciate is that the Court's frequently esoteric debate over Congress' power to adopt the ACA in essence rehashed issues that might reasonably be regarded as having been settled long ago. Since the Great Depression, as a society the United States has recognized without serious dissent the need to provide a national social safety net through programs such as Social Security. During the twentieth century, Congress recognized the need to extend that safety net to medical care for the elderly and poor, again without serious dissent. The ACA was an effort by Congress to modernize and extend the national social safety net. Many people understandably think that its basic constitutionality—as opposed to whether it was good policy—was settled nearly a century ago. From that perspective, in *NFIB v. Sebelius*, the Supreme Court was essentially permitting itself to be employed as a forum in which to refight that settled issue. The decision gave ACA opponents partial final victory despite having lost the substantive political debate in Congress, and they narrowly missed blocking the law entirely.

That leads to the further conclusion that the Supreme Court was only empowered politically (as opposed to legally) to rule on the constitutionality of the ACA because the elected branches of government were so deeply divided over its wisdom as national policy that the Court was able to step into the resulting political vacuum. The Court's ability to have the last word here is a striking symptom of the inability of our existing constitutional system to achieve politically legitimate results. In a sharply divided climate, Congress' passage of the legislation became a mere way station on the road to a lengthy court battle, since followed by continuing political controversy over the law. The Court's power to intervene decisively in this essentially political dispute, and potentially to bar permanently Congress' extension of our country's social safety net through creation of a national healthcare insurance system intended to serve all of our citizens, both rich and poor, should concern us all.

CONCLUSION

The Constitution's separation of powers no longer works. The presidency has become imperial; Congress is no longer a viable legislative body; and the Supreme Court has stepped into the political vacuum created by Congressional abdication and is deciding disputes that are fundamentally political and should be resolved by democratic means. Republican government cannot survive without an accountable Congress that is both willing and able to confront national problems and legislate to resolve them, rather than continually "passing the buck." It cannot survive unless the growing powers of the presidency are properly curtailed. And it cannot survive without limits on the Supreme Court's power to intervene finally in major political disputes in the guise of constitutional adjudication.

Indeed, given its deep existing flaws, the entire separation of powers concept needs to be reexamined, and alternatives such as parliamentary government or some hybrid system should be seriously considered. In any event, we unquestionably need to modify the incentives for service in all three branches of government in order to restore the interbranch competition that is essential for a separation of powers system to succeed. And we need to decide whether, in light of the enormous costs of separation of powers in lost government efficiency, the relations of various branches of government need to be rethought. These are very complex problems. And we know that creating the Constitution's separation of powers required extensive negotiations and occupied a good deal of the time of the Philadelphia Convention. These considerations alone strongly suggest that we cannot expect to repair these and other serious government dysfunctions through a single, freestanding constitutional amendment. Only a new convention can successfully reform this system as a whole.

4

The Constitution Has Failed as a Foundation for Representative Democracy

As is well known, the Constitution established a representative republic, not an Athenian-style direct democracy. But even at the 1787 Philadelphia Convention, delegates strongly disagreed about how republican principles should be applied in creating the new national government. They argued strenuously over how much voting power states should have in Congress, and over whether presidents should be directly elected, for example. There were frequent clashes between the view that elites, particularly the wealthy, should control most government decisions, and the conviction that ordinary citizens should have increased influence. The battle over the constitutional balance between elitism and populism continues in the United States today. But why does it matter?

Many people might answer that it matters because political equality is a human right. But though the Founders believed in civil equality generally, they did not believe in full political equality even for all white males, let alone for anyone else. Most of them did not believe that all citizens had a right of direct participation in government, or that they even had a right to an equal voice in shaping political outcomes. A majority accepted that ordinary citizens should not be allowed to vote directly for the president or Senators. Most of them thought that "gerrymandering"—partisan drawing of legislative and congressional district boundaries by states' ruling parties in order to maintain or increase their control of government—was acceptable. Racism, gender bias, and wealth discrimination were all seen by most Founders as acceptable bases for limiting or denying political participation to large parts of the population.

But within a generation or two after the Founding, Americans began to take a more inclusive view of the meaning of political equality.[237] During the nineteenth and twentieth centuries, the right to vote for the House of Representatives was expanded to include poor whites, free Blacks (in some states), and ultimately to women. Popular pressure forced the adoption of the 17th Amendment to directly elect Senators. Civil rights laws gradually expanded voting opportunity for Blacks and other minorities. Populist reforms such as the initiative and referendum further diminished elite power. But these reforms were not based merely on the belief that equality or justice required the liberalization of political rights.   They had an important instrumental basis as well.

The expansion of Americans' political rights has also been the result of a growing conviction that in the long run, representative government will make better decisions when there is less elite control of its institutions, particularly by the wealthy who often govern to advance their own interests.   The progressive democratization of political rights was intended to improve representative government's performance by requiring its leaders to consider a broader range of interests and views in making decisions, and by increasing its accountability.   That increasingly influential view has had powerful effects.

The growth of popular government has changed the very shape and direction of American politics. For example, popular pressure led to the creation of federal antitrust laws to control massive concentrations of economic power such as the Rockefeller-created Standard Oil Trust. That is to be expected: government institutions often change their policies when they are controlled by different groups. In fact, as we will see shortly, a wide range of important national policies would be fundamentally altered if institutions such as the Senate and the presidency more directly represented the will of the American people.

Yet despite earlier reforms, the Constitution still contains major structural features affecting the operation of its central political institutions that have two separate and equally fatal flaws: they violate today's standards of republican political equality, and they frequently have more anti-democratic effects than they did when created.

Constitutional and political scholars such as Sanford Levinson and Larry Sabato have carefully examined these deeply flawed features, which include lifetime tenure for Supreme Court justices; states' equal voting rights in the Senate; and the Electoral College.[238] This chapter focuses primarily on the harms caused by those defects, and provides new analysis and data concerning them. It also analyzes the ramifications of the Supreme Court's 2019 decision that the Constitution permits continued partisan election manipulation through gerrymandering.[239] Chapters 5 and 6 will examine the harmful results of another profoundly antidemocratic aspect of the Constitution, its rigid Article V amendment procedures. Finally, it is worth noting that earlier writers have also challenged other important structural features of the Constitution or its interpretation not discussed here, such as the presidential veto and judicial review, as undemocratic.[240]

THE SUPREME COURT

The Supreme Court was deliberately created as an undemocratic institution. Justices are not elected, but are appointed by the president and confirmed by the Senate. They serve for life terms and are removable only by impeachment, which requires a supermajority vote. These rules governing the Court have not changed since 1787. No Justice has ever been successfully impeached and removed from office. Hence, the Justices are politically unaccountable for their decisions. From a purely formal perspective, the Court is no more undemocratic today than it was then. And based on these rules, it is often claimed that the Court is and was intended to be "outside" politics.

In reality, though, the Constitution established a highly politically sensitive process for choosing Supreme Court justices. The Philadelphia Convention divided the power to appoint and confirm justices between the president and the Senate. That compromise allowed leaders with different constituencies to participate in making such decisions, in essence balancing local against national interests. From the outset, then, the Constitution envisioned a Court composed of justices chosen by elected political leaders. That meant that the appointment and confirmation of Supreme Court justices inevitably became part and parcel of the politics of the day. Long before today's claims of partisan Court rulings, President Thomas Jefferson and Chief Justice John Marshall fought strenuously for several years in the early 1800s over the Supreme Court's authority and judicial independence.

Their dispute began with a fierce struggle over the "midnight appointments" of Federalist judges made at the very end of his term by Federalist President John Adams, which Jefferson strenuously sought to block after succeeding Adams. Several years of warring legislation and related court decisions followed. They included the Supreme Court's acceptance in *Stuart v. Laird* of Jefferson's purge of Federalist judges, achieved through Congress' elimination of their positions by creating a new court system. And they included Marshall's now-famous 1803 decision in *Marbury v. Madison*, asserting the Court's power to decide the constitutionality of federal laws.[241] Their bitter contest eventually led to Jefferson's vigorous effort to impeach and remove the Federalist (and openly partisan) Justice Samuel Chase from the Supreme Court.

The Jefferson-Marshall dispute over the Court's power and what were legitimate grounds for removing Justices by impeachment had enormous ramifications for the Court's independence. In order to save the Court's authority, at one point during the 1805 impeachment trial of Justice Chase, Marshall considered proposing that Congress should be given appellate power to review Supreme Court decisions as an alternative to impeachment. Marshall's astute biographer, Senator Albert Beveridge, accurately called that "the most radical method for correcting judicial decisions ever proposed, before or since."[242] The titanic and highly partisan "midnight judges" and Chase controversies showed that early Americans uniformly recognized that grave political choices were being made through such lifetime judicial appointments. Remarkably, such choices may have an even greater impact today.

The Supreme Court has now become an even less democratic institution than it was in 1787, that is, an institution even less responsive to popular majority will. It is now possible for presidents to appoint justices who will routinely serve for far longer, on average, on the Court than its justices did earlier in American history. And thanks to the Senate's recent adoption of a majority vote rule (as opposed to a supermajority) for confirming justices, lifetime appointments to the Court can now be made on a purely partisan basis.

More remarkably still, the Constitution now enables partisan lifetime judicial appointments to be made even by a minority party. Its rules enable a Supreme Court justice to be chosen and confirmed for life even if the party in control of the Senate and presidency represents only a minority of American voters. In 2018, Justice Brett Kavanaugh was nominated by a president who lost the popular vote, and his appointment was confirmed by the votes of Senators who represented about 44 percent of the American population.[243] Would the Founders would have wanted to permit minority appointments even had they known that such appointments would enable justices to serve far longer today than in 1787? Should we want the Constitution to permit such appointments? To shed light on these questions, it is useful to look further at the historical context surrounding the Court's creation.

When Supreme Court justices were given life terms by the 1787 Constitution, average white life expectancies were much lower than today, but varied by social class among other factors.[244] In the white upper classes from which eighteenth century judges usually came, a reasonable estimate of average life expectancy would be fifty years beyond age 10.[245] Upper class life expectancy then was more than fifteen years lower than average American white male life expectancy today, and probably about twenty years lower than today's upper class life expectancy.[246]

The era's shorter average life expectancy meant that when the Constitution was drafted, justices' actual terms of service on average were likely to be in the range of twenty years or less. During the period from 1789 to 1970, in fact, the average length of service of Supreme Court justices was about fifteen years.[247] Justice Joseph Story, the youngest justice ever appointed to the Supreme Court, was 32 years old when appointed by President James Madison. However, most judges in the eighteenth and nineteenth centuries were a good deal older than Justice Story when appointed.

But as mentioned, average life expectancy has grown dramatically since 1787. As of 2017, average American life expectancy was more than 78 years.[248] That means that if Justice Story had been appointed at age 32 by president William J. ("Bill") Clinton, and had then died on the bench at today's average life expectancy, he would have served for about 45 years after his appointment. Justice Ruth Bader Ginsburg is now 87; if Justice Story had reached her age while serving, he would have been on the bench for 55 years.

The dramatic increase in American average life expectancy means that an average Supreme Court justice appointed in the twenty-first century even at middle age is likely to be able to serve far longer than would have been true of most justices in earlier times. And in fact, during the past five decades, the average tenure of Supreme Court justices has increased dramatically—to an average of more than 25 years (as of 2005).[249] At the same time, the power of the Court has increased, as we saw in chapter 3.

Today there are also distinguished judges who believe that because of the broad language in which many important provisions of the Constitution were written, Supreme Court justices are often free to decide cases in whatever fashion suits their political preferences.[250] As a result, long-serving judges will have far greater ability to substitute their personal political views for those of the people and their elected representatives than would generally have been true two hundred years ago.

The Court is therefore much more antidemocratic today than it was when it was created—and not because the Founders intended it. The emergence of such a "generation spanning" presidential appointment power is an important example of a way in which the Constitution has given presidents—not just Supreme Court justices—more power due to unforeseeable social change.[251] Do we want presidents and their appointed justices to continue to have such exceptionally large authority over the future of America's judicial system?

The Founders' goal in creating life tenure in office for justices was to protect the Court's political independence, not to give one president, or one political party, perpetual control of the Supreme Court for generations. Many observers agree that judicial independence could be protected adequately even by much shorter, fixed and non-renewable appointment terms for justices.[252] We should end the practice of allowing justices to hold office for generations.[253]

THE ANTIDEMOCRATIC SENATE

Over two centuries, the Senate has become a more democratic body in some respects, but far less democratic in others. Senators are now directly elected as a result of the Seventeenth Amendment. That was a major improvement over their election by state legislatures, which was originally provided for in the Constitution despite the facts that legislatures were often gerrymandered or readily corruptible by powerful companies or individuals. But states' equal voting power in the Senate, also mandated by the Constitution, now has even more pernicious anti-democratic effects than it did in 1787. As a result, the Senate has become a major stumbling block to effective government that confers illegitimate political advantages on small states and their dominant political and economic groups.

Many of the Founders recognized that the "Connecticut compromise" giving states equal votes in the Senate violated the republican principle of majority rule, which they saw as the bedrock of government's legitimacy under the new Constitution. For that reason, prominent leaders including James Madison, James Wilson, and others vehemently opposed it at the Philadelphia Convention. But they ultimately realized that they had no choice but to accept under duress what Wilson called a "vicious" principle that twisted the popular will to convince enough of the thirteen original states to agree peacefully to the Constitution. Unfortunately, the limited warping of the popular will these leaders believed that they were accepting has now been transformed into a far larger distortion than they intended.

As James Wilson pointed out at the Philadelphia Convention, the equal state Senate voting rule means that a minority of voters can block the will of the majority. That obstructive power is now unfortunately larger than it was in 1787. When the Constitution was adopted, the six smallest states had about twenty percent of the total population, but received forty-six percent of the Senate votes as a result of the Connecticut compromise. Today, the twenty-eight smallest states that contain twenty percent of America's population have fifty-six percent of the votes in the Senate. That voting strength increase has occurred because the disparity between states in wealth and population has grown dramatically over two centuries.

In 1787, the largest state, Virginia, had about 9 times as large a free population as Delaware, the smallest state. As of 2018, California's population was 69 times as large as Wyoming's. But thanks to the Constitution, California's Senators, who now represent about 39 million people, still have the same number of Senate votes as the Senators from Wyoming, who represent less than 2 percent as many people. The Constitution's "minoritarian" equal state voting principle has important policy consequences for American government, both in allocating money and in shaping national policies.

Senators from states where there are small, primarily rural populations often do not vote the same way on national issues as Senators who represent states with major cities such as New York and Los Angeles. That means that there are times when federal taxpayer money is clearly used to "persuade" small states' Senators to vote for policies preferred by large states. To put it more bluntly, small state votes are bought with appropriated funds. For example, a very careful study by leading political scientists showed that as a result of equal state voting, small states receive far more federal money than they otherwise would, particularly for infrastructure.[254]

But the pernicious consequences of artificially exaggerated small state power extend far beyond just wasteful federal highway spending and funding for other "bridges to nowhere" (spending on projects that lack economic or security justification). Their disproportionate power can warp the expression of national popular will and alter or frustrate important national policies. These distortions are especially significant with respect to partisan issues that cause the small states, which are disproportionately Republican, to oppose the views of large states, which are disproportionately Democratic (as discussed in chapter 2). The following "counterfactual" but nevertheless quite realistic analysis shows the dramatic policy changes that would occur if Senate voting strengths were modified (by constitutional reforms) to make them even somewhat more representative of the actual distribution of America's population and wealth.

A "New" Senate Would Dramatically Change National Policies

Suppose that for a constitutional thought experiment, we restructured voting power in the current ("Old") Senate in order to create a "New" Senate that somewhat more accurately reflected the national popular will. Voting in the New Senate would be based primarily on population, so that Senators from larger states would have more votes than Senators from smaller states. But for our experiment, we deliberately make only a moderate change in states' relative voting strength. It creates a New Senate that is a "halfway house" between the Old Senate and the states' voting strength in the Senate that would exist if it was instead based on directly proportional representation as in the current House of Representatives (see note for details).[255]

Now let's look at a series of actual "Old Senate" votes over about twenty years from the late 1960s to the 1980s and see the likely outcomes if the New Senate had voted on them instead. On a number of issues, national policy would have changed dramatically under the New Senate, often reaching the *opposite* result from the Old Senate.[256]

For example, in 1970 the Old Senate blocked a proposed constitutional amendment abolishing the Electoral College that had previously been adopted by the House of Representatives. But the New Senate would instead quite likely have agreed with the House of Representatives' decision.[257] In view of the fact that that proposed amendment had passed the House of Representatives by an overwhelming majority of 338-70, the New Senate would probably have approved its transmittal to the states. In light of the strong bipartisan support that existed then for direct election of the President (discussed later in this chapter), it is entirely reasonable to think that the Electoral College would have been abolished.

If presidents were directly elected, Albert Gore, Jr., and not George W. Bush, would have become president in 2000 (other things being equal). The Supreme Court would have had no say at all in that election's outcome. Former New York Senator and Secretary of State Hillary Clinton, not real estate developer and reality-TV star Donald Trump, would have become president in 2016. The creation of the New Senate would have significantly changed the course of American history over decades for that reason alone.

Moreover, a variety of important foreign and domestic policies would also have been modified by the New Senate in the 1970s and 1980s. In foreign policy, for example, the New Senate would have firmly rejected several major military policies proposed by the Reagan administration. It would have refused to permit the exceptionally controversial sale of powerful AWACS air battle-management airplanes to Saudi Arabia requested by the Administration. The New Senate would thereby have rejected a major escalation of the Middle East arms race. The New Senate would also have denied funding for deployment of the Safeguard Anti-Ballistic Missile (ABM) system, rejecting a major nuclear arms race escalation proposed by President Reagan.

The New Senate would also have fundamentally changed major domestic policies. It would have adopted legislation to set national "no fault" auto insurance standards to cut car insurance costs.[258] It would have refused to provide a massive federal loan guarantee to bail out defense contractor Lockheed Corporation in 1971. (The Lockheed Corporation bailout became the *only* peacetime precedent for the multibillion dollar 1979 federal loan bailout of Chrysler Corporation.)

The New Senate would also have adopted fundamentally different policies on several major environmental and civil rights issues than the Old Senate. The New Senate would have approved taxes on inland waterway barge fuel, requiring waterway users to bear more of the costs of such waterways—an economically sound environmental policy. The New Senate would have reduced government crop subsidies for both wheat and tobacco, requiring consumers to pay more of their real costs. And the New Senate would have refused to exempt the Tellico Dam in Tennessee from the Endangered Species Act. (The Tellico Dam exemption was the first time any development had ever been exempted from the coverage of the Act).

The New Senate would have adopted more liberal civil rights and labor policies than the Old Senate. It would have rejected South Carolina Senator Strom Thurmond's proposal to prohibit the Justice Department from bringing civil rights lawsuits to require school busing for desegregation. It would have permitted a Senate vote on 1980 legislation to strengthen federal laws to combat housing discrimination. And it would have permitted a Senate vote on important 1978 legislation to reform labor laws.

The New Senate thought experiment shows us that national policy is strongly adversely affected by equal state voting strength in the Senate, because the existing Senate's decisions often fail accurately to reflect the national popular will. Here is a more recent example of the adverse political effects of equal state voting. In the New Senate, fifty-three year old Judge Brett Kavanaugh would not have been confirmed to the Supreme Court. He would have lost by a wide margin (roughly 20 percent or more of the total vote) in the twenty-two larger states that account for about 80 percent of America's population. The proportionately stronger vote for Kavanaugh in the twenty-eight smallest states would not have been enough to overcome that margin. His nomination would have been defeated handily in the New Senate. In other words, Judge Kavanaugh's lifetime appointment to the nation's highest judicial office was entirely an artifact of the Constitution's equal state Senate voting rule.[259]

Should Americans today accept the very large distortion of popular will that results from continuing to use the Constitution's two-hundred-year-old compromise on Senate voting? Should we do so even though it increasingly adversely affects national policy and badly weakens Congress' legitimacy? In thinking about these questions, it is especially noteworthy that a reform of Senate voting would sharply dilute the power of special interest groups (or "factions") in Congress by properly balancing their frequently dominant influence in small states against that of many other interests in the larger states. As we will shortly see, that is one of the same very positive political effects that would flow from the abolition of the Electoral College.

THE ELECTORAL COLLEGE

America will elect its next President in 2020 using the Electoral College system created by the Constitution.[260] Under it, all actual votes for President are cast by "electors," not by popular vote. Presidents are elected by majority vote of the electors. A president can therefore be elected despite losing the popular vote, which has already happened twice in this century alone. It may happen again in 2020 if President

Trump is re-elected. The main justifications offered in 1787 for creating the Electoral College are no longer valid. And it is both far more harmful to our society today and more anti-democratic than it was when it was created.

The Electoral College was the result of tortuous negotiations at the Philadelphia Convention.[261] Popular election was deemed unworkable by many delegates for several reasons.[262] They thought that voters would usually not know candidates personally, and could not become adequately informed because of transportation and communications limitations, so they could not make an informed choice.[263] Popular election might lead to the choice of a demagogue who would become an American Caesar or a king.[264] Finally, James Madison and others were worried that popular voting would mean that states with larger free electorates (as opposed to those with larger populations that included many nonvoting slaves) would cast more votes. As the distinguished constitutional scholar Akhil Amar concludes, none of these arguments against direct popular election of the President is persuasive today. [265]

And the list of the Electoral College's harmful effects is also much longer now than it was in 1787. It violates today's democratic principles in several ways. It denies citizens the right to vote directly for president. It weighs the votes of citizens in some states (individually or collectively) far more heavily than those in others. It inherently creates a large risk that "accidental" minority presidents will be elected in close elections. It gives small states remarkably disproportionate influence in contested presidential elections decided by the House of Representatives (discussed in chapter 3). And it seriously distorts national policies by frequently giving exaggerated political influence to special interest voting blocs in battleground states.

Moreover, the Electoral College effectively creates a pernicious duopoly for the two major parties in presidential elections that deadens political discourse and thwarts policy reforms.[266] Finally, the Electoral College is increasingly dangerous to national security. In an age of global terrorism, foreign government interference in American elections, and potential nuclear war, America can no longer afford the luxury of electing minority presidents whose right to hold the office is questioned by many citizens. Some years ago, Professor Amar wrote that the College was "a constitutional accident waiting to happen."[267] Since he wrote, it has actually caused serious accidents, and it makes worse ones possible.[268] Let's take a closer look at some of its major harms.

As previously mentioned, the Electoral College periodically elects minority Presidents. Some dismiss the "minority president" problem not as a characteristic of the Electoral College but instead as an unpredictable minor fluke. But recent studies by political scientists show that unfortunately it is precisely when Presidential elections are most competitive that the election of a minority candidate is most likely. There is both historical and theoretical evidence supporting that view.

Of the twelve presidential elections through 2016 in which the leading candidate had a margin of less than three points, the Electoral College has chosen a candidate who did not receive a popular vote plurality in at least four (and arguably five) elections.[269] This means that we have elected a minority President in between one out of every three and one out of every four close elections. Unfortunately, it turns out that these results are not accidents after all. The Electoral College often produces minority Presidents when the country most needs a reputable leader who can command public support.

An extensive recent study concludes that the Electoral College's election of minority presidents is not a random fluke, but is instead inherent in its structure.[270] It shows that in very close elections where the popular vote difference is less than one percent, the probability of an "inversion"— i.e., an outcome in which the popular vote result is the opposite of the Electoral College result—is about 40 percent. Where the vote difference is less than two percent, the probability of an inversion is about 30 percent. In today's political environment, inversions favor Republican candidates. The average odds that a Republican will be elected president despite narrowly losing the popular vote are twice or more as high than the chance that a Democrat will win instead in very close elections. The Electoral College favors Republicans in close elections.[271]

Electing minority presidents is dangerous in an increasingly volatile world, because it can lead to the election of a President viewed as illegitimate by a large part of the American people. As discussed previously, when the United States suffered a terrorist attack in 2001, President George W. Bush needed to be able to perform his role as Commander-in-Chief without facing questions about his legitimacy. But even more than two years after the election and well after the 2001 attacks, thirty-eight percent of citizens still did not consider Bush the legitimate president.[272]

Moreover, the investigations of Special Counsel Robert Mueller III and the Senate Committee on Intelligence have recently established that the Russian government engaged in systematic covert activities in an attempt to influence the outcome of the 2016 presidential election.[273] Americans would be well-advised to expect that such secret foreign interventions will continue. That makes it more important than ever that our election outcomes reflect the popular will so that our leaders are nevertheless uniformly regarded as legitimate. By electing minority presidents, the Electoral College increases national security risks. Finally, it has even more anti-democratic effects today than it did in 1787.

The Electoral College works quite differently in practice now than it did two hundred years ago. Today, the population of California is about seventy times as large as the population of Wyoming, but Wyoming is guaranteed about 5 percent of the Electoral College vote given to California. While Wyoming gets one electoral vote for about each 190,000 of its residents, California receives one electoral vote for roughly each 720,000 residents. As the relative sizes of California and other large states have increasingly diverged over time from those of smaller states, the large states' strength in the Electoral College has not kept pace.

As of 2009, the nine largest states, which had 50 percent of national population, had only about 45 percent of the total votes in the Electoral College.[274] In sharp contrast, in 1792 the six largest states comprising half the population of the United States had 63 percent of the total vote in the Electoral College, or a 40 percent larger share of the total vote than today. As of 2006, "every single state with 2.8 percent of the national population or higher [had] less power in the Electoral College than pure proportionality would dictate."[275] At the same time, the winner-take-all system which is used to award electoral votes by nearly every state, largely due to the College's existence, gives voters unequal relative voting strength in different states.[276]

The Electoral College also causes very unfortunate distortions in national policy. It gives wholly unjustifiable political advantages to some bloc voting interest groups located in battleground states because they can "swing" the outcome of Presidential elections. Though varying interest groups have apparently benefited from this systemic bias during different periods of our history, whenever such strategically placed blocs exist their influence can distort national policy.[277] Moreover, the Electoral College-created need to confer special benefits on strategic voting blocs is especially troublesome in the national security and foreign affairs arenas.

Today's politicians are acutely aware that the Electoral College greatly increases presidential candidates' need to give deference or discrete political benefits to any special interest bloc strategically located in pivotal states. A good current example is the artificially exaggerated political influence of senior citizens, who vote heavily as a group (usually three times as heavily as 18-to-24-year olds) and who also vote as a bloc where issues such as the Social Security system's benefits for them are concerned. Taking the "wrong" position on Social Security reform would be likely to cost a presidential candidate in any close election the twenty-nine electoral votes of the state of Florida, due to seniors' bloc voting. And in any really close presidential election, the loss of Florida's electoral votes would inevitably mean the distinct likelihood of losing the entire election. In that light, it is not hard to understand why Social Security has been described as the "third rail" of American politics.

As a result of the Electoral College's exaggeration of senior citizen voting power, Social Security reforms opposed by any significant number of retirees will be far more difficult to achieve than they would be otherwise. When Congress finally acts to avoid the Social Security system's insolvency in the not-too-distant future, benefits for existing retirees—whatever their income level—are very likely to be politically untouchable. Congress will instead have no choice but to increase taxes on younger workers or to extend retirement ages. In fact, senior citizen bloc voting is likely to lead to political pressure to increase

Social Security benefits for existing retirees, thus necessarily imposing even greater burdens on younger workers.

If the Electoral College did not exist, of course, the power of senior citizen bloc voters would be substantially reduced. Their bloc votes in a state such as Florida would no longer sway an election by swinging large numbers of electoral votes. They would have no more influence on elections or national policies than any other similarly-sized group of voters. Their votes in Florida could be entirely offset by those of younger voters in Colorado, for example.

According to constitutional scholar Lawrence Lessig, there is also evidence that under the Electoral College system, presidents "bend their policies to benefit the battleground states." In 2008, for example, by one estimate, four states—Florida, Ohio, Michigan and Pennsylvania—received "more than a billion dollars in additional grant spending simply by virtue of being battleground states." And when the Trump administration lifted a ban on offshore drilling, the battleground state of Florida quickly received an exemption, while New Jersey, which is not a battleground state, did not.[278]

WHY THE ELECTORAL COLLEGE STILL EXISTS

If the Electoral College is as deeply flawed as this evidence shows that it is, why has it not been changed or abolished despite more than 500 proposals to modify it during our nation's history? After all, public opinion polling data as of the early 2000s demonstrated that over a period of fifty years, "a majority of Americans have consistently expressed support for the notion of an official amendment of the U.S. Constitution that would allow for direct election of the President."[279] The history of efforts to reform the Electoral College shows that the main obstacles to reform are the two-party system and the Senate's equal state voting rule.

Earlier efforts to abolish the Electoral College provide an insight into the obstacle created by small states' disproportionate Senate power. As mentioned above, in 1969, the House of Representatives passed a proposed constitutional amendment providing for the direct election of the President by an overwhelming vote of 338-70, or 83 percent of the House members voting.[280] But it died in the Senate in

1970. The amendment was killed by a filibuster coalition of small Mountain State and southern conservative Senators.[281] As we saw earlier, if the Senate voting system had been reformed to create a New Senate, the proposal would quite probably have passed the Senate and been sent to the states for ratification.

About ten years after the 1970 failure, the Senate voted again on a proposed amendment for direct election of the President. This time however, liberal Senators from large states, such as Senators Daniel Patrick Moynihan of New York and Bill Bradley of New Jersey, opposed reform. Their main reason apparently was that Black and Jewish organizations claimed that their influence in major swing states would be diluted by the change. Such group benefits from the College effectively created the other wing of a coalition of odd bedfellows that have opposed reform.[282] Apart from protecting small state interests (discussed below), why are today's Senators still willing to disregard the nation's long-term interest in making the presidency more politically legitimate and responsive?

The best explanation for many Senators' continued support for the Electoral College is that both major political parties and their special interest constituencies can periodically benefit from it while at the same time permanently preventing the rise of national third-party candidacies. The protection the College affords to the two-party system is so obvious that some political scientists have even described that as one of the "benefits" that justifies its continued use.[283] But the Electoral College affects regional and national third party insurgencies in distinctly different and politically dangerous ways. As one study concluded: "The Electoral College system is quite clear in its bias: it favors third parties with a sectional orientation, and it discriminates against those with a national orientation."[284]

For example, in 1968, if white supremacist George Wallace's regionally powerful candidacy had received as little as 13 percent of the total vote, it could have done well enough in the Electoral College to deadlock the election between the two major party candidates. That would have thrown the election into the House of Representatives, and allowed the openly racist Wallace to play kingmaker, profoundly damaging civil rights efforts.[285] But the political environment for national third party candidates under the College is far more hostile.

Their candidacies are seriously impaired by the need to compete nationwide in the major parties' stronghold states. In 1992, for example, businessman Ross Perot received more than 19.7 million votes—18.9 percent of the total vote—and did not receive a single vote in the Electoral College.[286]

The last redoubt for supporters of the Electoral College is the argument that despite all of this remarkably damning evidence against it, the Electoral College should be preserved because it protects the interests of the states, particularly small states, as distinct political entities by giving them added power in presidential elections. In evaluating that claim, it is important to remember that even in 1787, many delegates in Philadelphia thought that there was no legitimate reason whatsoever for a republic to give states special political advantages regardless of their population or wealth merely because they were states.

Quite to the contrary, leading Philadelphia Convention delegates such as James Madison believed strongly that in a republican government political power should not be based on states' mere identity as states, but should instead be proportionally allocated based on relative wealth or population (which at the time were closely correlated). Nor was this a new view. As discussed in chapter 2, John Adams had argued in Congress as early as 1776 that states should not receive equal representation merely because they were states. Everything we know about George Washington's views by 1787 suggests that he agreed with Madison as a result of his bitter experiences with the states. Washington thought that during and after the Revolutionary War the states' leaders were consistently selfish and unwilling to seek and uphold the national interest if it conflicted with their own.[287]

The small states were nevertheless able to force the Philadelphia Convention to protect their interests in various ways, such as equal voting in the Senate and in the Electoral College. But that was entirely a tribute paid to their bargaining leverage. The critical political and military situation then facing the Confederation had created a pressing necessity for consensus. When Convention delegate Gunning Bedford, Jr. of Delaware angrily threatened that his state would ally with a foreign power such as Great Britain if the Convention did not yield to small state demands, the other delegates were acutely aware that the Bay of Delaware alone was large enough to harbor the entire British naval fleet needed to invade the United States. They could not afford to have Delaware—and perhaps other states with similar interests—leave the Union, especially for a dangerous foreign alliance. Since then, of course, political and military realities have changed, and the nation has little to fear from Delaware.

In today's America it is no longer either necessary or desirable to give states qua states special influence in presidential elections. Presidents do not hold office for the purpose of representing states; they are elected to represent the nation. State power in presidential elections cannot be enhanced for some states without prejudicing the interests of other states and of individual voters. Allocating voting strength to states is a zero-sum game (i.e., for every winner, there is a loser). Regarding states as distinct entities might, on the other hand, be useful for analyzing what powers those governments should have if aspects of the Constitution's federalism were being reconsidered by a convention (see chapters 6 and 8). But the desirability of revitalizing federalism cannot serve as a rational basis for defending antiquated political institutions that have now become as obviously flawed as the Electoral College or equal state voting in the Senate.[288]

THE CONSTITUTION, DEMOCRACY, AND GERRYMANDERING

In its 2019 decision in *Rucho v. Common Cause*, the Supreme Court rejected efforts to have partisan "gerrymandering" declared unconstitutional because it violates current democratic principles of voter equality. The Court's ruling has important adverse implications for the future of our democracy.[289] I begin with some background that will be helpful in understanding the issues.

Gerrymandering is a common practice long engaged in by both major political parties. According to data cited by Lawrence Lessig, "in states where Republicans drew the lines, they won 72 percent of the seats with just 53 percent of the votes; in states where Democrats drew the lines, they won 71 percent of the seats with just 56 percent of the votes."[290] But because Republicans currently control a majority of state legislatures, they are its primary beneficiaries at present.[291]

A recent study concludes that in some of the past decade's elections, gerrymandering has shifted election outcomes for as many as 59 out of 435 seats in the House of Representatives. It claims that Republicans have made a net gain through gerrymandering of as many as nineteen seats in Congress in the past several elections, after offsetting the significant number of gerrymandered Democratic seats.[292] In recent years, gerrymandering has caused increasing controversy.

In *Rucho*, plaintiffs in two companion cases—one from North Carolina and one from Maryland—challenged those states' congressional district maps as unconstitutional partisan gerrymandering. The facts of *Rucho* provide good examples of gerrymandering. In North Carolina, Republicans who controlled its state legislature had redrawn its congressional district boundaries to maintain a 10-3 Republican congressional seat advantage, despite the fact that just a few years previously Democratic candidates had received a majority of the statewide congressional vote. In 2016, North Carolina Republicans won 10 out of 13 seats despite receiving only 53 percent of the statewide vote; in 2018, they won 9 out of 12 districts with 50 percent of the vote.[293]

In the Maryland companion case, Democrats in control of redistricting had intentionally revised congressional district boundaries to create a new Democratic congressional seat in a district long held by Republicans. They moved several hundred thousand voters into the new district, sharply decreasing the number of registered Republicans, and increasing registered Democrats. The facts of the North Carolina and Maryland cases left no doubt that they constituted partisan gerrymanders.

But in *Rucho*, by a narrow majority the Supreme Court washed its hands of responsibility for placing constitutional limits on partisan gerrymandering, no matter how much it distorts election outcomes. The Court held 5-4 along ideological lines that gerrymandering presented a nonjusticiable "political question." That meant, the majority held, that federal courts lack power to decide constitutional attacks on that practice based only on alleged partisan discrimination.

Writing for the *Rucho* majority, Chief Justice Roberts relied heavily on gerrymandering's political history in determining its constitutional status. He observed that partisan gerrymandering was known in the colonies before Independence, and that the Framers were familiar with it when the Constitution was drafted. In the first congressional elections held under the Constitution in 1789, well-informed observers such as George Washington and Thomas Jefferson believed that Virginia's highly influential leader Patrick Henry had engaged in gerrymandering to try to prevent James Madison from being elected to Congress.[294]

The *Rucho* majority argued that despite the Framers' clear knowledge of the practice, they had not created any objective standard a federal court could use to decide how much partisan gerrymandering was too much.[295] In addition, the Constitution contains specific provisions giving Congress supervisory authority over elections. Taken together, these considerations led the Court majority to conclude that gerrymandering claims were political questions to be resolved solely by political means.

However, the Court majority also made a striking concession to the Court's four dissenters. It stated explicitly that our understanding of democratic principles has changed markedly since 1787: gerrymandering is now "incompatible with democratic principles."[296] In what could also be seen as a significant tacit concession to the dissenting justices, the majority's opinion also discussed its view that under the Constitution, both individual states and Congress had authority to limit or bar partisan gerrymandering. The majority argued that Congress had actually acted in the past to limit it through measures such as requiring that members of Congress be elected from single-member districts.[297] And it noted that several states were considering barring partisan gerrymandering through judicial challenges or by creating independent commissions to draw district boundaries.[298]

Justice Kagan's vigorous—indeed scathing—dissent in *Rucho*, written on behalf of four justices, insisted that the Constitution required an end to partisan gerrymandering because it violated several provisions of the Constitution and directly undermined democracy. Most importantly, it was an unconstitutional form of discrimination in light of the Court's prior decisions mandating voter equality in other areas. In effect, Justice Kagan's dissent argues that the political history of partisan gerrymandering relied on by the majority is irrelevant, because the practice wholly fails to meet modern democratic standards.

The sharp clash between the majority's reliance on the country's political history as a sanction for gerrymandering and the minority's insistence that modern constitutional standards of equality must be controlling lays bare an important underlying disagreement about how the Court should interpret the Constitution as Americans' views of democracy evolve. That stark disagreement alone is worthy of debate and clear constitutional resolution if we want our political system to move toward consensus. But the *Rucho* decision also rewards a deeper look. It has even broader significance for our political future and for our view of the Court's appropriate role in the constitutional system.

At the heart of the debate in *Rucho* was whether the Constitution mandated proportional representation, at least of the two major parties. Gerrymandering is an important factor in preventing the emergence of such national proportional representation. It helps block changes in the partisan balance in government officeholding even if developing a better balance between the major parties is what many, or perhaps even most, voters in our divided country would prefer. By preventing a partisan balance that reflects voters' choices, it also hinders the development of more bipartisan, consensus policies by the national government, something many voters would quite likely also prefer. Notably, however, the Court's decision—and even the minority's sharp challenge to it—both also effectively sanction our existing majoritarian electoral system, i.e., a two-party system that political scientists agree effectively discourages require proportional representation of minority parties.

As Chief Justice Roberts argued, "Partisan gerrymandering claims invariably sound in a desire for proportional representation." Justice Kagan's dissent argues in substance that proportional representation of the two major parties should be constitutionally required. The majority contends that there is no such requirement in the Constitution, writing that "the Founders certainly did not think proportional representation was required."[299] In support of that view, the majority again relied on political history:

> For more than 50 years after ratification…many States elected
> their congressional representatives through at-large or
> "general ticket" elections….That meant that a party could
> garner nearly half of the vote statewide and wind up without
> any seats in the congressional delegation….When Congress
> required single-member districts in the Apportionment Act of
> 1842, it was not out of a general sense of fairness, but instead
> a (mis)calculation by the Whigs that such a change would
> improve their electoral prospects.[300]

The *Rucho* Court effectively held by a one-vote majority that the
Constitution cannot be used as a means to compel proportional two-
party representation. But if Justice Kagan's position had received only
one more vote, the Court would effectively have amended (or, some
would instead no doubt say, modernized) the Constitution to require
proportional representation for the two major parties.

What should ultimately concern us most about *Rucho*, however, is
that whichever way the Court had decided the case—for or against a
constitutional proportional representation requirement—there is
probably nothing that ordinary voters could do to change that
outcome. Once again, the Supreme Court has had the final word
politically, not just legally, on an issue of truly profound significance
for our political future. The majority's position maintaining the
majoritarian status quo is quite likely to be politically irreversible. We
can see the accuracy of that conclusion by considering the possibility
that gerrymandering will be ended either by Congress or by a
significant number of states in the foreseeable future through ordinary
political means.

Despite the *Rucho* majority's concession that Congress would have
effective power to mandate proportional representation (e.g., by
requiring creation of "nonpartisan" district boundaries), it seems
highly unlikely that a Congress divided sharply along partisan lines will
ever do that. While in theory whichever party gained majority control
of the entire federal government could pass such legislation, it is
unclear why a majority of that party's members would ever voluntarily
agree to do that, since they would very likely be lessening their own
political power as a result. Moreover, the *Rucho* majority's claim that

extensive gerrymandering reforms could occur at the state level tacitly concedes that Congress is unlikely to act.

Realistically, therefore, voters who want to create a proportional representation system will instead need to persuade individual state legislatures to require it, either directly or indirectly by supporting redistricting by judges or independent commissions. Such a process of state-by-state political trench warfare would take decades to achieve significant results. Moreover, it necessarily assumes that the dominant party in a particular state is likely to voluntarily relinquish its dominance, and that that will happen in enough states to make a difference. That seems more like a pious hope than a realistic political prediction. Thoughtful political scientists concerned about gerrymandering do not think that states will eliminate it. Neither did the four dissenting Supreme Court justices in *Rucho*.[301] And there is political history that persuasively supports their views.

The American political evidence from the past two centuries suggests that ordinary state-level political reforms will not end gerrymandering—instead, dominant parties at the state and national level will instead seek to maintain or expand their partisan control, just as they have in the past. A strong parallel is found in the fact that virtually every state uses a "winner-take-all" rule in presidential elections, thus shutting out both the losing major party and any third-party challenger from receiving any electoral votes if the winner gains a plurality (not a majority) of the vote. That rule is designed to increase the benefit of winning for the majority party at the cost of everyone else. For similar reasons, it is likely that states where either major party is dominant will strongly resist gerrymandering reform. As of this writing, 48 out of 49 two-house state legislatures elected on a partisan basis are controlled by one major party or the other. In 36 states, one party or the other controls the entire state government. In these circumstances, the odds that widespread gerrymandering reform will occur at the state level in the foreseeable future seem fairly slim.[302]

In that light, to create proportional representation and break up the two-party duopoly on a nationwide scale would, realistically speaking, require a constitutional amendment. But amending the Constitution solely for the purpose of altering the country's majoritarian electoral system is a political impossibility under the Constitution as it currently exists (for reasons discussed in chapter 5). Is it desirable that the Constitution currently gives the Supreme Court final authority to determine whether the United States uses a majoritarian election system or a proportional system?

Though it is widely used as an election system, particularly in Europe, proportional representation has both supporters and detractors. It appears that proportional representation systems may serve fundamentally different political goals than majoritarian systems such as our present one. For example, majoritarian or "Westminster-style" systems may produce strong party control of government, usually leading them to be more decisive than otherwise. On the other hand, proportional representation may result in including a more diverse range of political views in forming government policies, and some evidence suggests its use leads to lessened inequality.[303] The need to choose between such conflicting political values in designing an electoral system means that the future of our electoral system is just the kind of issue that would best be considered by a future constitutional convention. There it could be examined free from the political influence and enormous vested interests of the existing major parties, and also independently of the views of an unelected Supreme Court whose members are political theoreticians who have never had to face an election or run a government.

CONCLUSION

The Constitution's major political institutions are irreparably flawed as the basis for a modern representative government. They do not provide for adequate representation of the national popular will for two reasons. First, they do not meet modern standards for democratic representation. The constitution now provides increased "generation-spanning" political power to Presidents and the Supreme Court. It also allows both the presidency and the Senate to be controlled by minority parties. Further, the Constitution as now interpreted allows gerrymandering to continue and permits the two major parties to exclude minority voices entirely from representation in Congress. Second, under the Constitution's rules, presidential elections and the operations of Congress increasingly distort the popular will in ways that the Founders did not foresee, and very probably would not have approved. The Constitution's major institutions have failed as a basis for representative government. Nothing can be done to remedy any of these growing shortcomings by means of free-standing constitutional amendments. A new convention will instead be necessary to cure them, for reasons explained in chapter 5.

5

When Will We Amend the Constitution?
When Pigs Fly

This chapter considers the prospects for reforming the Constitution through individual amendments. It then examines popular legislative "workarounds" that supporters claim will avoid the need to amend the Constitution. It makes two central claims. The first is that due to the high hurdle imposed by Article V, no major "freestanding" constitutional amendment that does not have truly overwhelming public support—i.e., much greater than supermajority support—can be adopted in today's divided political climate. As constitutional scholar Lawrence Lessig found, except for the post-Civil War amendments, no constitutional amendment has passed when one of the two parties opposed it.[304] None of the main proposals to amend the Constitution popular today meets that demanding standard, with the possible exception of the Equal Rights Amendment. The chapter's second main assertion is that workarounds to avoid the need for amendments such as the National Popular Vote Initiative ("NPVI") or "court packing" legislation will either not succeed or are cures that are worse than the disease.

The numerous ways in which the Constitution fails to meet current national needs and democratic standards have led various groups to propose amendments. Recent examples include amendments to reverse the Supreme Court's *Citizens United* campaign finance decision or to abolish the Electoral College. In virtually every case, supporters of such reform amendments are unwilling to agree to any other constitutional amendments, so their proposals are best described as "freestanding" amendments.

Under Article V of the Constitution, amendments can be proposed by a vote of two-thirds of both Houses of Congress, or at a convention called for that purpose by Congress on the application of two-thirds of the states. Any amendment must then be approved by three-fourths of the states (38 out of 50 states today). Article V was written with requirements designed to ensure that the Constitution would be difficult to change.

James Madison expressed the view of many Founders when he argued in support of Article V's approach that hard-fought constitutional agreements about ground rules for national life should not be altered lightly or frequently. He thought that allowing frequent amendment would mean that fundamental political choices would be dominated not by "reason" or the wisdom of "patriotic leaders" but instead by "public passions." Thomas Jefferson strongly disagreed with Madison's view, arguing that constitutions should never be set in stone for generations. The dead hand of the past had no right to govern America's future in Jefferson's view.[305] Their profoundly clashing views of the process of republican constitutional change still deserve careful consideration in thinking about the path of reform today.

But Article V's high bar for amendments was erected due to political necessity in 1787, not based on a principled decision that one of those competing views of republican change had the better of that argument. The Convention had no choice but to propose Article V's restrictive approach. The Constitution could not have been ratified without it. The Philadelphia drafters anticipated that ratification would be a sharply contested process. They needed to provide strong—indeed, in some cases, ironclad—assurances that parts of the Constitution which ratification voters would view as necessary to protect their interests—such as its protections for slave states' interests—could not be easily changed under the new national government. Article V was essential to give those guarantees substance.

Article V's strong hindrance against amendments served its intended purpose in the short-term. Within a few years after it was adopted, for example, it became apparent that the Constitution's main structural protections for slavery could never be altered by peaceful democratic means because of Article V's requirements. Instead, it took the Civil War to remove them from the Constitution. And it also took the Civil War to add—in Sanford Levinson's apt phrase, "only at the point of a gun, during the military occupation of the defeated

Confederacy"—the Fourteenth Amendment, which is central to our modern conception of constitutional rights.[306]

The Civil War's deeply tragic events justify the conclusion that the Article V process ultimately backfired and was overly rigid, because it unyieldingly prevented the country from dealing peacefully with its central political and economic divide. Under Article V, the Constitution can be far too successful at preventing critically necessary political changes—and utterly cataclysmic consequences can occur as a result. Article V can indeed be a constitutional "iron cage," and as this chapter will show, today it is one from which there is no realistic prospect of escape on nearly all issues that matter.[307]

Worse still, today Article V can operate in ways even more restrictive than the Founders intended. As the country has grown and disparities in wealth and population between states have increased, and as it has become increasingly divided politically, amendments have become more difficult than ever. Article V ensures that even exceptionally small states are equal participants both in Senate voting on proposed amendments and during the ratification process. As a result, efforts to pass major freestanding amendments are futile, because virtually all such proposed amendments, whether desirable or not, will never pass without overwhelming public support.

Most freestanding amendment proposals fail. In fact, as of 2017, Congress had considered more than 1,000 proposed amendments over the preceding twenty-five years. All had failed.[308] Moreover, between 1789 and 2019, more than 11,000 amendments have been proposed; only 27 have been adopted.[309] The last significant amendment to the Constitution directly relating to electoral politics, the Twenty-Sixth Amendment which gave the right to vote to eighteen-year-olds, was adopted almost fifty years ago.

These facts amply support the conclusion of a knowledgeable observer that "the U.S. Constitution is the most difficult to amend of any constitution currently existing in the world today."[310] In fact, a number of leading political scientists have abandoned any real hope for constitutional change. In introducing an extensive 2019 study of American government's major problems, its editors wrote: "constitutional amendment and revision—challenging even during consensual eras—seem foreclosed by the persistent divides in

American politics."[311] That is also the conclusion reached by constitutional scholar Mark Graber. Graber thinks that the core reason for constitutional dysfunction is partisan polarization, but that polarized parties will never agree to constitutional reforms that may change the partisan balance of power, so meaningful constitutional reform cannot occur. Graber's specific concerns are addressed in chapter 6.[312] But in view of the number of reform proposals that have broad public support, it is worth taking a closer look at the nature of the problems created by Article V and why they occur to see if and to what extent such pessimistic conclusions are justified.

Even a brief glance at Article V's provisions shows that they do make it politically impossible to adopt certain kinds of freestanding amendments. For instance, Article V provides that "no State, without its Consent, shall be deprived of its equal Suffrage in the Senate." That permits any state to veto any change in the relative Senate voting strength of all fifty states that affects it, no matter what the other forty-nine states have decided they want. As a result, any freestanding constitutional amendment that alters the equal voting strength of states is doomed to fail.

Article V's requirement that states, not population (or some other measure), be used as voting units for ratification purposes has far broader implications, however. It also means, for example, that even without Article V's unanimous consent requirement, a change in relative Senate voting strength desired by thirty-seven states representing more than 90 percent of today's population could be defeated by thirteen states representing less than 10 percent of the population.

More broadly, by virtue of today's radically different national economy and geography alone, the terms "three-fourths of the states" and "three-fourths of the population" frequently have far less correlation with each other now than they did when Article V was written. That fact has profound political consequences. Today, when roughly eighty percent of America's population lives in twenty-two larger states, there are clearly times when the Article V requirement that three-fourths of the states—or thirty-eight states—ratify constitutional amendments imposes a much higher bar against ratification than the Founders intended. This is especially problematic when, as is often true today, widely desired reforms divide the United States along urban-rural or partisan lines (which are often overlapping).

One class of amendment that Article V also makes it impossible to adopt is any amendment that might modify relative partisan strength, such as an anti-gerrymandering amendment. That would also be true of any amendment to eliminate or even weaken the existing two major party duopoly by enabling the development of third parties. Any proposal that would have either of those effects, even if nominally nonpartisan, is highly likely to be viewed as adverse to the interests of at least one of the two major political parties. It follows that to successfully propose such an amendment in Congress under Article V, one party would have to have a two-thirds supermajority in both Houses.

But in the past fifty years, neither major party has had a two-thirds majority in both houses of Congress. In fact, there have only been a few congresses in the past 100 years where one party had a two-thirds supermajority in both houses of Congress. During one of those periods—the New Deal—despite the era's enormous constitutional controversies, the Roosevelt Administration chose not to propose any constitutional amendments. Roosevelt instead unsuccessfully proposed a legislative "court packing" workaround discussed below. In light the persistence of some level of partisan balance over the past century, any amendment to end gerrymandering or to increase third party competition and voice opposed by either major party is highly unlikely ever to be adopted by Congress.

Another type of freestanding amendment Article V makes it impossible to adopt is one perceived as significantly impairing the political power of small states. For example, no amendment would ever be adopted that took away the state "bonus," i.e., the right of any state to have at least three votes in the Electoral College. Under Article V, states constituting much less than twenty percent of the population could and would block it either in the Senate or in state legislatures. But in today's political climate, America's urban-rural divide and uneven distributions of population and wealth also mean that many other types of constitutional amendments will not be adopted. Let's look at a series of prominent freestanding amendment proposals, and consider their likely prospects, which are dismal indeed.

ABOLISHING THE ELECTORAL COLLEGE: "WHEN PIGS FLY"

There is no chance whatsoever that a constitutional amendment abolishing the Electoral College will be adopted under Article V. We can see this by looking briefly at the history of such efforts over the past fifty years and then considering the even more forbidding current political climate. In chapter 4, we looked at several unsuccessful efforts to get Congress to propose an amendment abolishing the Electoral College; here we take a brief look at them from a different perspective.

In 1970, a proposed abolition amendment was passed overwhelmingly by the House of Representatives. Remarkably, more than 80 percent of each major party's voting members supported it. Public opinion polls showed bipartisan support for the amendment as well. According to one study, "in May 1968, 66 percent of Americans approved of the idea of amending the constitution to replace the Electoral College with a popular vote system, according to Gallup. And there was no partisan divide: 66 percent of Republicans and 64 percent of Democrats approved."[313]

But even after the proposed amendment's overwhelming approval by the House of Representatives, it died in a Senate filibuster led by Senators from small mountain states and southern conservatives. In 1979, a similar proposal died in the Senate, this time due to opposition from several large state liberal Senators such as Daniel Patrick Moynihan of New York and Paul Sarbanes of Maryland who were influenced by opposition from Black and Jewish organizations whose members thought that their political interests would be damaged by Electoral College abolition.[314]

This political history shows us that in the 1960s and 1970s, proposals to abolish the Electoral College were being judged by elite leaders, as opposed to the public, primarily from the perspective of geographic or special interest group political advantage. Though abolition opponents were very probably in the minority, their opposition was enough to doom the proposals given Article V's stringent requirements. The same strong incentive to evaluate abolition proposals based on interest group advantage exists today, but its effects are worsened because there is now a large partisan split on the issue that did not exist fifty years ago.

As we saw in chapter 4, the evidence suggests that the Electoral College not only benefits small states disproportionately but gives a systematic advantage to Republican presidential candidates, who benefit from periodic inversions in close elections. At present therefore, both Republican partisans and small state representatives have incentives to oppose its abolition. And there is now a large overlap between partisan representation and geography in both the House of Representatives and the Senate, making intense partisan divisions in Congress on abolition likely. That conclusion is reinforced by the fact that current polling data show that a very large majority of Democrats support abolishing the Electoral College, while only a minority of Republicans support it.[315]

Those partisan realities suggest that it is highly unlikely that both the House and the Senate would pass proposals to abolish the Electoral College. Voting in Congress on any proposal to abolish the Electoral College would occur largely along partisan lines, and that would mean its defeat. Since 1980, Democrats, who are today's leading proponents of abolishing the College, have not controlled a large enough number of votes in both the House and the Senate for Congress to adopt such an amendment without Republican support. Even when Democrats had substantial (though not supermajority) control of both Houses in the 111th Congress during the Obama administration, they did not bring an abolition proposal to a vote; in all likelihood, it would have failed.

A 2019 Electoral College abolition proposal by Sen. Brian Schatz (D. Hawaii), S.J. Res 17, gained only three Senate co-sponsors in its first year. All were Democrats. Meanwhile, several Republican senators announced their opposition. All in all, these facts support one analyst's recent conclusion that an amendment to abolish the Electoral College will pass "when pigs fly." Or, as Jacob Levy, a political theorist at McGill University, concluded more formally in 2019: "There's no realistic chance of a Constitutional amendment to abolish the Electoral College."[316]

REVERSING *CITIZENS UNITED* OR ENABLING WEALTH TAXATION? NOT GOING TO HAPPEN

Proposals for a constitutional amendment to reverse the Supreme Court's *Citizens United* decision have been made almost since the day in 2010 when it was announced, but have gone nowhere. There is no reasonable prospect that a freestanding reversal amendment will ever be proposed by Congress or the states, let alone ratified, despite appearances to the contrary.

Citizens United opponents are no doubt cheered by the fact that on paper, every Democratic Senator in 2019 is on record as supporting a reversal amendment. As of the spring of 2020, 210 members of the House have also co-sponsored such an amendment. In addition, supporters claim that as of late 2019, many organizations and twenty states support a reversal amendment.[317] A 2018 survey showed that there was also strong public support for reversal.[318] According to the opinion study conducted by a University of Maryland organization, three-fourths of survey respondents—66 percent of Republicans and 85 percent of Democrats—back a constitutional amendment. Ironically, however, the same news story that reported these survey results said that a constitutional amendment was "highly unlikely" to happen.[319] That pessimistic conclusion is clearly correct for several reasons.

First, *Citizens United* is regarded as primarily favoring Republicans, so the issue is perceived in strongly partisan terms by elected leaders. In September 2014, a majority of U.S. Senators voted in favor of a constitutional amendment to reverse *Citizens United*. But the unsuccessful vote was entirely along party lines: all 42 "No" votes came from Republicans and all 54 "Yes" votes came from Democrats.[320] In 2019, there are no Republican cosponsors for the reversal proposal supported by all Senate Democrats. Only one Republican House member reportedly supports it. That stark partisan divide will persist.

At current levels of support in the House of Representatives in the spring of 2020, proponents of a reversal amendment are roughly 80 votes short of the necessary two-thirds majority. Virtually all its supporters are Democrats. But even if every Democratic House member ultimately supported the proposal, supporters would still be almost sixty votes short of the required two-thirds majority. Moreover, even if a reversal proposal passed the House, Republican opposition would probably prevent it from ever even being considered in the Senate, let alone adopted.

The evidence from the past decade shows that Congress will not propose a constitutional amendment to reverse *Citizens United* in the foreseeable future. As Lawrence Lessig concludes, "there is exactly zero chance that the United States Congress is going to pass by a two-thirds vote an amendment to effectively reverse *Citizens United*. Zero."[321]

Supporters of reversal also take heart from claims that twenty states have reportedly supported a reversal amendment. But that statistic very probably counts at least three states whose supposed "support" would eventually become the subject of litigation, because it did not stem from formal legislative action.[322] Realistically, ten years after *Citizens United*, only about half of the thirty-four states required under Article V even to request that Congress call a convention to consider the issue have acted in some manner in favor of an amendment. Even the states that have acted are badly divided on a critical strategic issue. Only six states have reportedly actually requested a convention; the others have instead asked Congress to propose an amendment, which will not happen.[323]

Wholly apart from these figures, however, there is the undeniable reality that despite reams of pious rhetoric, politicians of both parties continue to accept the expanded campaign financing support from the wealthy enabled by *Citizens United*. Elected officials of both parties still greatly benefit from money being raised and spent by "Super PACs," which are nominally independent of their campaigns, but which virtually all knowledgeable political observers believe operate in tandem with them. As noted in chapter 2, they have raised roughly $3 billion over the past ten years. Politicians are also still reaping windfalls from spending by so-called "dark money" PACs that do not need to disclose their donors. As discussed earlier, it is estimated that the top fifteen dark money groups alone have raised and spent $600 million since *Citizens United* was decided; some estimates of the total amount of dark money contributions by the end of 2019 approach $1 billion.[324]

There are both liberal and conservative organizations operating such "dark money" PACs. A list of such organizations compiled by the Center for Responsive Politics for the 2016 election cycle includes not just the National Rifle Association and the U.S. Chamber of Commerce, but the League of Conservation Voters, Planned Parenthood, NARAL Pro-Choice America, and the Environmental Defense Action Fund.[325] Both parties benefit from this dark money funding. As a 2017 article reported, "Democrats are following Republicans' lead by raising millions of dollars in so-called 'dark money' contributions, the origins of which are largely untraceable."[326] As noted in chapter 2, one dark money PAC alone, the Sixteen Thirty Fund, raised more than $140 million in the 2018 election cycle.[327] Instead of rejecting Super PAC and dark money funding, most Democratic and Republic political campaigns use the "nuclear arms race" defense for acquiescing in Super PAC and dark money funding—"we have no choice but to benefit from such expenditures because our opponents certainly will." The fact that Congress cannot even agree to pass campaign finance disclosure legislation to end dark money strongly reinforces the conclusion that it is highly unlikely to agree on proposing reversal of *Citizens United.*

The fate of a constitutional amendment permitting wealth taxation of the kind proposed by Senators Warren and Sanders in their 2020 presidential campaigns is fairly easy to predict from the fact that *Citizens United* will not be reversed. We can safely conclude that a constitutional amendment allowing wealth taxation will not be proposed, let alone adopted under Article V. Most elected officials opposed to reversing *Citizens United* will also oppose permitting wealth taxation. That level of opposition alone would probably doom a wealth tax amendment. But the actual opposition to a wealth taxation amendment may prove even broader than the opposition to *Citizens United* reversal.

Permitting wealth taxation will almost certainly be nearly uniformly opposed by wealthy individuals, and as discussed in chapter 2, they are major contributors to both political parties. Many of them will regard a politician's willingness to support wealth taxation as a political litmus test, and will refuse to contribute to anyone who supports such a tax. So, we can expect that wealth taxation will be opposed both by nearly all Republicans and either privately or publicly by many Democratic leaders under pressure from the wealthy. Consequently, neither Congress nor the states are likely to have supermajority support to propose a wealth tax amendment in the foreseeable future. That means, of course, that as often happens under the Constitution today, the Supreme Court will have the final word—in this case, on whether Congress has the power to tax wealth. As the next section shows, that may be equally true of the future of congressional power over gun control.

GUN CONTROL

Recent public opinion polls show that a majority of Americans support stronger gun control legislation, but that they are sharply divided on that issue along partisan lines. According to a late 2019 news report, "a Pew Research Center survey conducted in September found that 60% of Americans say gun laws should be tougher...eighty-six percent of Democrats and Democratic-leaning independents said gun laws should be stricter than they are today, compared with 31% of their Republican counterparts."[328]

As we saw in chapter 3, the Constitution plays an important part in preventing even clearly constitutional gun control legislation from being passed by Congress. This is partly a tribute to the political clout of gun owners and the NRA, but their influence is significantly exaggerated by the disproportionate Senate voting strength given by the Constitution to smaller states in which there are large numbers of gun owners. The twenty-nine states with the highest levels of gun ownership have 58 percent of the Senate votes, but only 46 percent of the population. If they vote as a bloc on gun control issues, they can prevent Senate passage of nearly any form of gun control legislation. In fact, by themselves they have nearly enough voting strength to prevent the Senate from even considering such legislation under the existing filibuster rule (which typically requires a minimum of 60 votes to adopt legislation).

These same political dynamics will prevent any proposal to modify the Second Amendment from succeeding under Article V. In view of the partisan divisions over the issue, and the political strength of gun owners in smaller states, Congress will not pass any such proposal by the necessary two-thirds majority of both Houses. Nor is it realistic to think that thirty-four states will petition Congress for a convention to consider a gun control amendment. As a result of these divisions, the Supreme Court majority will continue to have the power to determine the contours of permissible gun control regulation at the local, state and federal levels. In short, despite clear public sentiment for strengthening gun control nationwide, the Constitution is a major obstacle to any significant reforms in this area.

BALANCED BUDGET AMENDMENT

Congress will not propose a balanced budget amendment ("BBA") to the states under Article V. Supporters will be unable to obtain the required two-thirds vote of both houses in support of an amendment, recent congressional action shows. In April, 2018, BBA supporters in the Republican-controlled House of Representatives failed to obtain a two-thirds vote for an amendment.[329] The vote occurred along nearly perfect party lines, with Republican majority supporters receiving 55.8%. There is no reason whatsoever to expect a Democratic majority-controlled House to adopt such a proposed amendment given that partisan divide. Unless control of both the House and the Senate shifts exceptionally strongly in favor of Republicans, or a political earthquake dramatically changes the climate of opinion, Congress will not propose a balanced budget amendment.

Nor will Congress be willing to approve holding an Article V convention to consider a BBA unless political circumstances change dramatically. It is very unlikely that thirty-four states will adopt valid resolutions calling for one in the first instance.[330] In fact, as of mid-2020, BBA supporters appear to be conceding the defeat of their efforts to obtain the necessary state resolutions. BBA leaders are now reportedly developing an alternative that would add unrelated state general convention resolutions (some passed long ago) to state BBA resolutions to reach a nominal total of thirty-four states, and would then attempt to force a convention through litigation if Congress will not act.[331] That plan is virtually guaranteed to fail, as can be seen from the following analysis. Let's assume the best case for BBA supporters, that they succeeded in obtaining thirty-four state resolutions supporting a convention. Congress has never approved calling a convention for any purpose, and there are good reasons to think that a BBA convention will not be the first one it approves. At this writing, twenty-eight states have adopted resolutions on that subject.[332] These states contain about fifty percent of the population. All but one of them were controlled by the Republican party at the state level as of 2018, so the states' BBA convention call pattern exactly tracks the partisan split in the 2018 House vote. The BBA is perceived as a purely partisan issue.

If Congress received thirty-four state BBA petitions, under current circumstances opponents would still likely be in a majority in states that currently possess about 40 percent of House seats (roughly 175 seats) and almost one-third of the votes in the Senate. They would stoutly resist a partisan effort to obtain congressional convention approval. They would have plenty of ammunition. First, there are critical unresolved constitutional questions about whether under Article V Congress has power to limit the scope of a constitutional convention or to adopt rules that would govern it (these exceptionally important issues are discussed further in chapter 6). Therefore, notwithstanding efforts BBA supporters have made to address concerns about a "runaway" convention, opponents will undoubtedly argue that a runaway convention would result from congressional approval. They would also be quite likely to challenge the validity of various state resolutions seeking a convention (especially if they are unrelated general convention resolutions), and to propose legislative alternatives to a BBA, as well as encouraging litigation against the BBA convention proposal.

As a result, Congress will likely approve a BBA convention only if Republicans firmly control both its branches. A convention called by Congress by a vote on party lines would be perceived as an entirely partisan effort. I agree with Lawrence Lessig's view that that would by itself doom the convention's work to failure when ratification debates occurred.[333] I also agree with him that if Congress declined to call a convention and its inaction was then challenged in court by BBA supporters, it is exceptionally unlikely that the Supreme Court would be willing to intervene, deeming it a nonjusticiable "political question."[334]

In these circumstances, instead of approving a convention based on state petitions, it seems far more likely that Congress would adopt legislation to defuse pressure for a balanced budget constitutional amendment. That is just what it did successfully in 1985, when thirty-two states had petitioned for a balanced budget amendment.[335] BBA supporters today might well regard the passage of new legislation instead of a convention as a failure.   Past federal budget-control legislation failed to prevent worsening fiscal problems, and legislation can always be repealed.   Nevertheless, despite its supporters' efforts, the push for a BBA amendment is just as likely to fail ultimately as the rest of the currently popular amendment proposals.

THE EQUAL RIGHTS AMENDMENT

The Equal Rights Amendment to the Constitution was originally proposed by Congress in 1972, or forty-eight years ago as this is written.[336] The legislation Congress adopted when proposing the amendment contained in its preamble an explicit seven year deadline for state ratifications.[337] By 1978, thirty-five of the necessary thirty-eight states had ratified the amendment. Five of them had subsequently adopted rescission laws or resolutions.   In 1978, Congress adopted legislation by majority vote extending the deadline for three years—until 1982.[338] No additional states ratified the ERA before the 1982 deadline.

As of early 2020, on paper thirty-eight states have now ratified the ERA, if one disregards deadline and rescission issues. Two of the states that recently ratified did so in 2017 and 2018.[339] In early 2020, Virginia ratified the ERA—becoming the 38th state to ratify. Virginia's ratification will only result in adoption of the ERA, however, if: (1) Congress passes legislation to extend the deadline through Virginia's ratification; (2) that legislation is upheld against the certain constitutional challenge to it; and (3) all five prior state rescissions are also invalidated. The prospects for ratification through litigation are quite doubtful at best, particularly given the current conservative makeup of the Supreme Court. Moreover, Justice Ruth Bader Ginsburg has publicly expressed skepticism about the legality of late state ratifications, and said ERA advocates should "start over." Without her vote, defeat is "all but certain," but even with her vote, defeat is likely.[340]

Remarkably, however, even before Virginia's ratification occurred, the constitutional plot had begun to thicken further. Abortion rights groups and their right-to-life opponents have recently concluded that the ERA either should be, or might be, construed to include a constitutional right to abortion (of some dimension).[341] That new element of this chapter of the ERA controversy will inform all of the court challenges concerning ratification, and will guarantee that both sides will litigate the issue to the bitter end.

The ERA is the exception that proves the rule that today Article V prevents significant amendments unless there is overwhelming public support for them. During the almost fifty years in which the amendment has been pending, popular support for equal rights for women has grown to the point where it can fairly be described as nearly unanimous. Poll data from 2001 showed 88 percent approval of a constitutional provision. But by 2016, a poll showed overwhelming public support for the ERA: "94% of those polled said they would support an amendment to the U.S. Constitution that guarantees equal rights for both men and women. This extraordinary level of support was expressed by both men and women—90% of men and 96% of women polled...Democrats, Republicans and Independents all overwhelming[ly] support the amendment as well: 97% of Democrats, 90% of Republicans, and 92% of Independents."[342]

But even if the ERA were ultimately deemed ratified after this remarkably tortuous process, its history raises further questions about the value of Article V itself. In today's political climate there will be extensive future court fights over the ERA's implications, including the power it grants Congress to implement it by "appropriate legislation." Why would we want the process of adopting a single constitutional amendment to take more than fifty years, only to result in decades of additional litigation? Would it not be much better for us to reach a reasonably clear meeting of the minds about how a proposed amendment would change the constitution or significant laws during its original drafting, and then to have a political debate over its advisability that could be and should be resolved within one generation, rather than three or more? And why in any event is it desirable to let states, as opposed to voters, make such choices, particularly in a case like the ERA?

Because many significant constitutional reforms are blocked by the stringent requirements of Article V, reform advocates have increasingly looked for other ways to achieve their goals without amending the Constitution. The next section looks at the equally dismal prospects for some of these proposed "solutions" and the significant constitutional problems they will cause if adopted.

"Informal" Amendments and Workarounds

Some constitutional reformers claim that it is possible to avoid the need for amendments because the Constitution can be "informally" amended by Supreme Court adaptations of the Constitution to meet modern needs, by interpreting it as a "living" Constitution.[343] However, that approach will ultimately destroy republican government. That is true even assuming that for argument's sake here we deny any weight whatsoever to the claims of constitutional originalists that it rests on a mistaken view of the Founders' intent.

It is true, of course, that the Constitution has been "informally" amended, for example during the New Deal, when the Supreme Court ultimately permitted Congress to significantly expand its powers of economic regulation over the national economy.[344] There are constitutional scholars who believe that such an informal amendment process is all that is needed to make the Constitution adequately responsive to national needs and popular will. Moreover, they commonly believe that only informal amendment is desirable because otherwise the exercise of the popular will would have excessive and in their view negative influence on the Constitution. They almost uniformly regard allowing the Supreme Court entirely to control constitutional interpretation as preferable to an amendment or convention process because the Supreme Court's decisions are significantly influenced by elite lawyers and legal scholars, and are therefore supposedly not subject to what they see as dangerous, ill-informed popular passions.

But as Sanford Levinson has emphasized, such an informal amendment process is utterly incapable of making any of the urgently needed structural changes to the Constitution, such as abolishing the Electoral College or ending equal state Senate voting.[345] Advocates of informal amendment must therefore accept the Constitution's inherent, ever-increasing distortion of the popular will on a broad range of national policies in return for continued elite control of constitutional interpretation. And as a powerful recent critique by leading political scientists of the informal amendment approach emphasizes, "the commonsense pragmatism of the living Constitution threatens to unravel" "the framers' handiwork altogether" by depriving existing constitutional institutions of any substantial authority.[346] That tradeoff becomes a worse one every day, as national policies wholly fail to respond to rampant inequality and deteriorating economic and social conditions for America's poor and middle class which increasingly threaten America's ability to forge a peaceful future.

But the approach of such informal amendment or "living originalism" advocates will cause an even greater harm, because it has as its inevitable consequence the end of republican government. Congress' authority and willingness to legislate will continue to decline because living originalism will be completely unable to reform it. Therefore, living originalists must instead hope for an unbroken era of reigns by benevolent, far-sighted elected monarchs, a hope which our recent history suggests is wholly illusory. Instead, informal amendment, "living originalism," or other variants of those approaches are sure recipes for inevitable republican collapse in the wake of ever-increasing executive power.

As both our history and current politics show unmistakably, informal amendment also faces the insuperable difficulty that the Supreme Court is not truly independent of politics, especially in times of national division and social stress. Supreme Court majorities are entirely capable of making remarkably poor political decisions driven by ideology, and they can also unquestionably be captured by political factions. Anyone who thinks that the Supreme Court cannot err on constitutional issues in ways that severely damage the national polity need only consider the Court's *Dred Scott* decision just before the Civil War, which permanently denied United States citizenship to African-Americans and invalidated the Missouri Compromise on slavery.[347] That decision is often believed to have been motivated by a desire to lessen the chances of civil war, but instead very probably increased them.

Moreover, permitting constitutional interpretation and amendment to be the exclusive province of the Supreme Court will also inevitably damage not just Congress but representative democracy itself. The contrary view, that the Court should always have the constitutional "last word," means that as discussed in chapter 3, the Supreme Court can and will increasingly step into the vacuum created by failures of the political system, and make final decisions about what are ultimately choices about political values, not law. Ironically, as a result the Court will be increasingly dependent on the willingness of presidents to accept and enforce its decisions, ultimately strengthening the already imperial presidency (as discussed further below).

For these reasons, while one can certainly defend interpreting the Constitution as a living document in cases that require elaborating established constitutional principles, it cannot ultimately preserve representative democracy. In order to effect lasting change while preserving democracy, the Constitution must be amended through a representative process instead. The extreme difficulty of changing the Constitution through the Article V process has, however, instead led reform advocates to propose legislative "workarounds" that they think would avoid the need for constitutional amendments. Two leading workarounds are the National Popular Vote Initiative and "court packing."

THE NATIONAL POPULAR VOTE INITIATIVE WILL FAIL

The National Popular Vote Initiative ("NPVI"), a state-level legislative initiative, is founded on the idea that collective inter-state agreements to honor the results of the national popular vote in casting Electoral College votes can nullify the effects of the Electoral College, avoiding any need to abolish it through amendment. Under the NPVI proposal, each supporting state legislature passes a law providing that that state will join with other states in a reciprocal agreement that they will cast their state's electoral votes for the winner of the national popular vote. If states that have a total of more than 270 electoral votes agree to the NPVI, then their electoral votes should be sufficient to elect as president the winner of the popular vote.[348] It is easy to see why the NPVI appeals to many people. However, there are two compelling reasons why this particular workaround is very likely never to take effect.

The first is that the NPVI is increasingly perceived as a partisan political initiative being pursued primarily by Democrats. This is very unfair, since there is nothing inherently partisan about the NPVI proposal; but unfortunately, politics isn't always fair. Since its 2006 debut, the NPVI has been adopted by sixteen states that currently have a total of 196 electoral votes.[349] Of these sixteen states, fourteen were under Democratic control in 2018, and two were under split control.[350] As of mid-2020, not a single state legislature under Republican control has agreed to the NPVI. There is apparently also some backlash in states that have approved it. In one of the split states, Colorado, an approved 2020 ballot question will ask voters to decide whether to overturn the legislature's approval of the NPVI. As of late 2019, there are reports that there are also other states in which NPVI opponents are seeking to reverse earlier state approvals.[351]

The partisan pattern of state legislative NPVI approvals and resistance to it both strongly suggest that despite its nonpartisan nature, the Republican party at least increasingly views it as a partisan initiative. Because at present the Electoral College inherently provides an advantage to Republican candidates in close elections, it is not difficult to see why. In light of this partisan division, it is not clear what states the additional 74 electoral votes needed to meet the NPVI's minimum vote total will come from, even assuming that Colorado does not alter its position. And that division does not augur at all well for a higher hurdle the NPVI will need to meet in order to become law, which is that under the Constitution, Congress may have to approve it.

According to the Congressional Research Service ("CRS"), NPVI supporters have described its legal nature in various ways.[352] But a CRS expert thinks that the better view is that NPVI is an interstate compact.[353] That would mean that it is covered by the Compact Clause in Article I, Section 10 of the Constitution, which requires congressional approval of many compacts before they can become effective. NPVI supporters claim, however, that even if it is a compact, it does not require congressional approval.[354] Opponents claim that Congress must approve it.[355]

No matter which view on the need for congressional approval of the NPVI is correct, the Supreme Court is very likely to be called on to resolve that issue, and it will have little choice but to hear the case. The Court would then be faced with a remarkable political dilemma that might well permanently impair its institutional legitimacy. It would be forced to choose between "ducking" the issue on the grounds that it was a political question, on the one hand, or effectively destroying either the NPVI or the Electoral College entirely on its own authority, on the other.

If the Court rules that the issue of the need for NPVI's approval by Congress presents a political question and thus permits the NPVI to operate, that may simply defer the problem. Future presidential election results would then be litigated, and close elections quite possibly decided by the Supreme Court, just as *Bush v. Gore* was. If instead the Court rules that the NPVI does not need congressional approval, that is the end of the Electoral College. But if the Court holds that Congress must approve the NPVI compact, which may well be the Court's path of political least resistance, that will very probably lead to the compact's demise. Whichever way the Court decides the case, the losers will be convinced—whether events justify that view or not—that the Court has betrayed the Constitution for partisan ends.

If Congress does consider approving the NPVI as a compact, it is likely to encounter insurmountable opposition there, or to be vetoed by the president. NPVI supporters recognize that, which is why they are vehemently insisting that it does not need Congress' approval.

Opposition will occur for much the same reasons that Congress will not adopt an Electoral College abolition proposal. An interstate compact needs only majority approval by the two houses, not supermajority approval as an Article V amendment would require.

However, the Constitution has provided NPVI opponents with a huge advantage—equal state voting in the Senate.

Twenty-one out of the twenty-eight smallest states in the country have not ratified the NPVI at this writing. If the Senators from those states choose to vote against it, as is likely, their 42 votes will by themselves be able to block its approval by sustaining a Senate filibuster. To control a majority of the Senate and defeat the NPVI on the merits, the small states would only need the votes of Senators from five out of the thirteen larger states that have not yet adopted it; several of these states are quite unlikely to approve it. And, of course, any president who supported the Electoral College would be likely to veto a compact approval bill. If the president happens to be a Republican, a veto is fairly likely. It is highly unlikely that the necessary supermajority could be obtained to override any presidential veto.

The long-term partisan divisions in state legislatures and the divisive politics of the Electoral College together suggest that the NPVI cannot escape partisan controversy. Absent future large-scale partisan political shifts, it is quite likely never to gain full state legislative or Congressional approval. And the dispute over it may permanently damage the legitimacy of the Supreme Court. To abolish the Electoral College and end its harmful effects, it will instead be necessary to amend the Constitution.

COURT PACKING

Many constitutional reform advocates have realized in recent years that they will be unable to amend the Constitution to meet goals such as reversing *Citizens United.* They are also convinced that the federal courts, particularly the Supreme Court, are increasingly under partisan control. They therefore propose to achieve reforms instead through "court packing"—that is, by appointing additional judges who will then vote to overturn court decisions they oppose or favor reforms they support. There is precedent for that idea, since President Franklin Delano Roosevelt ("FDR") proposed court packing in 1937. But as we will see, Roosevelt's legislation failed.[356] Current court packing proposals are likely to fail for similar reasons; and they would severely damage the Constitution's separation of powers in the unlikely event they were successful.

In February, 1937 FDR, who had been greatly angered by the Supreme Court's decisions against the constitutionality of various New Deal programs, proposed legislation to allow him to "pack" the federal courts. Roosevelt's bill would have given him the power to appoint both additional Supreme Court justices and lower court judges. Under his plan, the President could appoint no more than six Supreme Court justices, and no more than two new judges on any lower federal court (up to a total of 50 new judges initially).

The obvious primary intent and effect of FDR's proposal was to give him immediate power to appoint enough Supreme Court justices to give him a Court majority that would sustain the constitutionality of various New Deal programs. (Although Roosevelt argued that the Court needed additional justices because it was overworked, it was very widely believed that that was a pretext). The political climate for his proposal still seemed highly favorable. Only a few months before making it, Roosevelt had won re-election in 1936 by a very large majority. Democrats, who were mostly fairly strong New Deal supporters, also had very rare supermajorities in both houses of Congress. Still, Roosevelt's proposal was resoundingly defeated both in the court of public opinion and in Congress.

Public opinion polls consistently showed that a majority of the public opposed the bill, despite Roosevelt's fireside chats supporting it. Both liberal and conservative Democrats opposed it. Senator Burton Wheeler of Montana, a strongly progressive New Deal supporter, became "the plan's chief opponent in the Senate."[357] New York Governor Herbert Lehman, a prominent liberal and one of Roosevelt's strongest supporters, publicly opposed the plan. Lehman's defection was seen as a "jolting blow between the eyes" to Roosevelt.[358] The Democratic chairman of the House of Representatives Committee on the Judiciary was so strongly opposed to the bill that Roosevelt's forces never sought House action.

The Democratic-controlled Senate Judiciary Committee heard extensive testimony on the bill. A leading witness opposing it, prominent legal scholar Erwin Griswold of Harvard Law School, made a concerted effort to show that there was no precedent for

FDR's proposal. Attorney General Robert Jackson strongly defended it. The Committee then reported against the bill's passage. Its report said: "The bill is an invasion of judicial power such as has never before been attempted in this country...." The Committee majority urged the Senate to destroy not just the bill but the concept of court packing itself: "It is a measure which should be so emphatically rejected that its parallel will never again be presented to the free representatives of the free people of America."[359]

The full Senate then gave the heart of FDR's plan its *coup de grâce*. It voted 70-20 to recommit the legislation to the Judiciary Committee with instructions to kill the parts of it that would allow FDR to pack the Supreme Court.[360] Nearly two-thirds of all Democratic Senators voted against FDR's plan. Roosevelt had not only suffered a remarkable defeat; Congress had gone on record against any similar proposal.

FDR's court packing plan was resoundingly rejected by Congress and the public despite the fact that there was strong majority support for his presidency and the New Deal. Protecting the federal courts from interference of the kind FDR proposed seemed more important to most people than advancing even the New Deal's very urgent reform goals. That conclusion is, of course, muddled by the fact that the Supreme Court is conventionally believed to have caved in to the political pressure created by Roosevelt's plan by changing its constitutional stance and agreeing to uphold various New Deal laws, the so-called "switch in time that saved nine."[361]

But the circumstances surrounding FDR's proposal strongly suggest that it would not have succeeded in any event. No president since has ever proposed anything even remotely similar. And the reasons for likely opposition are not difficult to find, since court packing would utterly transform the judiciary and simultaneously severely damage the Constitution's separation of powers. For the purposes of the following discussion, I assume that court packing by legislation would be constitutional, and that the real issue we need to face is whether it would be desirable given its unavoidable consequences for the Court and the Constitution.[362]

Court packing plans are based on the debatable assumption that it is desirable for the Supreme Court to continue to have the final word on all constitutional issues. But even if it is desirable for the Court to have the final word on some constitutional issues, as chapter 3 shows it is not at all clear that the Court should have the final word on issues of social policy such as national healthcare insurance or on presidential elections just because they can be framed as constitutional issues. And it turns out that court packing will have important consequences for both the Court and the Constitution's separation of powers.

Court packing plans are designed to increase the number of judges on a particular court who will be ideologically favorable to the positions of the political faction or party supporting them. Because of the resistance such plans will encounter, to succeed their supporters will almost certainly need to control all three branches of government. As a result, appointments made through a packing plan will be perceived as partisan choices. Court packing plans therefore guarantee unending partisan warfare over court appointments, as well as creating powerful incentives for adoption of alternative packing plans if political majorities change.

The creation of a partisan majority on the Supreme Court or a lower federal court will for many years, if not permanently, label it as a partisan institution in the eyes of the public. The Court's historic fundamental basis of legitimacy—the perception (entirely accurate or not) that its role is "outside politics"—will thereby be destroyed. (If we want to reform the Court's role in national government, chapter 8 suggests that there are much better ways to do that without impairing its legitimacy).

After the Court's politicization by packing, people who oppose the Court's decisions will have much less incentive to comply voluntarily with them, and will instead see it as legitimate to seek ways to frustrate them. Opponents of partisan Court decisions could well include future presidents, who might join with their allies in Congress in efforts to limit or nullify the effects of Court decisions. The serious danger to the nation of such political nullification where the president and the Supreme Court are on opposing sides of an issue will be clear to anyone familiar with the history of the conflicts between President Andrew Jackson and Supreme Court Chief Justice John Marshall during the 1830s.

During that era, controversies over the Cherokee Indian cases and the South Carolina Nullification Act directly threatened the heart of the Constitution—the core constitutional principle of the supremacy of federal law—and the federal government's ability to enforce its laws over state opposition. Those court disputes involved concerted efforts by the states of Georgia and South Carolina to resist major Supreme Court rulings protecting Native Americans and the enforcement of critically important federal tax laws, respectively. The epochal disputes were resolved in a way that protected federal authority only because Marshall and Jackson, who were normally strong political opponents, ultimately tacitly cooperated on them.[363] If either Jackson or Marshall had been unwilling to cooperate because they perceived their adversary as acting from partisan motives, the key power essential to the strength of the federal government—its ability to enforce its laws over state opposition—would have been gravely diminished if not destroyed.

Court packing would also turn the Court into a creature of Congress, destroying what remains of the separation of powers. Once court packing is approved, whenever the Court later considers an issue in which the Congressional majority prefers a particular outcome, the Justices will be well aware that if they do not follow the majority's views, they run the risk of further congressional tampering with the Court's membership or powers. In close cases at least, they will be strongly inclined to bow to the majority's wishes. That outcome would be similar to the result that would occur if the Constitution instead were changed to adopt the earlier British system in which Parliament had authority to revise court decisions. Great Britain's constitutional evolution on that issue sheds considerable light on the implications of court packing plans for the United States.

For centuries, the upper house of Britain's Parliament, the House of Lords, had the power to overrule the decisions of its highest courts. Parliament's authority stemmed from the fact that it was regarded as the supreme sovereign under British constitutional theory. Parliament's overruling of courts was seen a defensible method of controlling court actions because Parliament had to be politically accountable for such decisions. However, Great Britain recently decided to create a new Supreme Court with judges whose decisions would not normally be subject to Parliamentary review (though Parliament retained its sovereignty). The purpose of Britain's decision was to provide increased independence to its courts.[364]

If the United States adopted court packing legislation, it would effectively be adopting Britain's earlier practice by allowing indirect congressional control of the Supreme Court. Court packing would silently amend the Constitution to make Congress the supreme sovereign national political institution, eliminating a significant part of the Constitution's traditional checks and balances. However, court packing would subordinate the Court to Congress using a method that failed to provide even basic political accountability.

Under court packing, Congress would not review individual court decisions. Its members could therefore disclaim responsibility for changes in Court interpretations that proved politically inconvenient. Instead, Congress would content itself with threatening the Court with adverse consequences if it did not heed their views. That was what happened in 2019 when Senator Sheldon Whitehouse and several other Senators filed an amicus brief at the Supreme Court.[365] Their unsuccessful effort to "persuade" the Supreme Court not to hear a major gun control case by warning the Court that it faced packing if it did not follow their views provides a foretaste of the eventual effects of a court packing plan.

Court packing could be achieved by majority vote of Congress (and presidential approval). But altering the Constitution's separation of powers by majority vote would set a remarkably damaging precedent. It might well enable other alterations of the Constitution by pure majority vote that would be approved by a now-docile packed Supreme Court. If such majority vote alterations became common, they would undermine the political legitimacy of the Constitution itself. Court packing would, in short, thoroughly politicize the court system and damage the Constitution.

The broader lesson from the current re-emergence of court packing proposals, however, is that Article V is broken beyond repair. Chief Justice Marshall was probably right to think, during his fight with President Thomas Jefferson over the impeachment of Justice Samuel Chase (discussed in chapter 3), that giving Congress the power to review court decisions was preferable to having Congress impeach justices on purely political grounds (as Jefferson was certainly attempting to do to Chase). Similarly, congressional review of court decisions for which Congress could then be held accountable would be preferable to court packing. But of course, given prevailing constitutional thought on judicial review, Congress would not have the power to review Supreme Court constitutional decisions unless the Constitution were amended to permit that. Article V would be highly likely to prevent any such freestanding amendment from succeeding.

The harder Article V makes it for the popular will, or the people's elected representatives, to review and overturn a misguided Supreme Court constitutional decision, the more pressure there will be to pack the courts despite the destruction of the current relatively independent judicial system that would result. In fact, before proposing his court packing plan, FDR himself seems to have considered proposing a constitutional amendment that would have permitted legislative overrides of Court findings of unconstitutionality, but then to have rejected that approach in part because of the difficulty of amending the Constitution under Article V.[366] Roosevelt's court packing plan could be said to have been an unsuccessful effort to escape the iron cage of Article V, just as similar current proposals are.

CONCLUSION

It will not be possible to amend the Constitution under Article V's demanding requirements to meet any of the main goals of constitutional reformers. It is unfortunately futile to seek such amendments in today's political climate. "Informal" amendment or "living originalism" approaches will not bring about essential structural reforms, and will eventually lead to the collapse of republican government. Nor will it be possible to create viable legislative "workarounds" of the amendment process, whether through interstate compacts such as the NPVI or by court packing. Interstate compacts whose primary purpose is to circumvent constitutional provisions are likely to fail in the courts or in Congress. Court packing would permanently politicize the judiciary and destroy the Constitution's separation of powers. If we are going to reform the powers of the Supreme Court, chapter 8 shows that there are preferable methods.

Supporters of constitutional reform need to accept the unalterable reality that only a constitutional convention can remedy the ills they seek to cure. Because piecemeal reforms will not be adopted, reforms can be made only through a grand bargain that resolves a series of contested issues. Such a comprehensive agreement can be made only through collective deliberation at a convention. In the next chapter, we will consider how the Founders approached the delicate political task of creating a successful constitutional convention. That effort required them, among other things, to be willing finally to heed important political lessons drawn from their own earlier failed attempts at piecemeal reform of the Articles of Confederation.

PART 2

TOWARD A NEW CONSTITUTION

6

We Need to Hold a
Popular Constitutional Convention

Because piecemeal constitutional amendments will fail, only a grand bargain that resolves a broad range of contested issues can achieve true reform. A convention is the only place where such a comprehensive agreement can be reached. But as this chapter shows, Congress will not convene a convention under Article V. Americans will need to hold a popular convention instead. They have the power to do that without following Article V's deeply flawed procedures.

Widespread fears of dangerous results from holding a convention are greatly exaggerated. A popular convention will not become a Pandora's box of political mischief. To succeed, such a convention requires only strong enough support from ordinary citizens, not from elected officials or the wealthy who benefit from the status quo. Finally, there are strong reasons why supporters of a popular convention should not agree voluntarily to follow Article V procedures. (Chapter 7 discusses the politics and mechanics of planning for and holding a popular convention).

THE PEOPLE AND THE CONSTITUTION

In America, popular constitutionalism—the idea that the people play a "central and pivotal role in implementing their Constitution"—had antecedents even under British rule long before the Constitution itself was created. It had been expressed in various forms including the decisions of colonial juries reaching verdicts in defiance of judges' instructions to follow oppressive laws, and popular crowd actions. And it was strongly reinforced by the actions of ordinary Americans during the American Revolution.

Vociferous objections by colonial legislatures to British policies from the 1760s onward were strongly supported by extralegal popular actions such as commercial boycotts, the creation of committees of inspection and safety, and the Boston Tea Party, all designed to obstruct imperial rule. Major American leaders such as Samuel Adams in Boston saw that mobilizing popular support against British rule was the true key to successful American resistance.[367]

Americans began popular constitutional reform in the midst of their revolt against Britain. For example, in early June, 1776, a Pennsylvania "conference of committees" composed of representatives from each popular committee of inspection condemned the existing British-ruled government and called for a convention for the "express purpose" of framing a new government. The delegates to that extralegal convention drafted a new Pennsylvania constitution.[368] The new Pennsylvania constitution's creation was treason against Britain, since it formed a state government outside British control.

Thomas Paine later described the powerful implications of Pennsylvanians' exercise of popular power. He wrote: "Here we see a regular process—a government issuing out of a constitution, formed by the people in their original character; and that constitution serving, not only as an authority, but as a law of control to the government. It was the political bible of the state."[369]

In light of this longstanding tradition of popular action to bring about major political change, it should come as no surprise that in the Declaration of Independence, American revolutionary leaders explicitly endorsed the people's right to change their constitution. They declared that the only just form of government was government by popular consent. And they added that popular consent necessarily included the right of the American people to change their form of government whenever and however they chose. The Declaration's language on these points is crystal clear. Its drafters chose it quite deliberately, fully understanding its implications, in order to strengthen popular mobilization in support of the Revolution.

The Declaration said:

> We hold these truths to be self-evident:…governments are
> instituted among men, deriving their just powers from the
> consent of the governed; that whenever any form of
> government becomes destructive of these ends, it is the right
> of the people to alter or abolish it, and to institute new
> government, laying its foundation on such principles, and
> organizing its powers in such form, as to them shall seem
> most likely to effect their safety and happiness.

The amendment process established by Article V of the 1787
Constitution could be viewed as an attempt to limit this popular power
of constitutional reform by wealthy elite Founders, added to protect
their interests by making amendments very difficult. But the Founders
could only meet very strong objections to that Article during the 1787-
88 ratification debates by explicitly agreeing that the Constitution
could not and did not eliminate popular rights to take action for
government reform outside the Constitution, including by holding
popular constitutional conventions.

In defending the Constitution at the Virginia ratification
convention in June, 1788, for example, convention president Edmund
Pendleton explained to the delegates that Article V was not the
exclusive method of amending it. The people retained their sovereign
right to amend it if their elected representatives would not act,
Pendleton said:

> We, the people, possessing all power, form a government,
> such as we think will secure happiness and suppose, in
> adopting this plan, we should be mistaken in the end; where
> is the cause of alarm on that quarter? In the same plan we
> point out an easy and quiet method of reforming what may be
> found amiss [using Article V]. No, but, say gentlemen, we
> have put the introduction of that method in the hands of our
> servants [elected officials in Congress or legislatures], who will
> interrupt it from motives of self-interest. What then?

Pendleton continued that if that happened, the people would exercise their power to make reforms. He said:

> Who shall dare resist the people? No, we will assemble in Convention; wholly recall our delegated powers, or reform them so as to prevent such abuse; and punish those servants who have perverted powers, designed for our happiness, to their own emolument.[370]

Pendleton's defense of constitutional reform through a popular convention reaffirmed the position taken in the revolutionary leaders' 1776 Declaration. Pendleton was one of Virginia's most highly-respected legal authorities, who later served as the presiding judge of Virginia's highest court for many years.

James Wilson was a leading Pennsylvania delegate at the Philadelphia Convention who later became one of the earliest Supreme Court justices appointed by George Washington. Wilson told the 1787 Pennsylvania ratification convention that the people would retain their sovereign authority to change the Constitution despite its adoption and Article V. He said: "The truth is, that, in our government, the supreme, absolute, and uncontestable power remains in the people....The consequence is, that the people may change the constitutions whenever and however they please. This is a right of which no positive institution [such as Article V] can ever deprive them."[371]

As the distinguished historian Richard Hofstadter wrote, Wilson "said again and again that the ultimate power of government must of necessity reside in the people." Hofstadter added, "This the Fathers commonly accepted...To adopt any other premise not only would be inconsistent with everything they had said against British rule in the past but would open the gates to an extreme concentration of power in the future."[372]

The Founders' actions in adopting the Constitution strongly support the conclusion that the views they expressed on popular sovereignty during ratification were not empty political rhetoric, and that instead they believed what Pendleton and Wilson said about it. The Philadelphia Convention was actually a form of "popular" convention extralegally organized outside Congress by the states. From a legal perspective, theirs was what many people would later think of as a "runaway" convention.[373] The Convention established procedures for ratifying their proposed constitution that also unquestionably violated the Articles. If the Founders had not been willing to disregard the Articles by engaging in popular action, the 1787 Constitution would never have been adopted. Citizens today possess the same right to disregard Article V in creating a new constitution, and there are compelling reasons why they should do so to achieve needed reforms. Such popular action would be entirely in keeping with our history and America's democratic ideals.[374]

FROM THE ARTICLES OF CONFEDERATION TO THE PHILADELPHIA CONVENTION AND BEYOND

The Articles of Confederation provided that changes in the powers of the Confederation could only be made by unanimous consent of all thirteen states, and even then only after first being proposed by Congress.[375] After the Revolutionary War ended and the Confederation government wholly failed in its attempts to address a cascade of pressing national problems, Americans followed a turbulent road in 1786-87 to the Philadelphia Convention.[376] The heart of the controversy surrounding the Convention was not about whether to follow the Articles' procedures. Instead, as everyone understood, it was a struggle over the powers of the Confederation and the future of the Articles themselves.

The meeting of states commonly called the Annapolis Convention, held in September, 1786, had proposed that a national convention should be held to reform the Articles completely. Congress refused to act on its proposal. Separately in 1786, a "Grand Committee" of Congress, composed of representatives of nearly every state, had extensively considered Articles amendments and proposed several. But Congress failed to act on any of them. In fact, Congress was moribund by late 1786.[377] All of Congress' earlier piecemeal Articles reform proposals, such as those creating national tax powers, as well as state-led efforts to create a national commerce power, had been or soon would be defeated.

The movement for the Philadelphia Convention therefore actually began outside Congress in November, 1786. The Virginia legislature unanimously issued the state's call to the other states to meet with its delegates in convention in Philadelphia "on the second day of May next." Virginia leaders believed that a national convention was necessary because the Confederation was nearing collapse. Its legislature declared that it could "no longer doubt that the crisis is arrived."[378]

Virginia's call contained no limits on the proposed convention's agenda. State leaders had finally abandoned their longstanding insistence on accepting only their preferred piecemeal reforms. Virginia's resolution meant that it was asking the states to disregard Congress' exclusive power to propose Articles amendments. By February, 1787, as Congress remained gridlocked, six states, including the wealthy and populous states of Virginia and Pennsylvania, had already appointed delegates to meet in Philadelphia in May, 1787. Other states were actively considering joining the movement.

In several major states, however, by early 1787 there were efforts underway to prevent the Philadelphia Convention from ever meeting. Reform opponents in New York and Massachusetts were especially powerful, and in both states they nearly succeeded. New York's leaders were firmly opposed to any change that would give the Confederation power to impose taxes, a power then held by the states alone.

The New York delegation in Congress offered a resolution designed to prevent the Philadelphia Convention, but lost. James Madison wrote that even the tepid Massachusetts compromise resolution adopted instead, acquiescing to the Convention, was regarded as a "deadly blow to the existing Confederation" by both reformers and opponents.[379] Congress' vote accepting the Convention was a vote of "no confidence" both on the Confederation and on Congress itself.

But New York opponents of the Convention were not finished. Opponents in its legislature led by state senator Abraham Yates, Jr. then offered a proposal designed to prevent the Convention from granting any national government tax powers. State senator Philip Schuyler said that Yates' amendment "would have rendered their [delegates'] mission absolutely useless."[380] Federal tax powers, an essential element in the grand bargain ultimately reached by the Convention, would have been taken off the negotiating table. In that event, it is extraordinarily unlikely that the Convention would have agreed that the national government should be given commerce powers—another crucial element of the Convention's grand bargain. Yates' proposal was defeated only by the tiebreaking vote of Lieutenant Governor Pierre van Cortlandt.

In Massachusetts, leading revolutionary Samuel Adams also strongly opposed the Convention. He led powerful but ultimately unsuccessful state legislature efforts to block it from meeting and, failing that, to hamstring the delegates' authority. Massachusetts delegates later played a central role in creating the Constitution's central bargain because Massachusetts could not achieve its main reform goal—the creation of a strong national commerce power—in any other way. After Massachusetts agreed to an unlimited convention, the path to Philadelphia seemed clearer.

But the Philadelphia Convention faced a critical remaining hurdle—whether George Washington, the country's most widely trusted and admired revolutionary leader, would be willing to participate. Despite his firm conviction that the Confederation needed "radical" reform, even as of the spring of 1787 Washington still had serious qualms about the wisdom of holding the Philadelphia Convention. However, his concerns were strictly political.

Washington thought that the Convention was a last-ditch effort to save the union. He was deeply concerned that if it failed to agree on reforms, the Confederation would finally collapse—in his words, that there would be "an end put to Foederal Government."[381] As a result, for several months he closely studied states' decisions on convention participation. He eventually satisfied himself that the Convention would have an unlimited agenda, and would be attended by capable delegates from all major states with unrestricted negotiating authority, which would enable it to make a grand bargain on reforms.[382] Only then did Washington reluctantly agree to attend, after several earlier refusals. He accepted appointment at the end of March, 1787, just five weeks before the convention was due to begin.

The Constitution drafted by the Philadelphia Convention went far beyond making piecemeal amendments to the Articles of Confederation. Instead, it was based on a broad agreement that resolved a series of bitterly contested issues over the political structure and powers of the national government—particularly its powers to tax and to regulate commerce. As a result, the Convention proposed an entirely new, dramatically different, far more powerful government to completely replace the Confederation.

But the Convention then made an even more remarkable decision about ratification of its proposed constitution. Article VII of its proposal provided that "the Ratification of the Conventions of nine States, shall be sufficient for the Establishment of this Constitution between the States so ratifying the same." That brief sentence is one of the Constitution's most radical provisions; its implications deserve careful consideration.

Article VII ignored the Articles' requirement of congressional approval for its proposals. It also repudiated the Articles' requirement for unanimous approval by all states for changes in Confederation powers. Those were decisions made from political necessity. The proposed Constitution would very probably not have been agreed to by Congress. And it would unquestionably not have been ratified by all states.

The Philadelphia delegates were acutely aware that the Constitution was unlikely to be ratified in every state. Rhode Island had boycotted the Philadelphia Convention because it opposed fiscal reforms likely to be made there. North Carolina and Rhode Island both initially refused to ratify the Constitution because they opposed such reforms. In several other states, including the major states of Massachusetts, New York, and Virginia, Constitution supporters and opponents were so evenly matched that it was uncertain who would prevail. In the circumstances, the Philadelphia Convention could not afford to provide for unanimous ratification by the states, even though the Articles of Confederation plainly required that.[383]

THE CONVENTION'S POLITICAL LESSONS

What are the main lessons from the history of the Philadelphia Convention that apply to holding a popular convention today? The first is that the Convention was called only because it was widely enough recognized that piecemeal reform efforts had failed, and that a grand bargain to restructure the national government was necessary. It was deliberately organized with an unlimited agenda and broad delegate authority to enable such a broad agreement to be reached. Convention opponents focused their efforts on making it impossible for delegates to reach such a bargain.

Moreover, due to political necessity, the Founders were willing to cast aside the Articles' amendment rules. That history amply confirms Sanford Levinson's conclusion that the Founders "proved ruthlessly willing to ignore" the limitations of the Articles of Confederation.[384] Congress was compelled by pressure from states' independent actions to accede to a convention that it would not have permitted otherwise. It then also acquiesced to the Convention's ratification proposals, even though they deprived it of authority to approve the proposed Constitution. As one constitutional scholar wrote, "the procedures used to ratify the Constitution were impermissible under" the Articles.[385] Like the history of the American Revolution, the history of the Philadelphia Convention shows us that Article V can be disregarded in organizing and holding a popular convention today.

However, because they were proceeding outside the Articles, the Founders accepted the need to appeal to an alternative basis of political legitimacy—popular ratification—to obtain public support for their decisions. In that era, ratification for the Constitution had to be obtained by treating the states as decision-making units. The Founders proposed that supermajority approval by two-thirds of the states should be sufficient.[386] In other words, the Philadelphia Convention may have been extralegally organized, but there were major political safeguards that surrounded its work; from that perspective, it was not a "runaway" convention.

But the successful work of the Philadelphia Convention has not stopped today's opponents of holding any new constitutional convention from imagining that various horrible disasters would inevitably occur if a similarly structured convention were held today. Their misguided fears are discussed next.

COMMON FEARS OF A POPULAR CONVENTION ARE GREATLY EXAGGERATED

A remarkable number of opponents of holding a constitutional convention base their position on their fear that it might supposedly run amok. The most common response to indisputable evidence of the Constitution's severe flaws is to say that the cure of holding a convention would be far worse than the diseases identified. Opponents argue that the seriousness of the Constitution's flaws is overstated, while claiming that its critics understate the allegedly drastic risks of a convention. For example, constitutional scholar Cass Sunstein concedes that the Electoral College and states' equal representation in the Senate are "not easily defended."[387] But, he says, if a convention were held:

> Suppose that the entire Constitution were placed up for grabs? Would the new product be better than the current one? That would be most unlikely....If the United States had a constitutional convention, would it really focus on the composition of the Senate, the electoral college, the presidential veto...Or would it instead rethink symbolic questions and constitutional rights—for example, by reducing the protections given to criminal defendants, restricting freedom of speech, increasing protection of property rights, weakening the separation of church and state...It seems at least as likely that some such measures, rather than [Sanford] Levinson's structural [reform] proposals, would be the major results of a contemporary convention.[388]

Sunstein instead supports the informal amendment approach discussed in chapter 5. For him, the "existing constitutional framework" is to "a significant degree a democratic product." It follows that the case for changing the Constitution through a convention is "weakened." Moreover, that framework is a collective "product of many minds operating over time..." so there is "all the more reason to fear that any particular set of people, operating at any particular time and inevitably in the grip of current concerns, will make it worse rather than better." In all likelihood a convention can only harm the Constitution, not improve it, in Sunstein's view.

Another convention opponent, Professor Suzanna Sherry, argues that criticisms of various parts of the Constitution such as the Electoral College overstate the harms they actually cause, and that these relatively minor harms cannot justify the risks of a convention. A convention would be uncontrollable, she thinks. She worries that its delegates might decide to ban gay marriage and affirmative action, or to require supermajority approval for tax increases; to permit school prayer or declare the United States a Christian nation. She finds poll data that provide snapshots of the public's views on such constitutional issues "disturbing."[389]

Indeed, in some cases the fears of convention opponents are so great that they oppose even a convention created by state petitions to Congress under Article V. In 1979, constitutional scholar Laurence Tribe testified against a California resolution seeking a convention to consider a balanced budget amendment. He said, "I strongly believe that, as a practical matter, holding an Article V Convention...would be a needless and perilous undertaking...one likely to thwart rather than vindicate the will of the American people..."[390] In a similar vein more recently, a 2018 Common Cause memorandum was headlined: "U.S. Constitution Threatened as Article V Movement Nears Success." Literally read, that means that in Common Cause's view even the states' use of Article V as written would undermine the Constitution. What Common Cause apparently fears most is that "the result of such a convention could be a complete overhaul of the Constitution..."[391] Let's take a look at the opponents' main fears about holding a convention, and examine whether they're real or imaginary.

THREAT OF A RUNAWAY CONVENTION

Professors Sunstein and Sherry, Common Cause, and many others at all points on the political spectrum fear that any convention, even if called to consider only one proposed amendment, would become a "runaway convention," with the Constitution "up for grabs." Of course, not all "runaway" conventions are unfortunate—after all, legally the Philadelphia Convention was a runaway convention. But as opponents argue, it is theoretically possible that a convention might focus not on structural flaws such as the Electoral College but instead on "symbolic questions and constitutional rights"—or perhaps both.

The legal possibility of a runaway convention cannot be ruled out, even if it had been called by Congress under Article V. Even if a convention were convened pursuant to a congressional call intended to limit its scope, for example by limiting it to consideration of one topic such as a balanced budget amendment, some prominent scholars believe that it would possess unlimited authority to propose other amendments.[392] But the possibility that a "runaway convention" might occur is not a realistic reason for concern once one grasps a few fundamental points about the inherent legal and political nature of a convention (discussed further in chapter 7).

A convention's work cannot bind anyone, because it has no authority of its own to change laws or the Constitution. Nothing any convention (runaway or not) does has any binding force on anyone until its work is ratified.[393] Moreover, if a convention does not propose a ratification mechanism that requires a sufficiently high level of supermajority public approval for its proposals, its work will not be regarded as legitimate, and will not become part of the permanent constitutional landscape. Instead, political resistance to the results of the convention's work will continue, much as popular opposition to the 1787 Constitution's omission of a Bill of Rights vigorously persisted even after it was ratified, forcing Congress to propose a series of constitutional amendments to include those rights.

The fact that durable constitutional changes must rest on supermajority approval means that there is a major built-in political safeguard for the convention process.[394] A convention will have no choice but to proceed with great caution before proposing any radical change. In light of that, conventions will propose bold reforms only when their delegate majorities are convinced that they are essential. The history of the Philadelphia Convention itself shows that a convention is highly unlikely to agree to any proposed amendment that would prevent its work from being ratified.

The Philadelphia delegates debated and rejected numerous proposals. Some were rejected not because they lacked sufficient support but instead because delegates were convinced that they would threaten the Constitution's ratification. For example, the Convention debated requiring uniform national voting qualifications, and rejected the idea because delegates were concerned that some states would reject the Constitution if it imposed such a requirement.[395] Similarly today, if a new convention included politically extreme proposals (e.g., ending the right to a jury trial) in its work, it would very probably doom its entire effort to failure in a supermajority ratification process.[396] There is little reason to fear such ill-judged actions. Convention opponents' claims that putting the Constitution "up for grabs" would inevitably be disastrous are unfounded.

UNDUE INFLUENCE OF SPECIAL INTERESTS

Convention opponents often claim that holding a convention would be a bad idea because it will inevitably be dominated by special interests. These concerns take two different forms. One variant is that delegates controlled by special interests will be elected because the election process will be either corrupted or ineffectual. Such concerns can be laid to rest by a well-designed election process, an issue discussed in chapter 7. A second variant of this concern has much broader implications. Writers such as the respected constitutional scholar Mark Graber argue that a convention will necessarily be dominated by the same special interests that control politics today— in effect, they contend that holding a convention would be futile because it could not escape the confines of "ordinary" politics.

Graber thinks that the main reason for today's constitutional dysfunction is partisan polarization, since in his view the Constitution works only when parties are "non-ideological."[397] But, he argues, polarized parties will never agree to constitutional reforms that may change the partisan balance of power, so meaningful constitutional reform cannot occur (at least by formal means, as opposed to through continued partisan struggle on specific issues). This argument is overly broad for several reasons.

The first difficulty it faces is that today's constitutional dysfunction is not caused by partisan polarization, though polarization may worsen it. The Constitution is first and foremost a decision-making system for national policy, and many of its decision-making flaws have nothing to do with partisanship. Many profoundly important decisions that the federal government makes or fails to make through drift—for example, foreign policy and defense issues; modernizing national infrastructure including public health protection, highways, railroads, postal and communication systems; and many others— cannot usefully be described as raising "partisan" issues today. But Congress' flawed structure discussed in chapter 3 means that it either does not act on such issues, abdicates its authority to the president, or makes short-sighted decisions about them.

Even where partisan alignments do strongly influence government decisions, what frustrates effective decision-making is not partisanship per se, but the fact that partisan forces are evenly balanced and that the Constitution's rules do not force an end to the resulting partisan stalemate. Instead, as we saw in chapters 2 and 4, the Constitution's structure and Supreme Court decisions disproportionately reinforce Republican partisan strength, making tie-breaking in political disputes considerably more difficult than it otherwise would be. And as constitutional scholar Stephen Griffin's work shows, by enabling inaction not just by one partisan group but by both major parties on various issues, the Constitution encourages policy disasters such as Congress' failures to improve American intelligence before 9/11 and its willingness to permit the banking industry to operate without essential regulation for decades, leading to the 2008 financial collapse.[398] Reforming Congress must include steps to avoid that type of drift and its capture by the wealthy, and that is not a partisan issue.

Further, many of the most important structural reforms the Constitution needs either are not reforms that will alter partisan strength or are reforms that can be made through a broad convention agreement that can overcome strong partisan opposition. For example, changing the voting strength of states in Congress to reflect population will face intense opposition, but it will primarily pit large states against small states, not purely Democrats against Republicans. Congress needs major reforms, and that is not a partisan issue. In addition, as Stephen Griffin points out, major constitutional reforms such as the initiative and referendum were made despite resistance from dominant parties.[399] That will be equally true of a variety of other desirable reforms discussed in chapter 8.

Professor Graber's argument is strongest with respect to voting system changes such as proportional representation to end the current two-party duopoly, which the major parties are certain to resist strenuously.[400] However, whether a convention can successfully force such a change over "bipartisan" opposition as part of a grand bargain will depend on the nature of the other elements of the bargain and the degree of overall popular support for it, which means that the outcome on that issue cannot be predicted in advance.

Ultimately, this type of concern about vested interests rests on the view that popular action against them can never be successful, even when reforms have broad public support. But as we saw earlier, the Philadelphia Convention was vigorously opposed by powerful special interests in various states, who wanted to maintain their control of state powers and revenue sources. One of the convention's main achievements was to bring those special interests under national control. And as Stephen Griffin's work shows, powerful popular reforms to strengthen democracy such as the initiative and referendum have been made even in the face of strenuous opposition by major economic monopoly powers such as the railroad barons who bought and sold entire state legislatures. Such reforms were deliberately designed to end government capture by private power.[401]

Throughout our history, popularly initiated reforms have repeatedly overcome special interest opposition. The creation of the Interstate Commerce Commission and federal antitrust laws over the concerted opposition of rich and powerful railroads and oil and other industrial monopolies; the Sixteenth Amendment enabling the income tax despite several decades of opposition by the wealthy; and the Seventeenth Amendment providing for direct election of Senators are all examples of popular reforms achieved by overcoming strong vested interest opposition. As will be discussed shortly, more recently popular opposition forced the federal government to abandon the

Vietnam war to which elites were firmly committed, despite having spent more than $1 trillion on it.[402]

Of course, no constitutional convention can occur entirely outside the influence of the day's politics. The history of the Philadelphia Convention shows that if peaceful reform is to occur, constitution drafters must be willing to make compromises that reflect the strength of existing interests that are too powerful to be limited by such a consensual process. The Constitution's drafters very reluctantly compromised with state elites who wanted to preserve their power, and they compromised with major slave states to protect slavery. But recognizing that some compromises will need to be made by any convention is far different from accepting the view that a convention will inevitably fail to make fundamental beneficial changes in the structure and operation of government. After all, that is precisely what the Philadelphia Convention did. If a new convention makes a comprehensive agreement that gains the support of a sufficiently broad reform coalition, it too will be able to fundamentally reform government. In particular, it will be able to reach an agreement that will impose effective limits on the power of our wealthy oligarchy to control government, as is discussed further in chapter 8.

In broader perspective, the dynamics of constitutional convention politics are analogous to the well-understood problem of launching a space rocket into orbital trajectory around the earth. The rocket must have enough takeoff power to accelerate into an orbit; it must travel stably through the orbit for long enough to achieve its mission; and it must finally safely re-enter earth's atmosphere. Similarly, a convention must be backed by strong enough demands for change to overcome powerful opposition to holding it at all; it must be attended by capable delegates who can design reforms and discern how much political baggage a package of them can carry; and its work must then survive supermajority ratification. Whether the convention can achieve its reform goals will largely be a function of the quality of the organizing process and public support for it discussed in chapter 7. But uncertainty about the ultimate extent of reforms is not a sound reason to despair and oppose a convention.

LACK OF CONVENTION RULES

Critics point out that there are no rules provided in advance for a convention.[403] Therefore, they say, an entirely new constitution might be created, just as happened in 1787. This argument fails first and foremost because the creation of the 1787 Constitution had everything to do with the irreparable defects of the Confederation government, and nothing to do with the Philadelphia Convention's lack of rules. This claim also overlooks the fact that many of the rules created by the Philadelphia convention for its work materially assisted its efforts (as discussed in chapter 7). Finally, it ignores that the 1787 convention's work was decisively shaped by the need to receive supermajority ratification for it, a very powerful though informal rule.

LEGAL DISPUTES

Convention opponents argue that the prospect that a convention might be held, or the lack of rules governing a convention or ratification of its work, would lead to legal disputes and could cause "chaos." Undoubtedly there will be legal disputes before, during, and after a convention, but they will be driven by political opposition, not well-founded legal claims. In view of the fact that a convention has no binding authority, it is difficult to see how such challenges will be successful in preventing or interfering with its work or with the ratification process (this issue is discussed in detail in chapter 7).

POSSIBLE UNEQUAL REPRESENTATION

Convention opponents point out that it is unclear how conventions would choose delegates, under what rules delegates would vote, or under what rules their proposals would be ratified. Such rules could in theory prove to be unfair or unequal. But a convention held under what are widely seen as unfair rules, or that proposes ratification of its work under unfair rules, will fail to effect any lasting political change. The fact that a popular convention will be able to create rules for its organization gives it the ability to be inclusive, and that is desirable, not to be feared. Chapter 7 recommends rules for a popular convention's organization that address delegate allocation and election as well as rules for delegate voting, all of which can be fully publicly debated well in advance of a convention.

WHO ARE "THE PEOPLE" WHO WILL HOLD A POPULAR CONVENTION?

Some writers claim that the idea of "popular sovereignty" is either a fiction or too general to be useful. That leads them to ask who "the people" really are, and why Americans should be willing to empower someone claiming to represent them to write a new constitution. However, America's history from the Revolutionary era onward shows that popular sovereignty is not a fiction. Throughout our history, different groups of ordinary citizens have periodically acted together to exercise their authority to reform government. As discussed above, both key features of the Constitution and major federal laws and institutions have been changed as a result of popular action.

Some observers are concerned, though, that there is no widely admired, charismatic public leader today who advocates holding a popular convention, suggesting that a movement supporting one lacks necessary leadership. But as Alexander Hamilton himself discovered, someone always has to be the first to step forward to lead such a cause, and at first that leader may be alone. Hamilton was one of the first advocates of a national convention to fundamentally reform the Articles of Confederation. He was elected to Congress in 1783 by the New York legislature primarily to seek one. But he faced so much opposition to his plan in Congress that within a few months he quit in disgust and returned to private life. Remarkably, one of Hamilton's main opponents was Virginian James Madison. Only four years later, Hamilton found himself serving with Madison at the Philadelphia Convention. So although Hamilton began as a lonely prophet, he soon gained the necessary company to succeed. But how will such leadership emerge today?

As chapters 3 and 4 show, today's elected leaders have been thoroughly co-opted by the current political system and its rewards. Most of them benefit greatly from the constitutional status quo, including its incumbent protections. There is no reason to expect them to take the lead on constitutional reform. Instead we should look for reform leadership to unelected citizens who are capable of assessing the long-term future of the country and who have no vested interest in preserving the Constitution's flaws. Yet leaders in private life will often be reluctant to participate in a convention, just as George Washington was, for both personal and political reasons. A critically important task of a popular convention's organizers will be to develop a national organizing committee, and through it a convention call and a delegate election process that will attract private leaders to serve (discussed in chapter 7). There is no question that the country has enough talented individuals to deliberate productively together on a new constitution. Several such individuals are listed as examples in chapter 7. A well-structured convention process will successfully encourage them to participate, and the popular movement will have gained the necessary leadership.

Ultimately, though, popular movements do not depend for their success on charismatic leaders; they succeed because they have strong enough popular support to enable leaders to press forward to their goals. Despite America's traditional enthusiasm for heroes as leaders, our history shows that a popular movement like constitutional reform doesn't "need another hero," in the words of the famous song sung by Tina Turner. What such a popular movement needs instead are many ordinary citizens (such as readers of this book) who decide to lend it their support. A good example supporting this conclusion is the course of opposition to the Vietnam War.

Originally, there was strong bipartisan elite support for the Vietnam War. There were extremely few elected leaders who opposed the War when President Lyndon Baines Johnson and Secretary of Defense Robert McNamara began large-scale bombing of Vietnam. War opposition outside Congress was confined mostly to the American left, such as members of Students for a Democratic Society. But within a few years, as LBJ's military escalation cost growing numbers of American soldiers' lives and devastated Vietnam and its people, the war steadily became a more divisive issue in domestic politics. Hundreds of thousands, and eventually millions, of ordinary Americans began to participate in public protests against it.

Within four years of Congress' nearly unanimous Gulf of Tonkin resolution authorizing the war, by the 1968 presidential election campaign, Vietnam war policy had split the Democratic party and forced LBJ's resignation. By late 1969, after the election of president Richard M. Nixon, in a period of slightly more than one month a political tidal wave of more than two million Americans took part in public demonstrations against the war in Vietnam. It was obvious even to the country's conservative national leaders that American policy must change. President Nixon's loyal adviser Patrick Buchanan told him two days after the October, 1969 Moratorium marches and teach-ins: "The war in Vietnam will now be won or lost on the American front."[404]

The Vietnam War was ended a few years later despite the nation's massive investment in it. Popular pressure on elected leaders—who were nearly all followers, not true leaders—led to the United States' withdrawal from Vietnam. Similar popular pressure can lead to a new constitutional convention. When a sufficient level of popular support for a new convention develops, that issue will attract the support of ambitious elected leaders as well. But they will join a popular movement whose strength will ultimately derive from its support by many ordinary citizens.

It is apparent from this review that the fears expressed about holding a popular convention are all greatly exaggerated. Playing on such fears in opposing a convention is a pretext. The real reason for opposition is actually that a convention may make substantive decisions opponents do not like. We should ignore such opponents. As constitutional scholar Mark Tushnet points out, the absence of guarantees that a democratic political process will have a result we like cannot serve as an argument against that process.[405] However, there are observers sympathetic to holding a convention who think that Article V's procedures should be followed voluntarily. That issue is discussed next.

SHOULD WE FOLLOW ARTICLE V TODAY?

Some writers who advocate holding a new convention think that the call for a convention either must or should originate with Congress.[406] As we have seen, popular sovereignty makes recourse to Congress unnecessary. However, a deeper look at this issue is still desirable.

Organizers of a popular convention might voluntarily seek congressional approval, hoping perhaps that their efforts would gain added legitimacy. That approach will prove futile.

To date, Article V has never been used by Congress to call a convention even when numerous states supported one. Over the years, 743 requests for article V conventions have been made; virtually every state has petitioned for an Article V convention at some point. Congress has never approved a request.[407] Nor is there any prospect that Congress will agree to permit even a convention called by state petitions to occur in the foreseeable future. Congress is exceptionally unlikely to approve any convention, particularly a popular convention, due to the enormous uncertainty about its Article V powers.

Some writers claim that if thirty-four states petition Congress for a constitutional amendment, under Article V Congress has no discretion, and must approve holding a convention.[408] While Congress' Article V duty in calling a convention may look ministerial on paper, it would actually involve considerable discretion and have the potential to create enormous, lengthy controversies in which the courts would very probably refuse to intervene on "political question" grounds.[409]

Congress would first need to determine whether it has received thirty-four "valid" state petitions. Congress would also have to decide what the scope of the convention it calls should be, since many state petitions seek a convention limited to one subject, and might use differing language in their requests. Decisions about scope could include how long a deadline would be permitted for ratification of any convention proposals.[410] Congressional debates about a convention's scope will almost certainly be accompanied by strong disagreements over whether and how any scope limitations Congress attempts would be enforceable. In any event, there is serious dispute about whether Congress has any authority under Article V to call such a limited convention.[411] These deeply contentious issues will arise whenever Congress is asked to call a convention.

Congress' decision on a convention's scope might by itself determine its outcome. At the same time, if Congress cannot constitutionally limit a convention's scope, fears of a "runaway" convention will remain available for profitable exploitation by convention opponents. It is also uncertain whether Congress has power to make rules for a convention. The only significant effort to create such rules by North Carolina Senator Samuel J. Ervin, Jr. and others roughly fifty years ago failed.[412] Even assuming that Congress had power to make convention rules, its debates over them would often be little more than veiled efforts to "rig" the convention or to prevent it from ever meeting at all.

Because of these considerable uncertainties, seeking to achieve any reasonable consensus on congressional approval of either a popular convention or a convention based on state petitions would be a futile endeavor which will at best delay and at worst prevent holding the actual convention. Congress is exceptionally unlikely to be willing to call a convention, except perhaps in extraordinarily difficult political circumstances such as the New Deal (and perhaps not even then). Instead, it will seek to prevent either type of convention in order to maintain its control of the amendment process. That is clear both from Congress' past actions and from the political realities surrounding congressional approval.

In the past, whenever significant political pressure for adoption of a constitutional amendment developed, Congress took steps to deflate it without acceding to a convention. In some cases, Congress adopted legislation it hoped would satisfy demands for an amendment. In others, it proposed constitutional amendments, but did so in a form it chose, including limitations on ratification procedures. For example, by 1912, nearly enough states had submitted petitions to Congress to require a second convention on the issue of direct election of Senators. Seeking to prevent a convention, the Senate finally acted after years of delay and sent the Seventeenth Amendment for direct election of Senators to the states for ratification.[413] In 1985, Congress adopted deficit control legislation that successfully defused the movement by thirty-two states seeking a convention on a balanced budget amendment.[414]

As these examples suggest, and particularly since virtually all constitutional amendment proposals lack supermajority support in Congress today, it is exceptionally unlikely that Congress would now be willing to relinquish its control of possible amendments by authorizing any convention, especially a general convention. If Congress will not call a general convention, meaningful structural reform cannot possibly occur under Article V. As we have seen, the Founders recognized that popular sovereignty could always be exercised to change the Constitution if necessary. The same type of political necessity that confronted the Founders exists today, and fully supports holding a popular convention.

But is there some other substantive reason why we should nevertheless defer to Article V's procedures and seek state resolutions approving a convention, as opposed to organizing a popular convention and seeking popular ratification? To put this another way, is Article V's reliance on the states for reform still a desirable policy to follow voluntarily? To view Article V as still viable necessarily requires us to conclude that all states continue to be equally valid political decision-making units today, even though the small states are now the principal obstacles to a great share of especially desirable constitutional reforms. To consider this further, let's look first at the fundamental problem state equality creates under Article V, the minority veto.

ARTICLE V, THE MINORITY VETO, AND THE STATES AS POLITICAL UNITS

Article V creates an increasingly serious minority veto problem. To illustrate its importance, let's suppose that the following amendment to Article V itself was proposed. It would change the number of states required to approve constitutional amendments from three-fourths of the states (38 states) to two-thirds of the states (34 states). Some people would argue that under Article V, three-fourths of the states would need to approve such an amendment. That would mean that if thirteen states opposed the amendment, it would fail. Today, the thirteen smallest states—those by far the most likely to oppose the proposed amendment—constitute around 5 percent of the country's total population, and their objections alone would veto the amendment. Would it make sense to allow 5 percent of the population to veto a constitutional change that the other 95 percent of the population had agreed they wanted to make?

Some people might answer that a good deal would depend on what constitutional change was being considered. For example, suppose 95 percent of the population wanted to do away with the constitutional right to trial by jury. Perhaps the other 5 percent should legitimately be able to veto a change to an individual right such as that. On the other hand, if 95 percent of the population believed that the Constitution should provide for a universal right to adequate healthcare without regard to ability to pay, should the other 5 percent be able to veto that choice?

However, Article V creates a one-size-fits-all rule for answering such questions. It allows the small states to veto any change to the status quo they dislike. A new constitutional convention would have much more flexibility in deciding how a future minority veto should operate. For example, it could decide that a minority veto should apply in certain specific cases, but not in others. Or it could decide that a minority veto must represent the views of a sufficiently large part of the country to be effective in some cases, but not as large a part in others. There is also another serious difficulty created by the Constitution's provisions statically protecting states' power.

Under the Constitution, states with very small numbers of voters are guaranteed seats in Congress, the Senate, and votes in the Electoral College. Today, about ten percent of the population located in seventeen states has 34 percent of the votes in the Senate, for example. Even if these states actually lose population over the next few years, becoming an even smaller part of the national total, they are guaranteed to keep their political privileges. As a result, even if the seventeen smallest states eventually have only 5 percent of the population, they will still have 34 percent of the votes in the Senate, for example. Under Article V, the thirteen smallest states will still be able to veto constitutional changes even if they represent much less than 5 percent of the population.

The Constitution's increasingly artificial protection of states' voting power suggests once again that using existing states as basic political decision-making units in various parts of the Constitution is a fundamentally flawed idea. Should we accept the legitimacy of the Article V state minority veto? In the following section we will see that there are good reasons for thinking that we should choose a different method of allocating political power, such as relative population, that is more consistent with modern views of democracy.

WHAT ARE STATES GOOD FOR TODAY?

The Articles of Confederation were based on the idea that states were sovereign entities. Article II provided that "Each state retains its sovereignty, freedom, and independence, and every power, jurisdiction, and right, which is not...expressly delegated to the United States." The view that states were sovereigns voluntarily joining together in a confederation supported the idea that they were equals that should have static equal rights within the Confederation.

The opposing dynamic conception of states' political power in a federal government, advocated by James Wilson and others in Philadelphia, flatly rejected the idea that states were and should remain equals merely because they were states. These leaders agreed with John Adams that in a republican national government, political power should be distributed based on the relative contributions to the operations of the government expected to be made by different parts of the country, which could change over time.[415] As is well-known, the Constitution compromised between the static and dynamic views of state power, giving all states some share of influence without regard to their wealth and size. But for the most part it also rejected the Articles' minority veto principle, providing that majority will should govern most important decision-making about the use of critical national powers.[416]

Today the static conception of states' equality has lost its validity for two reasons. Although the Constitution is based on federalism, the reality of our federal system is that the relationship between states and the federal government has changed markedly since 1787. And many states today are no longer as functional as government units as states were then.

Despite the Constitution's so-called "dual federalism," states are not "sovereign" entities in the same sense in which the federal government is sovereign. If they were, the Constitution would not have given the full right to control national tax or military powers to the federal government, or stripped states of their powers to make treaties, to print paper money, or to abolish previously contracted debts. The Civil War established that states do not have the ability to secede. It also settled that states have no right to maintain social institutions that the national government has decided to outlaw because they violate constitutional rights, such as slavery.

So, although the states retain independent governmental powers, their authorities are now subject to very substantial constitutional and federal policy limitations that can be enforced against them in the national interest. If they are going to continue to be treated as political equals with each other under the Constitution, it must be for some other reason. This leads us to ask how the states' place in the union today compares functionally to their position in the 1780s when the Constitution was adopted.

At that time, states (and the local jurisdictions they controlled) were for nearly all purposes the single most important political authorities in their citizens' everyday lives. Prior to the Constitution, they controlled most forms of taxation. They decided how the limited state and local public services that existed then would be provided. Public services consisted mostly of military defense, law enforcement, and some infrastructure provision, as well as limited social and economic regulation. States operated largely independently of each other, except to some extent in wartime. They were expected to stand on their own footing financially, not by receiving any direct or indirect financial assistance from the general government.

Today state government functions have changed dramatically. We no longer expect states to have viable freestanding military forces. Moreover, state and local government functions have now expanded to include a very large range of social services, including public education and hospitals, most of which were not provided by any government in the 1780s. But the tax revenue base available to many states has not kept pace with these greatly increased demands for government services.

Today as a result, many states would effectively be bankrupt but for federal financial direct and indirect assistance to their citizens.[417] The states as a whole receive about twenty-five percent of their total revenues from federal transfers.[418] But some of them are far more dependent on federal funding than that average suggests. For example, let's look at a sample of five states—Kentucky, New Mexico, West Virginia, Mississippi, and Alabama—that are heavily dependent on federal assistance. These states and their residents collectively receive nearly twice as much in net federal direct and indirect assistance as the size of their *entire* state budgets combined.[419] They could not possibly substitute increased state tax revenues for that federal assistance without causing many residents to move out of state to flee taxes. Without large amounts of federal assistance, they would have far larger populations living in poverty than at present. Nor would many of them be able to provide adequate public services or be able to meet their state pension obligations.

In fact, a very large percentage of the fifteen American states that are most heavily dependent on federal financial assistance are among the twenty-eight smallest states that collectively contain less than twenty percent of the total American population. These federally dependent states often receive thousands of dollars per resident annually in net federal assistance after deducting the money their residents pay in federal taxes. Many of these states cannot realistically be regarded as financially viable independent units today.

As Alexander Hamilton was the first to recognize clearly, it is in the national interest to disregard such fiscal "balance of payments" issues between the states for many purposes. But it is entirely unreasonable to ignore them entirely in allocating political authority. If we were drawing political boundaries for America today, they would be drawn quite differently for functional and financial reasons than they were in the eighteenth and nineteenth centuries when most states were created. There is no sound reason to continue to observe functionally obsolete state boundaries to the extent that they confer disproportionate political power where major decisions such as amending the Constitution are concerned.

A final important consideration in thinking about whether states are validly regarded as equal political units is that some have a much higher than average potential for being corrupted by special interests than others do. Corruption can either be illegal public corruption, involving misuse of public funds or resources (e.g., bribery), or legal corruption.[420]

There is plenty of public corruption in state and local governments. A 2014 report from the Safra Center on Ethics at Harvard University stated: "According to the Justice Department, in the last two decades more than 20,000 public officials and private individuals were convicted for crimes related to corruption and more than 5,000 are awaiting trial, the overwhelming majority of cases having originated in state and local governments."[421]

One type of legal corruption is political corruption, in which a government is dominated by a special interest or faction. Historically, factional domination was feared because factions were expected to use their power to reward factional supporters, for example by shifting tax burdens unfairly onto opponents, or by making taxpayer-funded infrastructure investments that favored factional supporters. There is political corruption at every government level.

But experience suggests that James Madison's famous argument in *Federalist* No. 10 that enlarging the republic was the best way to control political corruption by factional dominance was basically correct: the federal government is more difficult to corrupt on a long-term basis than state governments. There are two reasons why it is harder for special interests to dominate the national government than state governments. First, a special interest must have a broader socioeconomic and geographical constituency and much larger financial resources if it wants to successfully control both Houses of Congress and the presidency than if it wants to dominate a part-time, poorly paid and poorly staffed state legislature and governor. Second, a special interest is far more likely to face concerted opposition from other special interests with conflicting objectives at the national level than at the state level. The coal industry's history illustrates these points.

A single major coal company or industry group of such companies may be able to heavily influence or even control a state legislature (or a court) in a state such as West Virginia where the industry is a major employer. In 2009, for example, the United States Supreme Court decided a remarkable case concerning the 2004 West Virginia judicial election.[422] At the time of the election, Don Blankenship was chairman and principal officer of the A.T. Massey Coal Company ("Massey"). Massey was facing $50 million in damages in a case on appeal before the West Virginia Supreme Court. During the campaign, Blankenship spent $3 million to unseat an incumbent state Supreme Court justice. Blankenship's direct and indirect contributions to his preferred candidate Brent Benjamin exceeded the total amount spent by all other

Benjamin supporters and Benjamin's own campaign committee.[423] Benjamin won the 2004 election by 50,000 votes.

Justice Benjamin then refused to disqualify himself from the pending case involving Massey, claiming that he had no "direct, personal, substantial, pecuniary interest" in the case.[424] Massey won in the West Virginia Supreme Court by a 3-2 vote, with Benjamin in the majority. During a rehearing of the case that followed, two West Virginia Supreme Court justices disqualified themselves, one because photographs had surfaced of him vacationing with Blankenship on the French Riviera while the case was pending, the other because he had attacked Blankenship.[425]

A sharply divided United States Supreme Court then held in 2009 that West Virginia Supreme Court Justice Benjamin must recuse himself based on the "extreme facts" that created a "probability of actual bias," in order to protect constitutional due process. It reversed the West Virginia Supreme Court's decision and remanded the case to it.[426] A *USA Today* editorial about the case said: "Blankenship has inadvertently done what no reform group ever could: He has vividly illustrated how big money corrupts judicial elections. It puts justice up for sale to the highest bidder —or at least raises that suspicion."[427]

In sharp contrast to Massey's influence in West Virginia, even the entire nationwide coal industry has had great difficulty influencing much of the decision-making in Congress over the past several decades. Over strenuous industry opposition, Congress has tightened air pollution laws and subsidized alternative energy sources. That has been possible in large part because the coal industry's nationwide finances and total employment have sharply declined, limiting its political resources. In 1950, the industry had about 400,000 full-time equivalent workers; by 2020, this had declined to 53,000 in a much larger total labor force.[428] Coal's share of electricity production declined from more than 55% of the total in the 1990s to 30% by 2020.[429] Between 2011 and 2016, U.S. coal producers lost more than 92% of their market value.[430] The industry has declined under pressure from several forces, including increased competition from other energy industries and challenges from the environmental community.

This coal industry example, though anecdotal, suggests that James Madison's argument in *Federalist* No. 10 was generally correct. Even though there are occasions when at least for some period of time a special interest can control the national government, it is far more likely that states will be captured over the long-term by special interests than that the federal government will be. And in reality, smaller, financially weaker states are more likely to be captured and corrupted more readily by special interests than larger states can be, though the problem exists in many states.

These functional, financial and corruption considerations all support the conclusion that today states are not equals. Today states are not equally able to contribute to the costs of national government. Nor do they face even remotely equal social welfare and law enforcement burdens. Yet the Constitution still dictates that all states be treated as equals in making critically important decisions. Its requirement for state equality is unfortunate enough when it distorts how we choose presidents and make national policies through legislation, as we saw in chapter 4. But it is fatally flawed when it creates a minority veto over constitutional change, as Article V does.

States should no longer be treated as equals for purposes of amending the Constitution. The Philadelphia compromises that led to treating states as equals under Article V were not based on principles of republican government that we accept today; they were based on political necessity. There is no sound reason for the American people to continue to treat them as valid today by voluntarily holding a convention under Article V. Instead, we should organize a popular convention and then ratify its work outside Article V. One purpose of such a convention, to be discussed in chapter 8, should be to consider whether changes are needed in the relationship between states and the federal government to revitalize federalism.

CONCLUSION

Because piecemeal amendments are destined to fail, major reform of the Constitution will not be possible unless a convention is held. Congress will not call a convention under Article V. A popular convention therefore must be held because it is the only means of reaching a grand bargain to resolve the necessary range of outstanding constitutional issues. Both the principle of popular sovereignty and strong policy arguments support the view that this can and should be done outside Article V. The Founders did not treat the Articles of Confederation as binding on them when they organized and held the Philadelphia Convention and sought ratification of the Constitution. They ignored the Articles due to political necessity, and justified their disregard by seeking supermajority ratification for their work. The same considerations apply to holding a convention today.

The fears of a new convention expressed by its opponents are in substance a defense of the status quo based on an exaggerated "parade of horribles." A dispassionate look at their claims suggests that there is no more reason for concern about a new convention than there was to fear the Philadelphia Convention in 1787. That convention faced special interest opposition, and a new one will as well; but that is no reason why we should accept the status quo. The leadership needed for effective reform will emerge from a well-managed process for organizing and conducting a convention. Article V's requirement that states be treated as equals in calling a convention and ratifying proposed amendments can no longer be deemed valid in view of the fact that states are, in reality, no longer equal and in many cases no longer even viable entities.

We have the power to make a new constitution, and now is the time exercise it.

7

Popular Convention Organization and Procedure

Let's suppose that after reading this far you agree that holding a popular convention will be essential to achieve constitutional reforms vital to our country's future. You and others who share your view will need to decide how you can organize and conduct it. As comparative studies of past constitutional conventions have shown, during the reform process conventions often face a series of fairly similar issues, several of which are discussed in this chapter.[431] This chapter does not, however, comprehensively discuss the full range of issues that might arise in the course of conducting a constitutional convention and seeking ratification. Instead, it discusses the main flash point issues that convention supporters will have to confront.

The histories of the 1787 Philadelphia Convention and the French Constituent Assembly of 1789-1791 show us that the fight over whether to hold a convention or not may by itself actually determine the fate of constitutional reform. It follows that properly resolving the central issues that will face convention organizers and garnering support for the convention while doing so may well determine a new convention's success or failure. To the greatest extent possible, these problems need to be considered and addressed in advance because reform opponents will unquestionably seek to defeat a convention before it ever meets. The first task for convention organizers will be to create a nationwide convention coordinating committee ("NCCC") to manage the convention process.

NATIONWIDE CONVENTION COORDINATING COMMITTEE

The NCCC should be a relatively small national committee organized to run all phases of the convention. The first critical task for organizers will be to recruit its members. Choosing suitable members of the NCCC can help to build public support for the convention and the need for reform, as well as creating a solid reputational base for the fundraising necessary to support the convention's work. The NCCC's members should be a diverse group of well-respected citizens committed to the idea of holding a convention to achieve constitutional reform, but it is not necessary for them to agree on what reforms need to be made.

Just as a few examples and without intending in any way to limit the possible field, there is good reason to think, based on their achievements and on their established ability to recognize and withstand special interest pressures, that people such as Mary Barra, Oprah Winfrey, Henry Louis Gates, Jennifer Granholm, Yo-Yo Ma, Barbara Corcoran, Raj Chetty, Mark Cuban, Colin Powell, Bill Gates, Richard Posner, Leon Panetta, David Souter, Rahm Emanuel, Pete Buttigieg, Andrew Yang, David F. Levi, Madeleine Albright, James Mattis, Anthony Fauci, Deborah Birx, Kwame Anthony Appiah, Mark Shields, David Brooks, and many others would be suitable members to serve on the NCCC, if they chose to do so.

NCCC organizers will have to decide whether to include elected officials as members, or whether its membership should instead be composed entirely of private citizens to avoid bias and emphasize that the convention will occur outside the normal political process. It would probably be desirable to have both types of members, but to ensure private citizen majority control and take precautions to avoid conflicts of interest. NCCC members must be well-enough regarded professionally to make it possible for them to organize a fundraising campaign to support the convention's work, but should not be expected to make any significant personal financial contribution. Once the NCCC is organized, its first task should be to develop the "call" for the convention. The call will embody the NCCC's overall convention strategy, seek public support for it, and provide a basis for fundraising.

THE CALL FOR A NEW CONVENTION

If a new constitutional convention able to consider a range of possible reforms is going to be held, it will need to be based on a popularly issued call, not one approved by Congress. To be successful, a popular call will require exceptionally careful planning and design to surmount the inevitable legal and political challenges a convention will face. Following is a discussion of the main issues that the NCCC should anticipate and address before they issue their call. While some of these issues may seem procedural or technical, they all involve pressure points that opponents may use to attempt to defeat a convention movement.

The call for a popular convention must be properly framed to achieve four goals: (1) to choose a suitable place and time for its meeting; (2) to present an agenda for public debate during delegate elections of reform issues that organizers believe that the convention should consider; (3) to provide the fundamental terms for the election of delegates; and (4) to gain public support for the convention and raise funds for its work.

TIME AND PLACE

The call should provide sufficient advance notice so that predictable legal and political challenges to the convention can be resolved and delegate elections can be held in sufficient time before it meets. That suggests that it would be desirable for the call to provide at least a year's notice before the convention's proposed meeting. It may also be desirable for the convention to be held in a federal non-election year, since that would dampen efforts to turn the convention into an election issue or a surrogate election contest. The proper timing of resulting ratification efforts needs to be considered as well, since they too could become entangled in an election. A central location such as Chicago should be chosen to make it easy for delegates to attend. But the convention's meeting time and place, though quite significant, are less important than the NCCC's critical decision about whether it should seek to limit the convention's scope in the call.

THE CONVENTION'S SCOPE

Many people today on both the political left and right who support a convention will nevertheless argue strenuously that a call for a new convention should voluntarily limit its scope. They think that doing so would mollify convention opponents who claim they fear an unlimited convention. They may also themselves prefer that certain issues be ruled out of convention consideration.

In theory, it might be possible to limit the scope of a popular convention in its call. As discussed further below, a privately-funded popular convention will essentially have the legal character of any other private expressive association, and will have broad powers to control its membership and internal governance, much like a political party.[432] As a condition of their election, delegates could therefore be contractually required to agree to accept a limited convention scope as provided in the call without violating their rights.[433] It is reasonable to think that such an agreement would be enforceable by a court, though there are no guarantees.[434] But limiting the scope of the convention may create significant difficulties of its own.

For example, convention supporters may well argue, as Larry Sabato does, that it would be much better for convention organizers to announce that the convention will not consider any changes to the Bill of Rights.[435] But excluding any such changes would make addressing issues such as campaign finance reform, social media regulation, and gun control reform technically impossible, since doing so would require modifications to the First and Second Amendments. If, those specific issues were permitted to be considered but other changes affecting the Bill of Rights were excluded, both supporters of other reforms and reform opponents would contend that an arbitrary, partisan line had been drawn. Fortunately, it may be possible to avoid this sort of dilemma.

There is a compelling argument to be made that the convention's work should not be limited by the NCCC's call to begin with. For a popular convention to have the best chance to be successful, an unlimited convention agenda is necessary, because that is one of the essential preconditions for its ability to reach a comprehensive agreement. That is true even though delegates may—and probably should—voluntarily decide at the convention to limit its ultimate agenda in order to gain ratification for their proposals. Both historical and current examples support that view.

The creation of the 1787 Constitution offers an important precedent showing the need for an unlimited agenda for a new convention. The Constitution was built around a comprehensive agreement reached at the Philadelphia Convention resolving several major constitutional reform issues on which it was possible to reach consensus.[436] Before the Convention, individual states had spent four years after the Revolutionary War insisting that they would only accept the specific piecemeal Confederation reforms they wanted, and had therefore failed to gain any reforms at all. The Philadelphia Convention was able to meet with an unlimited agenda—and to reach a grand bargain—only when the states had accepted that their piecemeal reform approach could not succeed, and that the Confederation faced imminent collapse if reforms did not happen.[437] The United States faces a similarly demanding political situation today, and for a convention to succeed in making needed reforms, it must meet without an agenda that has been limited in advance. Let's look at a current example that confirms this point.

A limited scope convention is the approach now being pursued by proponents of the balanced budget amendment ("BBA"), who want Congress' approval for it under Article V. But though they apparently do not recognize it, not only is their ability to achieve such a scope limitation in Congress constitutionally in doubt (as discussed in chapters 5 and 6), but such a limited call is actually a deadly political trap for their proposal. We consider its effects here because the BBA has the largest current level of state support and because its supporters' approach illustrates the flaws of limited convention proposals generally.

On the one hand, in the unlikely event that a convention call limited to the BBA were issued by Congress and then observed by the resulting convention, that would make it impossible for delegates to agree to any other reforms. That would in turn rule out an agreement to resolve a broad range of other unresolved issues. That should cheer BBA supporters in particular.

But their joy will be short-lived when they realize that it would also gravely impair the chances that a BBA would ever actually be ratified.

We have already seen in chapter 5 that virtually every significant freestanding amendment will fail to be proposed by Congress under Article V, including a proposed balanced budget amendment. Even in the exceptionally unlikely event that Congress did eventually approve a convention limited to the BBA amendment, that would only occur in the face of sharp partisan divisions. A convention limited to that issue would then in all probability fail to reach a consensus agreement on a BBA amendment because its delegates, many of whom would certainly strenuously oppose the BBA, would be unable to incorporate any other issues into their negotiations. If a sharply divided convention then proposes a balanced budget amendment for ratification, I agree with Lawrence Lessig's view that the convention will very probably fail to obtain ratification by the necessary Article V supermajority.[438] That would mean that the convention had been futile. The limited convention call would ultimately have led to the permanent demise of the BBA.

On the other hand, a convention call with a scope limited to a BBA that was then ignored by the convention would allow opponents to charge that it was a "runaway" convention. That would create a grave political risk that all of the convention's work, including any agreement on the BBA, would be condemned as illegitimate and defeated by reform opponents on that basis alone. To avoid this inescapable political trap, not just for the BBA but for all other freestanding amendments, the call for the new convention should be unlimited.

However, the NCCC's call for a popular convention should nevertheless present a reform agenda for public debate during the election of delegates, while also making it clear that organizers have no intention of prohibiting the discussion of other possible reforms during either elections or the convention. (Chapter 8 presents such a possible reform agenda). The NCCC could also support preparation of a set of background briefing materials discussing the pros and cons of possible reforms to be made available to the public during the elections. It could consider using either the deliberative polling technique or even shadow conventions to aid it in preparing such materials and an agenda.[439] This aspect of the call can also serve as part of the basis for the NCCC's effort to gain public support for the convention. The knowledge gained through public discussion and debate on a range of reforms during the election of delegates will assist voters in choosing delegates, and will also assist the elected delegates substantially in performing their convention duties. Next, the call should establish key terms for the election of delegates.

DELEGATE COMPOSITION AND ELECTIONS

The call should begin by establishing the total number of convention delegates. One leading commentator supporting a convention has suggested that there be about the same number of delegates as there are members of the House of Representatives—435. Another suggests an even larger number, such as 700, to permit greater representativeness.[440] Two considerations argue against numbers that large, but there are countervailing arguments as well which the NCCC will need to consider in making its decision.

First, generally speaking, the smaller the convention is, the more prestigious and hence more desirable it will be to serve as a delegate. This is analogous to the fact that being a Senator is almost uniformly regarded as a "step up" in a political career from being a member of the House of Representatives. Senators serve in a far smaller body; have longer terms; generally have greater influence; have larger responsibilities and staffs, and so on.[441] Making delegate service as desirable as possible is important to induce the country's most capable individuals to serve.

Second, it is essential that the number of delegates be limited to a total that will permit serious deliberations on issues both by convention committees and by the convention as a whole. Based on the current sizes and relative deliberative performance of the existing houses of Congress and of their working committees, a maximum of about 225 delegates seems desirable to meet those goals.[442] That is about four times as many as the fifty-five delegates who attended the Philadelphia Convention. The Philadelphia delegates were able to durably restructure the entire national government completely in four months of meetings. Although I prefer the smaller number I've suggested, the middle-ground figure of 435 delegates would probably be the maximum workable convention size. Any much larger delegate total risks creating a largely ineffective political circus of the kind that often occurs at national party conventions. But there are some prominent legislative bodies, such as the United Kingdom's Parliament, as large as 650 members. The NCCC will need to balance deliberative quality against considerations such as broadened representativeness and diversity (discussed below) in making its final decision.

The logistically simplest method of electing delegates would be to provide that they were elected from states. But some delegates should instead be elected at-large either regionally or nationally. If the convention were to have 225 total delegates, I recommend that forty to fifty delegates be elected at-large, preferably nationally. The remaining 175-185 delegates should be allocated between the states proportionally based on population following "one person, one vote" principles, as recommended by Larry Sabato.[443] If the total number of delegates were enlarged to 435, the same allocation system should be used.

The NCCC will need to decide whether some delegate positions should be reserved for election based on membership in specific social or demographic groups. In my view, half of the delegates should be women, in order to assure that women's concerns are fully represented and debated by the convention. Beyond that, as is true under the existing rules of the Democratic Party for its national conventions (for example), I believe the NCCC should take affirmative steps to ensure diversity and delegate service by minority group members, which I think should include providing some amount of election campaign funding, discussed below.[444] However, there are also arguments (discussed later) for selecting some delegates by lottery, and at least in a larger-sized convention, I recommend that a portion of the delegates be chosen on that basis.

The proportional allocation of delegate strength between the states based on population is a linchpin to the success of the proposed convention in achieving reforms. Proportional allocation will not guarantee particular outcomes on issues that come before the convention. But failure to allocate most if not all delegates proportionally would be the death knell for a large number of the most significant reforms that the convention might well otherwise consider. Among the reforms that would in all likelihood be precluded by an allocation that did not fairly reflect relative population would be abolition of the Electoral College; changes in the structure of the Senate and probably that of the Supreme Court; campaign finance reform to curb the influence of the wealthy; and gun control reform. Foreclosing such structural reform proposals by the convention would also inevitably make reaching any agreements there either on fiscal reforms such as a BBA or on creating a modernized federalism that would assist smaller states (discussed in chapter 8) far more difficult as well, if not impossible. All of those issues would be fundamentally important elements of a convention grand bargain; without them, it might well be impossible for the convention to reach one.

If such badly needed reforms of the Constitution could not be given full consideration and a fair vote by the convention, the convention would be likely to fail. It would fail either because without the ability to make a grand bargain it could not reach agreement on a range of other issues, or because its work would not be ratified by voters. Voters might decline to ratify by the necessary supermajority either because they believed that the convention had failed to address many of the Constitution's basic flaws, or because the convention's proposals were not sufficiently appealing absent structural reforms many of them would support.

There is little question that small state representatives will strenuously object to "one person, one vote" allocation of convention delegates. But they will have no legal basis for objection for reasons discussed below. And they will have no practical way to object, if we leave aside for a moment their ability to stage a boycott, also discussed below. The stakes involved in this single decision by the NCCC cannot be overstated—they are enormous. This is not a place where convention organizers can afford to compromise, and there is no reason whatsoever for them to do so under modern democratic theory.

DELEGATE ELECTION PROCEDURES

The NCCC convention call should require that delegates be chosen by popular vote, rather than by state legislatures. In view of the convention's legal character as a private expressive association, there is no legal requirement or sound policy reason to permit state legislatures to elect delegates. The NCCC can create a website that will allow all delegate candidates to provide information to voters. The election period designated by the call should be brief; no more than three months of campaigning should be permitted. A longer campaign would be both unnecessary and wasteful.

Some writers believe that a traditional election system for choosing delegates will not result in the choice of sufficiently disinterested delegates because efforts by special interests—including single-issue reform groups—to control them will succeed.[445] That fear is misplaced. If the convention call is well-conceived, a very large majority of the people attracted to possible service as delegates will be people working outside traditional politics who will have little interest in becoming career politicians. They will not need to cater to the whims of particular interest groups in seeking election because they will not aspire to permanent office, and because allying themselves with such special interest groups may limit their appeal to other groups of potential voters.

Moreover, most capable candidates will be people who are quite used to dealing with various forms of pressure in their current lives and occupations, so they will be well-equipped to resist the efforts by special-interest groups to capture them. As constitutional scholar Stephen Griffin notes, most of these people have been deliberately "holding themselves offstage." If they decide to participate in reform, Griffin thinks they could "appear on stage rather rapidly, shifting the entire debate from whether we will reform to evaluating which reforms are best." He adds that in this light, "the social and economic resources that could be summoned to undergird a reform effort have been dramatically underestimated."[446]

There have been some suggestions that delegates should be chosen by lottery to avoid concerns about special interest influence and for reasons of fairness and representativeness. There are certainly reasonable arguments in favor of selection by lottery.[447] But it is also true that using it involves a tradeoff. A lottery is the anthesis of the ability principle that George Washington thought it was essential for states to employ in choosing the Philadelphia Convention's delegates. Americans will be able to choose similarly capable delegates from a range of candidates today. However, the NCCC might decide to permit a limited number of people who had been chosen by lottery to serve either as delegates or delegate-advisers.

I recommend that the NCCC's call for a new convention suggest that voters use two main broad criteria for the choice of delegates. First, the delegates they choose should be the people they deem most capable of deliberating on constitutional reforms based on their skills, knowledge, openness of mind, fairness, experience and leadership ability, without regard to their social or economic status or occupation. For example, there is good reason to think based on their achievements that the individuals listed earlier in this chapter as possible NCCC members and many, many others would be much better delegates to a convention than most if not all state or federal career politicians and officials.

Recent studies of citizen participation in possible future constitutional conventions in Great Britain conclude that it would be desirable to have a citizen majority in them.[448] Current career politicians and appointees hold office because they are favored under the existing constitutional system. They will have a strong bias toward protecting the parts of it they see as politically advantageous to themselves and their institutions.[449] But the experience of Iceland's recent failed popular constitutional reform process suggests that there may be value in permitting elected officials and judges to serve as convention delegates.

From 2011 to 2013, Iceland engaged in a constitutional reform process. Iceland's constitutional drafters, called the Constitutional Council, excluded parliamentarians as members. The Constitutional Council was directly elected by the general public,[450] conducted its deliberations in an exceptionally transparent manner including extensive use of social media, and gained substantial majority support for its recommended constitutional changes in an advisory popular referendum. But its proposals nevertheless failed to gain the required approval by Iceland's politically divided parliament.[451]

Iceland's experience suggests that including at least some elected officials as delegates can add legitimacy to the reform process as well as providing the convention with insight about what reforms will be politically possible. But the NCCC might nevertheless conclude that there should be a "term limit" on elected officials' eligibility for service under which particularly long-term officeholders would be excluded.[452] Delegates at the convention will in any event be able to solicit the views of excluded officeholders about proposed reforms as needed.

A second essential criterion for delegate elections is that delegates need to be chosen without any restrictions on their authority to negotiate imposed by anyone, including voters, Congress, or state legislatures. Since delegates will ultimately make a proposal to be submitted for supermajority voter approval, and will have no other authority, there is little need for concern about the fact that their authority would be nominally unrestricted. Concerted efforts will undoubtedly be made by convention opponents to restrict delegates' negotiating authority, either in advance by instructions or by seeking to provide for their recall during the convention if they exceed their supposed authority. Such authority-limiting efforts are in reality little more than efforts to control the convention's work, and should be rejected.

The purpose of delegate selection should be to choose the highest quality representatives capable of the best collective deliberation at the convention, not to designate ministerial agents who will simply follow pre-ordained instructions. Delegates should be elected to serve as trustees for the public and the nation as a whole, not as agents for specific groups of electors or states. This is the same view of office that British leader Edmund Burke advocated when he famously wrote to his Bristol constituents saying that it was his duty to serve as a member of parliament on behalf of the British nation, as opposed to serving as an agent for Bristol.

Burke wrote:

> Parliament is not a congress of ambassadors from different
> and hostile interests, which interest each must maintain, as an
> agent and advocate, against other agents and advocates; but
> Parliament is a deliberative assembly of one nation, with one
> interest, that of the whole... You choose a member, indeed;
> but when you have chosen him he is not a member of Bristol,
> but he is a member of *Parliament.* [453]

Another reason to reject efforts to limit delegates' authority is that
no conceivable set of instructions to delegates can correctly anticipate
the entire course of convention deliberations. Their intended purpose
or effect can therefore only be to block disfavored convention actions.
Similarly, there is little purpose to be served by a recall mechanism
except to create a behind-the-scenes means for exercising "string
pulling" control over delegates by persons or groups outside the
convention. Balanced budget amendment advocates, for example,
have adopted such recall provisions at the state level, which they
apparently hope will serve as—or at least be perceived as—a means of
restricting convention delegates' "unauthorized" actions.[454] However,
imposing such constraints on delegates will defeat the primary purpose
of holding a new convention, which is to resolve as many outstanding
constitutional issues as possible through a grand bargain. All efforts
to tie delegates' hands should be opposed.

The NCCC's convention call should provide that the convention
may choose not to seat delegates if it concludes that their authority to
negotiate has been restricted as a condition of their election, including
by any form of recall mechanism. The call should prohibit delegate
recall from the convention under any circumstances, though the
convention may choose to exclude delegates for misconduct such as
failure to make full financial disclosures required under the call.

CONVENTION FUNDING FROM SMALL DONORS

A rough but conservative estimate of the overall costs of holding a
convention and ratifying its work would be $300-$500 million.[455]

About one-third of the total amount would be needed for each major phase of the convention's work: initial organization and delegate elections; conducting the actual convention; and the ratification contest. The first two-thirds of these funds at least would need to be raised after the call is issued but before the delegate election process begins in order to ascertain that the convention is ready to proceed.

Some people may think that it would not be possible to raise that amount of money from small individual donors, as would be very desirable to avoid having any "strings" placed on the convention's work or undue influence by wealthy donors. But that concern is likely to be sharply diminished if the amounts involved are placed in context. For example, the "GoFundMe" crowdfunding website alone has raised more than $9 billion over ten years, or an average of $900 million per year.[456] As constitutional scholar Stephen Griffin points out, charitable foundations have billions of dollars they could use to support constitutional reform efforts (including the NCCC's work) if they chose to do so.[457] As one example of public interest group support, four leading environmental groups in 2018-2019 received public contributions totaling roughly $250 million.[458] Most of the contributions to GoFundMe and the environmental organizations are relatively small "public interest" contributions, and together they amount to more than $1 billion per year. This suggests that if there is strong enough public support for a convention, providing the funding for it should be quite feasible. And this conclusion is greatly strengthened when we look specifically at political donation patterns.

During a single month—May, 2020—the progressive fundraising platform ActBlue reported that it had raised $178 million from more than 5 million contributors, with an average contribution of $34. ActBlue also reported that it had raised a total of more than $5 billion in small donor contributions since 2004. More than $1 billion of that amount was raised in the six month period between late 2019 and mid-2020.[459] Looking at convention costs in this political donation context, if 10 percent of registered voters nationwide—about 13 to 15 million voters, depending on the election—contributed $35 each to support the convention's work, the entire convention cost would be covered.[460] If the average contribution was $50, contributions by 6-8% of registered voters would cover the entire convention costs.

By comparison, in 2016, 15% of adults nationwide reported making a political contribution, which would actually constitute nearly 25% of registered voters.[461] Even if we assume conservatively that a significant fraction of potential political donors would be deterred from contributing by the unfounded claim that holding a popular convention was an illegitimate activity, it appears that there would easily be sufficient support for the convention's work available. That would be particularly true if donation limits were increased from $35.00 to $100 or even perhaps $1,000. Because it would require three to five hundred thousand $1,000 donations to fund the entire convention, it is highly unlikely that even permitting $1,000 donations would lead to undue influence for any individual donor or even a group of related donors.

This data strongly suggests that private small donor funding is a realistic source of financing for the convention's work. In fact, today it is far easier to raise election campaign funds through small donations using the Internet and social media than it was only a few years ago. As only one recent example of the potential for raising such private funds, the 2018 United States Senate campaign of Representative Beto O'Rourke in Texas raised approximately $80 million in contributions from 800,000 individuals, or an average of about $100 per contribution. At the same time, more than 1.5 million Americans donated more than $200 per person/household to finance various political campaigns in 2018, accounting for more than $4 billion in contributions that year alone.[462] Holding a popular convention and ratifying its work will cost about 8 to 12 percent of that amount. These considerations suggest that the availability of small donor funds to support the convention's work should not be of great concern.

True, many campaigns do fail to raise as much money as the O'Rourke campaign, which took place in a very large state and involved a challenge to a nationally unpopular incumbent. But those facts point us to the real issue raised by convention funding, which is not whether there is a large enough pool of small donor funding available. The real issue facing convention organizers is instead whether there is sufficient public support for the convention. Asking through the NCCC convention call for small contributions to fund the convention's work is one very useful way of determining and demonstrating the breadth of its public support.

There is a useful analogy to be found in other forms of citizen action as well. In a recent book, constitutional scholar Lawrence Lessig presents several case studies of successful state level reforms that were organized by private citizens and overcame intense partisan opposition. For example, in Michigan, a citizen volunteer group that began its work at the prompting of a single individual, Katie Fahey, obtained more than 400,000 petition signatures and raised $2 million from 14,000 contributors (an average contribution of $140) to support an initiative to end gerrymandering there. The citizens' group overcame concerted partisan opposition, including the spending of $4 million in advertising and lawsuits seeking to block its work, and then received 61 percent of the vote for the initiative.[463] As this and Lessig's other examples show us, private citizens are able to put substantial energy and resources into reforms they support. There is no reason they cannot or will not do so in support of a popular convention.

FUNDING OF DELEGATE ELECTIONS

Some writers who support a convention advocate public campaign funding for candidates in delegate elections.[464] That is understandable because in theory it enables a broader range of people to seek such positions. However, the use of taxpayer funds for such purposes would require approval by some government body such as Congress or state legislatures. But it follows from the unavoidably controversial nature of any convention that any government's representatives would be extraordinarily unlikely to provide tax funding for convention delegate elections without imposing "strings" ultimately intended either to influence the election or to control the convention's actions. To avoid such biased control, it would be better to use privately raised funds for delegate elections, and we have just seen that such funding should be available.

I recommend that part of the NCCC's funds be used to finance election efforts of some leading delegate candidates. In light of the small donor data discussed above, allocating something in the neighborhood of $50-100 million to assist in financing a reasonable number of delegate election campaigns, perhaps on a matching basis, should not be especially difficult. Candidates who receive funding from a pool consisting of large numbers of small one-time donations are unlikely to feel obliged to follow any particular donors' views on reform.

Convention-sponsored funding could be made available to candidates who demonstrate a reasonable level of public support through polls or petition campaigns. Campaign funding could be made available preferentially to assist campaigns by minority group or low-income candidates with such support in order to bolster convention outreach efforts. Candidates whose financial net worth exceeds a set amount could be made ineligible to receive campaign funding, in order to make the allocated funds more widely available to candidates of modest means.

Outside contribution amounts to delegate campaigns should be limited by the convention call. Donations to delegate election campaigns should be limited to those from domestic sources. Candidates should be permitted to contribute their own funds up to specified limits. All donations to delegate elections including personal funding should, however, be required to be publicly disclosed in an easily accessible form within a very brief time. All delegates should be required to file full public reports on the funding of their campaigns before the convention. Any delegate who receives any funding from any undisclosed source should not be seated by the convention.

The inevitable outside efforts to influence delegate elections and later the activities of the convention will complicate the election and convention process. Under current constitutional free speech doctrine, though, it may not be possible for the NCCC to prevent outside groups, parties, corporations, or individuals from engaging in political spending such as advertising to advocate or oppose possible constitutional amendments, even though that might indirectly influence delegate elections. There would probably also be outside efforts to spend money for advertising and organizing to support or oppose individual delegate candidates, and such spending might also be protected, though that is open to greater doubt.

In any event, it should be possible for the NCCC to require third parties engaged in such forms of spending to make it clear to voters by a prominent visible disclaimer that any such spending or advertising is not authorized by the NCCC or by any delegate candidate.[465] Any delegate candidate who coordinates in any way with any outside funding group should be denied seating by the convention. The legality of outside funding efforts of various kinds should be carefully reviewed by the NCCC, and a detailed legal strategy should be developed and funded in advance of the call to make it possible to compel outside funders to follow NCCC's requirements.

Throughout our political history—including the formation of the 1787 Constitution—wealthy individuals and special interest groups have sought to influence elections and government, and they have sometimes succeeded. We can be fairly confident, however, that such special interest efforts can be frustrated by a carefully-planned election process for a popular convention, though under current law there may be no "magic bullet" to prohibit such influence efforts beyond disclosure requirements and delegate seating restrictions outlined above. Ultimately, the best protection against pernicious outside influence on delegate elections and the convention itself is political: voters need to elect delegates capable of recognizing and withstanding such influence. If voters choose able, suitably experienced individuals as delegates, we can be reasonably confident that despite any individual failings and special interest pressures, their collective deliberations will be sufficiently independent.

ANTICIPATING AND RESPONDING TO CHALLENGES TO THE CONVENTION

Once the NCCC has completed the convention call but before it is issued, it will need to prepare for legal and political challenges intended to prevent the convention or to hamstring its work. The first and most important point for the NCCC to appreciate is that there will be concerted efforts to "strangle the convention in its crib." Because a new popular convention might well propose major changes to the American political status quo, it is certain that vigorous efforts will be made to prevent it from meeting at all or to prevent it from proposing various amendments. These efforts will probably resemble the kinds of sprawling political fights that typically occur during the California popular initiative process.[466] They will include lawsuits, actions in Congress and state legislatures, and campaigns against delegates because of their views on possible reforms.

As to legal challenges, there will doubtless be claims that permitting the convention to meet under the call, or even electing delegates to it, would violate the Constitution or federal law in some fashion. However, because it will be a privately funded nonprofit organization, the Convention will in legal contemplation be nothing more than a lengthy meeting of an expressive association of people with common interests for the purpose of peacefully considering a range of public issues. That type of gathering should be fully protected by the First Amendment. A long line of Supreme Court cases involving public interest organizations, beginning with *NAACP v. Alabama* (1958) and extending into state efforts to regulate political parties such as those found in *New York St. Board of Elections v. Lopez Torres* (2008), uniformly protect private freedom of expressive association. These precedents will render frivolous challenges to various aspects of the convention, including delegate elections and its meetings.[467] They should fail if the courts are willing to entertain them at all, though of course that will not stop people from trying, so organizers need to be fully prepared.

The political challenges to the convention will be far more extensive and more serious. The easiest opposition approach would be to seek Congressional action to block the convention. That was essentially what Philadelphia Convention opponents tried in 1787 when they realized they were likely to fail to prevent it at the state level. Fortunately, the results of that approach are likely to be equally unsuccessful today.

Congress is going to be faced with a difficult dilemma when it is asked to block a popularly called convention. Here the well-known political saying, "you can't beat something with nothing," would apply.[468] Congress cannot politically afford simply to oppose the holding of a convention that is supported by many people in many states without offering any alternative to it. Congress might try first to avoid this problem by taking its own legal action against the convention.

Congress might go to court claiming that Congress' approval of the convention was required under Article V. But its members would probably be sharply divided over whether to bring such legal action if the convention had a reasonable level of public support, so such a lawsuit seems relatively unlikely. If it did sue, however, Congress would be forced to make the unpopular argument that it had exclusive authority to authorize any meeting held to consider constitutional reforms. That argument should fail for reasons discussed in chapter 6, and also because it flies in the face of the First Amendment's protections for free speech and association discussed above.

In lieu of court action, congressional opponents of a convention will be forced to propose legislation to take the place of constitutional reforms, and it must be attractive enough to deflate the convention movement. As discussed in chapter 6, that was the approach Congress took successfully in 1985 by passing the Gramm-Rudman-Hollings debt control legislation in order to defeat efforts by thirty-two states to seek a balanced budget amendment to the Constitution.[469] If the NCCC's convention call explicitly contemplated that the convention could consider a broad range of constitutional reforms, however, Congress would be exceedingly unlikely to be able to agree on a series of legislative proposals sufficient to end the pressure to hold a convention to consider all such reforms.

Alternatively, convention opponents could seek hearings and legislation in Congress to have it impose scope limits and rules on the convention similar to Senator Ervin's unsuccessful legislation (discussed in chapter 6). Such efforts would consume considerable time and (purely coincidentally) delay the convention. However, it is likely that Congress would not have any constitutional authority to impose scope limits or rules on a popular convention called outside Article V. In any event, Congress is exceptionally unlikely ever to reach agreement on matters of scope and rules with respect to a general convention.

These considerations together suggest that Congress is very unlikely to be able to deflect or delay convention efforts aimed at achieving a range of fundamental reforms. The NCCC should treat opponents' attempts to persuade Congress to block or control the convention as nothing more than dilatory tactics that will ultimately fail, and move steadily forward with arranging the convention while resisting them.

STATE BOYCOTTS

Convention opponents in some states will argue that their jurisdiction should simply boycott a popular convention. They will contend that holding it is illegal under Article V or federal law. Or they will claim that it will inevitably make undesirable changes, for example, by altering their state's voting strength in the Electoral College. They will charge that a convention will be a political "stacked deck," and assert that the best way to respond is for the state to boycott it.

For example, as discussed in chapter 6, Rhode Island boycotted the Philadelphia Convention, because its governing party had adopted state fiscal policies that its leaders knew were widely condemned in the rest of the country and that were likely to be outlawed by a new federal constitution—as they indeed then were.[470] Today, the fact that states will not have equal state voting rights under the NCCC convention call (as discussed above) may well cause certain states to boycott the convention before it begins, or to seek to instruct their delegates to withdraw after it convenes. Some state boycotts are therefore likely for these and other reasons. The resulting boycotts will be a price well worth paying to make certain that the Convention's actions broadly represent national public opinion rather than the views of state elites or special interests who control particular state governments.

A convention will have several ways to respond effectively to a boycott. First, it can disregard the states that boycott, and conduct its deliberations without them, which is what happened in the Philadelphia Convention. Rhode Island ultimately was forced to agree to the 1787 Constitution anyway in 1790, after the new federal government made clear that it would adopt policies to make it costly for Rhode Island not to do so.[471] If either the Convention or the federal government had instead made any concessions to Rhode Island's boycott, they would have handed the state an enormously powerful minority veto over the new form of government created by the Constitution. And that would have strongly encouraged other states to seek their own vetoes.

Similarly today, a convention boycott by one or even several of the smaller American states is unlikely to meaningfully affect a national popular convention's work. Ultimately, their boycotts may be ignored without great cost. After all, if they are unhappy with the convention's eventual proposals, they can seek to defeat them either during ratification or in court. But if they fail in those efforts, which is likely if the convention reaches a sound reform bargain that gains widespread public support, they will very probably have no realistic alternative but to conform to the new constitution's requirements because they will have little political leverage at the national level.

CONVENTION ARRANGEMENTS AND PROCEDURES

CONVENTION FUNDING

Some writers who advocate a convention support providing public funding for its work. However, as discussed previously, public funding will not be provided without inevitable strings attached to control the convention's decisions. The convention should be brief, lasting no more than six months and preferably less. A reasonable estimate is that it would cost at most about $1 million/day, and probably significantly less, to hold the convention. That would include the costs of providing air and in-city transport, hotels, food, compensation, and a secure convention site for 435 delegates and 100 staff. Over five to six months, convention costs would probably total under $100 million, and about $150-$180 million at most.[472] For the reasons discussed above, if a sufficient number of people support holding the convention, it should not be difficult to raise a pool of small donor funds adequate to support its work. If convention funding is based on small donor contributions, it is difficult to see how delegates would be unduly influenced by any particular contributor's views. The NCCC convention call should prohibit delegates from using any other source of outside funding (other than limited amounts of personal funding) to support their convention participation, and they should be excluded from the convention for violations.

CONVENTION RULES

The convention should establish its own rules of procedure once it convenes, since its delegates will be in the best position to decide what rules will best suit their work and because efforts to dictate rules in advance will inevitably often be sub rosa efforts to control the convention. However, it will be worthwhile for the NCCC to consider in advance some contentious rules issues that will probably arise during the convention, and to prepare background information about them for delegates to use in considering the convention's rules. In particular, despite the very different political circumstances today, some of the rules used by the Philadelphia Convention should be given careful consideration for possible use, because they would be helpful to almost any convention faced with divisive issues.

For example, the Philadelphia Convention adopted a very liberal rule on reconsideration of issues, which permitted any delegate who changed their mind about an issue to ask the convention to take a second look at it. According to historian Richard Beeman's authoritative account, the rule "proved to have far-reaching consequences. It would enable the Convention to function not like a legislative body, with strict rules for the recording of votes and the bringing of business to the floor, but rather as an informal 'committee of the whole.'" Beeman says that this allowed "delegates the opportunity to take 'straw votes'—to measure the relative strength of opposing opinions on particularly contentious issues and, when appropriate, to change their minds as they groped their way toward compromise and consensus."[473] Such a generous reconsideration rule seems well designed to permit convention delegates not just to reach decisions but to reach well-considered decisions with which they are all as comfortable as possible. Such decisions are more likely to provide a solid basis for supermajority approval of the convention's work.

On rules for delegate voting, I agree with Larry Sabato's recommendation that each delegate have a separate vote, rather than requiring state delegations to vote as a unit. Giving delegates individual voting rights reflects the constitutional principle of voters' independence. It prevents efforts to hamstring delegates to protect parochial special interests. It also recognizes the reality that the United States is a modern nation, not a fortuitous collection of independent states. As Sabato wrote:

> In a "one-person, one vote" world...there is only one politically acceptable choice...and that is to choose "one person, one vote" for delegates on all matters coming before the convention. In 1787 the United States may have been little more than a "league of friendship" entered into by thirteen semiautonomous states. After more than two centuries, though, it is a well-integrated nation that respects state powers and traditions but acts as a unified whole.[474]

In general, the convention should make decisions by majority vote. But given the political sensitivity of various issues to be considered, there may be circumstances under which it will decide that a specific proposal should not be approved by the convention unless it receives supermajority approval from delegates. Among other things, adopting such a practice would enhance the Convention's ability to develop a set of constitutional reforms that has an increased chance of receiving supermajority approval from ratification voters—the acid test of the convention's ultimate success.

As to convention deliberations, as is well known, the Philadelphia Convention adopted a rule requiring secrecy, which was nearly uniformly observed by the delegates. As Richard Beeman points out, "the rule of secrecy, however alien to our twenty-first century values, helped make the Constitutional Convention of 1787 an agency of deliberation rather than partisan debate. It allowed the delegates to take risks in debate, float only partially developed ideas, or disagree vehemently, but ultimately reconcile their views." James Madison later argued that "no Constitution would ever have been adopted by the convention if the debates had been public."[475]   Some commentators today conclude, however, that it was the Philadelphia Convention's secrecy which enabled delegates to make tragic bargains, such as the ones that protected slavery and extended the slave trade until 1808.[476]

By comparison, the French constituent assembly debating reforms to the French constitution during 1789-1791 permitted widespread public access to its deliberations. Debates were open to the public, and were "constantly interrupted" by the public. "Patriot" forces pushed for moving much of the convention's business from committees into the full assembly, where "'souls become strong and electrified, and where names, ranks and distinctions count for nothing.'" Voting by roll call "enabled members or spectators to identify those who opposed radical measures, and to circulate lists with their names in Paris." According to the constitutional scholar Jon Elster, as a result "the [French assembly] discussions...were heavily tainted by rhetoric, demagoguery, and overbidding."[477]

Constitutional scholar Mark Tushnet points out that there is an inevitable tradeoff between a convention's transparency and its ability to strike politically necessary bargains. He writes:

> Modern constitution-making faces an imperative of transparency....Transparency at the drafting stage has the important advantage of inducing deliberation and rational argument, but perhaps the equally important disadvantage of discouraging bargaining. Public discussions typically invoke basic principle, thereby educating the observing public about the choices being made...Speaking in public, advocates must take responsibility not only for their arguments but for the provisions they support. Public sessions, though, make it difficult to strike what might be essential compromises that can be defended only as necessary to get the constitution adopted but not as based on fundamental principle.[478]

Of course, a popular convention held today will not be able to proceed in secret as the Philadelphia Convention did. There is no doubt that any convention held now will receive intense public scrutiny, including demands that all its proceedings be open and televised. But as Tushnet's analysis suggests, transparency can have adverse effects on convention bargaining and decision-making.

Here again the Icelandic constitutional reform process is instructive. The Constitutional Council ("CC") that drafted the proposed constitution engaged in what might fairly be described as hyper-transparency in its work. According to a study of the reform process the CC enthusiastically embraced the use of social media, "at the expense of a professional distance that would have been more typical of such assemblies….At almost every stage of the process the public was involved and often actively so."[479] CC use of social media was so extensive that some have referred to its draft constitution as the world's first "crowd-sourced" constitution. CC members had public email addresses and responded to individual public letters and emails. An outside "semi-formal collective" "stress tested" the draft constitution for gaps and tweeted the results in real-time. The CC adopted as a principle that it would provide "equal access" to its work for everyone to dilute special interest influence, which meant that no interest groups or members of parliament were invited to private meetings. The CC considered any attempt to win political support for its proposals outside its mandate.[480]

But the Constitutional Council failed to persuade Iceland's parliament to adopt its proposed constitution, or even to agree to put it to the binding popular referendum the Council advocated to determine whether it would be adopted.[481] The CC had steadfastly refused to cooperate with either parliament or the political parties, seeing such actions as inconsistent with transparency. Some commentators believe that that refusal was why its proposals failed to gain the support of majorities in either government or the parties.[482] Iceland's parliament refused to act on the Council's proposals even after a nationwide advisory referendum made clear that there was supermajority support for most of them.[483] The lesson of the Iceland experience is that extensive transparency in a constitutional reform process may shape the drafting process but is no guarantee that effective reform will occur.

With the inevitable tradeoffs between transparency, consensus, and national unity in mind, the right balance will need to be struck by the convention between keeping the public informed concerning its work and making certain that the convention can deliberate effectively despite substantial public and special interest pressures designed to influence it. The convention should consequently reserve the right to close its proceedings to the press and the public by an appropriate vote when needed, just as Congress does.[484] There are alternative ways of ensuring that ratification voters are adequately informed about the convention's work.

These would include the fact that the convention will have the ability to draft a final report on its work that can provide an additional basis for public debate during ratification. Congress has throughout its history prepared "conference reports" after its two houses have met to confer and agree on legislation. Such conference reports have usually been regarded by courts as a major basis for their later interpretation of federal statutes.[485] A final convention report on its proposals could serve much the same function during ratification. But of course, the convention should decide for itself how it wishes to proceed in this respect and not be bound by an advance decision.

Some writers suggest that the convention should have subpoena power.[486] That is unnecessary because if the delegates are capable, they will collectively already be in possession of sufficient information about both government's operations and society's difficulties to make it needless for them to seek to extract information under legal compulsion. They can hold public hearings to shed light on particular issues without subpoena power. In any event, as a private association, the convention will not have the legal authority to issue subpoenas. Seeking a grant of subpoena power for the convention from one or more government bodies would be virtually certain to result in strings being attached to its use.

RATIFICATION

The most fateful decisions facing the convention will concern the process for obtaining ratification of its work. Seeking congressional approval of a popular convention's work would be futile and self-defeating. In 1787, the Philadelphia Convention transmitted its work to the Confederation Congress as a face-saving formality. But the proposed constitution's supporters had no real desire to permit Congress to do anything more than to rubber stamp the Convention's work and transmit it to the states without amendment. After some debate, Congress ultimately agreed to do nothing beyond that. Today, there is nothing to be said for letting Congress even be involved in transmitting a new convention's work to the states, since the people, not the states, should make the ultimate decisions on ratification.

The convention should seek supermajority approval of its work from voters nationwide to gain the maximum legitimacy for the result of its efforts, not from state legislatures. The states are not valid units for ratification purposes for reasons set forth in chapter 6. The Constitution's requirement that three-fourths of the states approve constitutional amendments under Article V will permit reforms to be vetoed by less than ten percent of the American population. Such a veto would be especially harmful if the convention decides it would be desirable to restructure federalism by revising the decision-making roles of the federal and state governments (see chapter 8). Permitting such a powerful minority veto to operate during ratification of a new convention's work will inevitably prevent the adoption of a range of vitally necessary constitutional reforms, even those favored by an a very large popular majority.

The convention's most difficult decisions will concern first, what level of supermajority support ratification should require, and next, whether to submit its entire proposal as a package for an "up or down" vote, or to permit one or more aspects of its work to be the subject of separate ratification votes. The final decision about what level of supermajority should be proposed for ratification of the convention's proposals should not be made in advance of the convention, since it is best made by the delegates themselves. However, the NCCC should consider proposing a minimum level—perhaps 60% or slightly more—in the convention call as a means of structuring public debate during delegate elections. Some general considerations that the convention decision should take into account can also be suggested here.

Essentially, supermajority approval has two basic purposes: (1) to require the existence of a broad consensus before constitutional change occurs; and (2) to safeguard minority rights and interests. Both of those factors must be given appropriate weight if the reforms adopted during ratification are to be widely enough regarded as politically legitimate and to become enduring features of government, as opposed to engendering endless opposition even if ratification occurs.[487]

Taking the need for durable political legitimacy into account, the size of the gap between the convention's reform proposals on the one hand, and existing constitutional provisions and their interpretation on the other, informed by an understanding of public opinion concerning various proposed changes, will determine how large a supermajority the convention decides to propose for ratification of its work. Broadly speaking, it would be reasonable for the convention to propose a lower level of supermajority approval if its proposals concerned only changes that are already the subject of a very broad social consensus, and a higher level if they were more controversial.[488]

Another major ratification issue a new convention will inevitably face is whether to seek a single up-or-down vote on its proposals, or to propose separate votes on some of them. If the convention adopts a very controversial reform—such as creating federal tax powers was in 1787, for example—as part of a grand bargain, then permitting only an up or down vote on the entire reform package is likely to alter significantly the voting dynamics on the entire proposal. A package voting structure could positively affect the prospects for adoption of a controversial reform and yet negatively affect those for the convention's proposals as a whole. The convention will need to decide how to strike the proper balance.

It was precisely because the structure of ratification voting can affect its outcome that Anti-Federalist opponents of the Constitution almost uniformly opposed an up-or-down vote on it. They wanted instead to be able to strip out from the Philadelphia Convention's proposals those to which they and many others strongly objected, such as the broad new federal tax powers, which they expected could then successfully be voted down (or force a second convention to reconsider them). Pro-Constitution Federalists, on the other hand, insisted as strenuously as they could that the proposed Constitution that should be voted on only as a package during ratification, since that voting procedure protected their most controversial reform proposals, which they viewed as essential to the new government.[489]

RATIFICATION VOTE PROCESS AND FUNDING

The costs of conducting the ratification vote should also be paid through private funds from small donors. If the convention has been successful in reaching a reasonable consensus agreement, it should be easier to raise funds for holding the ratification vote than it was for the earlier stages of the effort. The convention should seriously consider providing for only a brief ratification period after it completes its work and has sufficiently publicized it. That will avoid delay tactics from opponents intended to defeat ratification by dragging the process out. The convention will inevitably face a large array of political and legal efforts to defeat its work during and even after ratification. But if the convention process has been handled well, and if the convention has proposed sound reforms and a reasonable, well-structured ratification process, these efforts should fail, and the process of integrating the convention's reforms into the operations of government can proceed without undue delay.

CONCLUSION

As this review of issues facing a popular convention's organization and procedure shows, there are no insurmountable obstacles that would prevent a well-organized popular convention effort from succeeding, including practical concerns such as the necessary fundraising. A popular convention will inevitably face strenuous opposition throughout its development and work, which will take the form of various legal and political challenges, but it can be defeated. It is perfectly realistic to think that Americans can hold a popular convention—all that is needed is a widespread enough conviction that the times demand one and a very carefully thought out plan for its meeting.

8

A Constitutional Reform Agenda

To this point, this book has made two basic claims: the Constitution is dangerously broken, and a popular convention can and should be held to revise or replace it. This chapter proposes convention reform priorities, and offers some specific reforms. But its proposals are entirely independent of the claims made in earlier chapters, so even if you disagree with every reform it recommends, the book's first two claims will still stand. And the book's earlier claims are what matter fundamentally to achieving constitutional reform. After all, the convention delegates themselves will ultimately decide on reform priorities and what specific proposals they will support, so this chapter presents only suggestions for readers' consideration. Before discussing reforms, however, let's take a brief look at the enormous potential transformative power a new constitution could have, by looking at the changes wrought by the 1787 Constitution.

THE 1787 CONSTITUTION, POLITICS, AND SOCIETY

To meet the political crisis it faced, the Philadelphia Convention chose to create a radically different, potentially far more powerful, form of government. The government the Convention proposed could not have been created except through a grand bargain, because its proposal made a series of fundamental reforms that had each individually been successfully resisted by one part of the country or another for years before it met. The resulting Constitution had profound implications for American politics, but it also initiated and fostered a fundamentally important process of social transformation that delegates had not foreseen.[490]

Some revolutionary leaders were deeply shocked by the Philadelphia Convention's proposals. Virginia leader Patrick Henry decried them as a betrayal of republicanism intended to create a "great and mighty empire." Richard Henry Lee of Virginia wrote that it was "really astonishing" that after having fought a "long and cruel war in defence of liberty," Americans "should now agree to fix an elective despotism upon themselves and their posterity."[491] Even friendly critics, such as Thomas Jefferson, were extremely unhappy about some aspects of the proposed Constitution. Jefferson said that he thought it might ultimately create a king, and he lambasted its failure to include a Bill of Rights.[492]

The new federal powers granted by the Constitution had enormous implications for the economic and social development of the United States. The federal government quickly went from complete insolvency to becoming by far the most financially solvent government in the country. It could repay the nation's massive Revolutionary War debts. New revenues also supported national institutions, particularly the military, needed both to deter foreign powers from aggression and to protect westward expansion.

Alexander Hamilton, Washington's first Treasury Secretary, realized that the nation's large new resources could also be used to wholly restructure the states' finances. Many of them were facing serious financial difficulties after years of war, recession, and growing population losses to western emigration. Hamilton's 1790 public finance plan proposed the assumption and refinancing of all state debts in addition to restructuring the federal debt. Among other things, Hamilton's proposal successfully induced wealthy federal and state government creditors to reduce the size of their claims.

Hamilton's plan greatly assisted the federal government in building a new American social contract. His financing system was an enormously influential means of gaining allegiance to the national government from citizens who soon realized that their post-war tax and debt burdens had been greatly lightened by it. The plan helped foster a powerful sense that the expanding nation was now operating as a strong collective entity.

The federal government's new stability and the nation's abundant land and other resources strongly encouraged immigration. Eventually, the strong allegiance of many citizens to the Union, combined with its massive constitutionally-enabled financial resources, allowed the United States to survive the Civil War. That devastating war would have torn many other countries to shreds. The Constitution deserves much of the credit for creating a federal government both strong and resilient enough to withstand its enormous carnage and incessant political strife, guided by Abraham Lincoln's courageous and farsighted statesmanship.

Despite the Constitution's real achievements, however, there is more substance to many criticisms of its corrosive effects on America's republican government than its leading Federalist supporters thought. The United States has become a de facto empire and now has a wealthy oligarchy. To protect it, much as Patrick Henry feared, we now possess the world's most powerful and costly standing military forces. We have an imperial presidency and a supine "do nothing" Congress, a relationship which increasingly resembles an "elective despotism." In recent decades, several presidents and Supreme Court justices have been chosen by partisan minorities. Politically unaccountable federal courts now often make irreversible decisions about major political issues such as presidential elections on tenuous constitutional grounds.

The Constitution also sustained a bitter legacy of racial oppression. Millions of African-Americans lived as slaves under its authority. They and their descendants were then subjected after "emancipation" to an entire era of racist oppression, sanctioned by the federal courts and effectively by a majority of Congress as well. Many Americans justifiably believe that racism continues to influence heavily important aspects of social life and minority opportunity today. As we saw in chapter 1, today there are still persistent large gaps in wealth and opportunity between white Americans and minorities, especially Blacks.

The 1787 Constitution is no longer able to meet either America's social and political needs or the standards of modern democracy. It is in dire need of major renovations, if not wholesale replacement. In a troubled world, America needs a new social contract to regain its citizens' allegiance and to address pressing social and economic problems discussed throughout this book that we continue to ignore at our peril. A new constitution can provide the foundations for that social contract, just as the Constitution helped government build a new social contract during the early Republic. Following are reforms for consideration by a new convention dedicated to that task and some pitfalls a convention will need to avoid. Earlier writers have developed a broad range of specific reforms that a convention may wish to consider; the proposals discussed in this chapter are not intended to be either comprehensive or exclusive.[493]

As to pitfalls, the convention will inevitably need to decide how much political baggage its proposals can carry. For its work to be successful, some reforms that might be desirable will need to be left for another day. The convention's ability to make a grand bargain will mean that it can act boldly and creatively, but public opinion including supermajority ratification will inevitably impose limits on the scope of even such a bargain.[494] Among other things, to obtain ratification a package of proposals will need to be "cross-partisan," in the sense that they can receive support across a wide part of the political spectrum. As Lawrence Lessig points out, all individual constitutional amendments after the Fifteenth Amendment have depended on cross-partisan support.[495] But a grand bargain can create a much broader cross-partisan coalition than individual amendments ever could.

In considering this reform agenda, convention supporters should appreciate one other fundamental point. Establishing a new constitutional right without a clear constitutionally-based enforcement mechanism is merely a handoff of a political problem, not its resolution. Otherwise, new rights will be the sorts of "parchment barriers" or "paper rights" for which James Madison understandably had little regard, because he believed that such rights would not be observed whenever a popular majority wanted to override the rights of a minority. History supports Madison's view. If we want rights to be protected, the constitution itself must provide tools to make it possible even for individuals or small groups of citizens to insist on their effective enforcement over majority opposition.[496]

I believe that collectively the reforms presented here contain the elements needed to create a grand bargain at a new convention, because they include proposals that will appeal to a broad range of political groups. Many of these proposals are nonpartisan and are designed to improve government decision-making and to protect or enhance democracy; others will appeal to liberals or conservatives, but not both. However, various proposals should appeal to the following groups whose interests will lead them to become allies of reform: large states; both large and small city mayors; businesses that seek clear, coherent, and stable federal policies at home and abroad; both younger and middle-aged Americans concerned about education, health care, environmental protection including climate change, and retirement security; minority group members; and fiscal conservatives.

STRENGTHENING SOCIETY

Many of our citizens—often based on harsh personal and community experience—know that our country's professed desire to create equal opportunity for all has not actually provided them with equal opportunities in life. To regain their allegiance, we need to make reforms needed to realize fully our goal of creating and preserving freedom for all by redefining and ensuring equal opportunity. We have made commitments of various kinds under federal law intended to meet that goal. But it is time now to make certain that these abstract goals become concrete realities. That will require the creation of new constitutional rights. As the political scientist Emily Zackin has shown, Americans have long understood the need for such positive constitutional rights, and have included such rights on issues such as education, labor protection, and environmental protection in state constitutions throughout much of our history.[497] We need now to establish such rights for the benefit of all Americans, and to ensure that legislatures and Congress will implement them.

To provide the social and economic basis for real equal opportunity for all, the new constitution should provide that all Americans have the rights to an adequate quality primary and secondary education (including appropriate vocational training), childcare, environmental protection, and healthcare. The constitution should also require that the responsible units of government provide the funding necessary to meet these commitments (see federalism discussion below). In order to make certain they are carried out, it should create a clear means of citizen enforcement of those rights without any required showing of direct personal legal harm (i.e., it should waive federal legal standing requirements), including entitling prevailing parties to court-awarded attorneys' fees and treble damages. And it should similarly expand citizens' power to enforce laws against all forms of discrimination.

One of the most important achievements of the New Deal was to create a national social safety net to protect many, though unfortunately not all, Americans. The New Deal safety net is now failing badly, as we saw in chapter 1. A new constitution should strengthen the social safety net, by requiring that children in foster care, the elderly and disabled, the homeless and other vulnerable groups receive adequate care. Responsibility for the care of vulnerable groups should be clearly assigned to the proper level of government (see federalism discussion below), and responsible governments should be constitutionally required to provide adequate funding for such care. These rights should be made fully enforceable by citizens.

RESTORING PUBLIC CONTROL OF PRIVATE WEALTH AND CORPORATE POWER

A new constitution should restore public control over private wealth and corporate power in our technological society. During the nineteenth century and the Progressive era, as emerging forms of energy were incorporated into new industries such as railroads, electric lights, and the telephone, Americans decided that such new industries would either be subject to public regulation or publicly owned. The creation of such public utilities was a victory for the principle that new technologies should be brought under social control and be made widely accessible to the public at reasonable rates, rather than creating private wealth through monopolization. Such government authority to prevent capitalism from becoming predatory by monopolizing essential new technologies was essential to maintaining capitalism's public acceptance.

Today's technology companies such as Facebook, Google, and Apple, on the other hand, have grown into phenomenally wealthy private entities with virtually no public oversight, ownership, or regulation. American consumers pay far higher prices for technology such as broadband cable internet than do many Europeans as a result of what are often technology oligopolies or monopolies tolerated by government. Not only do their excessive costs damage average consumers, they sharply limit access by the poor to technology increasingly essential to participate in most aspects of modern life, including job markets.[498]

Moreover, many Americans today have legitimate concerns about the potential for social harm posed by leading new digital technologies, including artificial intelligence. These technologies have the potential to distort election outcomes nationwide; seriously violate individual privacy; cause social and emotional harm to individuals; and inflame mass passions, among other ills, even while destroying important traditional mediating instruments of democracy such as the print news media. A new constitution should either require creation of a system to regulate technology company oligopolies or monopolies in the public interest, including rate regulation, or order them to be broken up under the antitrust laws.[499] The convention should also decide whether the federal government should be able to regulate speech on technology platforms in the public interest, including imposing platform liability for false or otherwise defamatory speech by third parties.[500] The new constitution should also provide that where local technology oligopolies or monopolies exist, state and local governments may acquire them as publicly-owned companies at reasonable prices.

As another necessary step to rebalance public and private power, the constitution should expand the nation's authority over today's immense concentrations of private wealth. This problem has two aspects: wealth personally acquired by individuals, and inherited wealth. As to the former, if the government adequately controls predatory conduct by business, in theory, it would be unnecessary and probably counterproductive to establish a limit on the amount of private wealth that could be acquired. It would instead be limited through marketplace competition. The convention will need to decide whether it believes strong enough competition exists or can be restored in key economic sectors, or whether some limit should be placed on the amount of private wealth that can be acquired by individuals in certain industries (e.g., defense contracting).

Limits on wealth that is inherited rather than earned by individual efforts are needed to preserve republican government. As leading Founders knew, the unhindered ability to pass unlimited private wealth down from generation to generation will inevitably create a permanent American aristocracy. As a country, we already have a wealthy oligarchy, and we are directly headed toward allowing it to become a permanent de facto aristocracy, whose members will inevitably destroy republican government as they dominate politics. It is no answer to say that many wealthy heirs use their money to support philanthropic causes, because there is no requirement that they do so and because wealthy individuals rather than public institutions make decisions about how to invest those resources. There will doubtless be disagreements about what limit on inherited wealth should be established. But the convention should recognize that if it does not impose limits, it is highly unlikely that Congress will ever do so. Congress and the legal profession have been captured by the wealthy; they will not adopt or willingly enforce such limitations.

Finally, Congress should be given clear constitutional authority to tax wealth directly. To avoid future doubt, it should be made explicit that it possesses the power to tax unrealized capital gains as well. Essentially, Congress should have the same power to tax forms of property held by the wealthy that states and cities already employ to tax middle class property such as people's homes. (Granting Congress such power is not the same as endorsing its use; but it will then be available without delay or debate if needed, much as a windfall profits tax is needed in times of war). The convention should also consider whether the constitution should establish a maximum level of wealth taxation that Congress may impose.

POLITICAL AND INSTITUTIONAL REFORMS

The constitution needs several important political and institutional reforms. These include abolition of the Electoral College; restructuring state voting strength in the Senate to reflect population, in a manner similar to the allocation of seats in the House of Representatives; campaign finance reform; and measures to increase political competition for seats in Congress and to make Congress more focused on representing the country as a whole, rather than parochial interests. Political reforms should include voting reforms.[501]

POLITICAL REFORMS

The abolition of the Electoral College is unquestionably justified (see particularly chapter 4). The country cannot afford more presidents elected by popular minorities. A major benefit of abolition would be that in executing his or her office in the national interest, a future president would never be politically beholden to any electoral minority, including those in small states and those in strategically located special interest large-state voting blocs whose power is artificially exaggerated by the College.

There is little doubt that the redistribution of state voting strength in the Senate will face enormous opposition, including outraged claims that Article V of the Constitution flatly prohibits this change without the consent of every affected state. For reasons detailed in chapter 6, a popular convention can and should ignore that provision of Article V. It relies entirely on the utopian and anti-republican idea that states qua states should be deemed equal—not just for a long time but eternally—for purposes of structuring the entire national government.[502]

Restructuring Senate voting to reflect population is one of the most important reforms that can be made to transform Congress into a viable legislative body once again. First, a restructured Senate will mean that federal legislation will increasingly be tailored to meet the needs of larger states, which contain most of the nation's population and much of its wealth, but which also experience many of its most difficult social problems, including much of its urban congestion, violence, and poverty. Second, it will mean that Supreme Court appointments cannot be made by political minorities, and over time that shift will favorably influence the Supreme Court's decisions toward achieving equal justice. Justices whose appointment must be approved by Senators representing a majority of the population are more likely to have views that take into consideration a broader range of opinion about legal and constitutional issues, rather than being captive to a narrow ideology that is acceptable only to a political minority. Third, the United States is likely to make more effective and durable treaties and foreign military commitments under a restructured Senate. Fourth, a Senate that accurately reflects the needs of large states will almost certainly be more responsive to the country's environmental protection needs, particularly those resulting from climate change, because those areas of the country are likely to experience much greater hardship and incur considerably greater costs from environmental damage than others will.

After the convention proposes a restructuring of the Senate and a national voter supermajority approves it, even in the unlikely event that the Supreme Court proves willing to decide the political question raised by the inevitable challenge to that decision, it is highly improbable that the Court will conclude that the convention or voters lacked authority to make the proposed change in state voting strength, notwithstanding Article V. The predictable sharp controversy surrounding this badly needed reform to end grossly distorted congressional decision-making should not deter the convention from proposing it.[503]

The convention should also consider whether to prevent the Senate from continuing to use a filibuster rule that effectively requires supermajority consent to adopt legislation. Prudent leaders will not adopt legislation that is firmly opposed by a large political minority unless the need for action is clear and the case for the policy change is equally clear; but giving a shrinking minority a broad legislative veto is overkill. The numerous past abuses of the filibuster to prevent desirable reforms strongly suggest that it should be eliminated.

The convention should expand the size of the House of Representatives to increase its representativeness, as recommended most recently by the American Academy of Arts and Sciences ("AAAS") after a two year nationwide study that included forty-seven listening sessions around the country.[504] The convention should also decide whether House of Representatives members should continue to have two-year terms of office. Electing members of the House to three or four-year terms would give the House somewhat greater ability to withstand short-term political pressure, and also limit fundraising demands on members.[505]

The constitution also sorely needs to be amended to "take money out of politics" in order to end the disproportionate influence of wealthy Americans on government. But that unfortunately cannot be done successfully simply by overturning the Supreme Court's *Buckley v. Valeo* and *Citizens United* decisions and their progeny. Congress has been captured by the wealthy. Even if it is given clear constitutional authority to legislate broad campaign finance reforms, it is readily foreseeable that it will not use its power to actually bring campaign funding by the wealthy under effective control. Instead, Congress will engage in "window dressing" reform, even while claiming that it is making major changes.

The easiest way to grasp that point is that the "bipartisan" Federal Election Commission ("FEC") created by earlier "bipartisan" congressional campaign finance reforms is actually one of the most toothless federal agencies ever created. It is run by six commissioners, of whom no more than three can come from one party, and it can only act with the agreement of four out of six commissioners, which means that representatives of both parties must agree to act. The FEC's structure therefore makes partisan deadlock almost inevitable, which is unsurprising because many in Congress did not want it to be powerful. As a result, the FEC's efforts to control campaign financing have repeatedly been deliberately evaded with impunity by both major parties in an era where campaigns involve billions of dollars each election cycle.[506] As of this writing, this utterly ineffectual agency lacks even a quorum needed to do business due to lack of appointed commissioners, a clear sign of both parties' utter lack of interest in effective regulation.[507]

Perhaps the domination of campaign financing by the wealthy could be ended by moving to a new system of public campaign financing that barred all private funding, as some advocate. But such a radically different system has its own complexities and shortcomings, including the possibility of stifling desirable political competition, particularly against incumbents. Whatever approach is chosen, delegates must bear in mind that it is unrealistic to expect Congress to adopt meaningful campaign finance legislation, even if it is given clear authority to do so. It makes no sense to ask the fox to guard the henhouse. The convention must resolve this issue if reform is to occur.

If the convention wants to achieve successful campaign finance reform based on continued private funding, it must establish limits on campaign contributions by all entities and individuals that might provide funding. Limits must not be capable of being evaded by the multiple formalistic legal devices such as super PACs developed over the past several decades. The convention's proposal must include harsh civil and criminal sanctions for violations. The best way to enforce proposed limits will be through public and citizen court enforcement, aided by treble damages and attorney's fees and waived legal standing requirements. Public enforcement should not be permitted to displace citizen enforcement where both are sought, however, because of possible political or financial conflicts of interest and "sweetheart" deals.

The convention should also seriously consider whether the new constitution should end the two-party duopoly in American politics. Abandoning single-member districts and winner-take-all voting, and moving instead to proportional representation or another system, such as ranked-choice voting and multi-member districts as recently recommended by the AAAS, that will enable significant minority party representation in government, would increase political competition.[508] It would also be a seismic political change. There are reasonable arguments for and against such changes.[509] But one thing is clear: if the constitution does not end the two-party duopoly, Congress will never do so. The two major parties both have been willing periodically to commit temporary political suicide by choosing party nominees that the broader electorate then firmly rejects, but as constitutional scholar

Mark Graber argues, they will not voluntarily agree to commit permanent political suicide.[510]

The convention should end gerrymandering, as recommended most recently by the AAAS report.[511] Professor Sabato argues that ending it will significantly increase competition for congressional seats.[512] But it is important that the convention be clear about precisely what system of drawing congressional district boundaries is to take its place. It will need to establish clear criteria to be used in creating districts; decide whether legislatures or independent bodies should be authorized to create them; and finally, to decide whether and on what specific grounds federal and state courts should be authorized to intervene in future gerrymandering disputes.

If the new constitution does not ban gerrymandering, Congress and most of the states will never do so. Both parties significantly benefit from gerrymandering, though in different states and at different times. Which party receives the greatest political advantage from it may change over time in the future, as it has done in the past. For these reasons, as Professor Sabato concludes, and as Justice Kagan and her three dissenting colleagues in *Rucho v Common Cause* recently agreed, neither party will voluntarily "disarm" by agreeing to ban gerrymandering.[513]

The convention should adopt measures to equalize the cost of voting for federal offices across America. Based on extensive recent studies of the actual relative costs of voting in different states, constitutional scholar Lawrence Lessig concluded, that "the costs of voting are not born[e] equally in America. Instead, they burden the vote of Democrats more than they burden the vote of Republicans....Thus increasing the costs of voting is a simple technique for suppressing Democratic votes, and thus increasing the chances for Republicans to win."[514] The experience of the pandemic shows that America's election system is broken, and needs reform. The new constitution should mandate that voting for federal offices be based on uniform national election requirements so that voters' cost of voting for those offices is equal no matter what part of the country a voter casts his or her vote in.

The new constitution should also establish uniform rules for determining voter qualifications and eligibility, including voting rights restoration after completion of prison sentences.[515] These rules should be designed to prevent voter suppression, which Hoover Institution Senior Fellow and former Stanford professor Larry Diamond recently wrote is an increasing problem: "The hard truth is that there has been a rising tide of voter suppression in recent U.S. elections. These actions — such as over-eager purging of electoral registers and reducing early voting — have the appearance of enforcing abstract principles of electoral integrity but the clear effect (and apparent intent) of disproportionately disenfranchising racial minorities."[516]

The convention should consider whether the new constitution should provide for the use of one or more of the "direct democracy" mechanisms that were adopted by California and other western states roughly one hundred years ago. These include the citizen initiative and the referendum. These devices were adopted as ways of allowing popular forces to overcome the complete corruption of state legislatures by powerful economic monopoly interests such as the California railroads. While these direct democracy mechanisms have been criticized, particularly by progressives, for some of their results, they have also led to some useful government reforms, such as California's environmental protection laws and its nonpartisan legislative redistricting system.[517] Constitutional scholar Stephen Griffin, argues that if such devices are carefully limited in their use and powers, their availability could actually strengthen representative government.[518] The convention would be able to impose conditions on the use of any of these devices it authorizes in order to protect against their perceived harms.

INSTITUTIONAL REFORMS

The constitution should be amended to include several institutional reforms. These include modifying the rules for the separation of powers if it is retained; limiting the powers of the president and the Supreme Court; and additional reforms to restore Congress' effectiveness.

SEPARATION OF POWERS MODIFICATIONS

Although it is clear that the separation of powers system does not work at present, the ultimate question for the convention is whether it can be made to work at all, or whether some form of parliamentary government would instead be preferable. Of course, shifting from a presidential system to a parliamentary government would be a dramatic change in American politics. However, the American presidential system is increasingly an outlier compared to many democratic governments around the world that established their current forms of government more recently than the United States. According to recent studies, a very large share of the world's democracies that existed in the late twentieth century had adopted a parliamentary government. About a third of the world's population lived under such governments as of 2004.[519]

There are substantial arguments both for and against changing the United States to a parliamentary system.[520] Claims in favor of the current system emphasize its stability, since the president has a fixed term and does not depend on a vote of confidence from Congress to continue in office. They also stress the virtues of presidential leadership independent of Congress because the president is separately elected. Those who argue for a change to a parliamentary government, particularly one that employs proportional representation, point to what they claim is more efficient and inclusive decision-making and greater accountability to voters.[521] Even if the convention decides to continue the existing presidential separation of powers system, however, I recommend that it consider modifications to its principles that would informally limit presidential power and at the same time improve the operations of both Congress and the executive branch. Two possible reforms are discussed here.

The convention should consider whether members of a president's cabinet could be—or perhaps even should be required to be—chosen from among sitting members of Congress. At present, American cabinet officials are often figureheads whose policies in their agencies are determined by White House staff. A cabinet composed of members of Congress would instead have an independent political base supporting its work to which its members would need to be accountable. That would both permit and encourage them to respond to the president's policy proposals with a much greater degree of freedom. The president would be able to draw continually on a much wider range of political knowledge and experience. He or she would have close advisers who intimately understood Congress' concerns. The president's cabinet would also be far more likely to discuss executive branch policies informally with other members of Congress than at present, and would be more capable of obtaining congressional support for the president's policies.[522]

I also recommend that the president and his or her cabinet be required to participate in a congressional version of Parliamentary "question time." In the United Kingdom, question time is a regular part of Parliament's weekly business which requires cabinet ministers and the Prime Minister to attend and answer questions from Parliament.[523] In the United States, on the other hand, existing institutions for the public exchange of information and debate between Congress and the President have become far less useful. The annual State of the Union address is increasingly a formality that is now little more than a political stage show for television audiences. Media questioning of presidents is generally of limited value because it is entirely at the discretion of the president; it occurs in a highly controlled environment; and there is an enormous disparity between the press and the president in relative access to information. These outdated, staged public dialogues need to be replaced.

The president should be required regularly to face direct questions from members of Congress and debate policies with his or her political opposition's leaders. That would increase the stature of Congress vis-a-vis the president. It would allow—and indeed require— presidents to hear Congress' concerns directly, avoiding repeated mediation, deflection, and negotiation of such concerns by staff and special interests. And it would compel presidents to defend their policies personally in front of a national audience. Voters could then decide for themselves how well those policies fared in debate without needing to rely on "spin" from either side or third-party interpretation.

LIMITS ON PRESIDENTIAL POWERS

A new constitution also needs to impose added structural limits on the power of the president. First, presidents should be made removable from office on broader grounds than at present. The criteria for impeachment and removal should be broadened to include incompetence or malfeasance in office, even if no crime has been committed. Impeachable offenses should also include authorizing troop engagement (directly or indirectly, as in the cases of aerial bombing or drone use) without the advance consent of Congress, except in cases of imminent danger of attack on the United States itself. Finally, a president's systematic refusal to enforce any constitutionally valid law should be an impeachable offense.

To avoid partisan removals and protect presidential authority, a two-thirds vote requirement for impeachment and removal should be retained (unless the convention decides to propose a parliamentary government). However, as an exception to that rule, in the case of impeachment for authorizing military action without congressional consent, I recommend that only a sixty percent vote should be required for impeachment and removal. I also recommend that no court review of a congressional impeachment and removal process or vote be permitted on any grounds, since Congress will be making a political decision for which it should be fully accountable.

The president's constitutional powers as commander-in-chief should also be limited in one other major respect. The constitution should recognize that United States use of nuclear weapons presents unique dangers to world peace and national safety and survival. Presidents should be prohibited from authorizing the use of nuclear weapons, even in wartime, without the advance consent of a war council consisting of the four top party leaders in the House and Senate, except in the case of imminent threat of attack by nuclear weapons on the United States itself. Failure to observe these procedures should be an impeachable offense, requiring only a majority vote for impeachment and removal.

The president's powers as head of the executive branch and chief law enforcement officer also need considerable clarification in order to avoid continued wasteful, time-consuming disputes over their extent based on vague, all-encompassing claims such as the "unitary executive" theory or the supposed requirements of the Administrative Procedure Act.[524] Following are questions about presidential powers it would be desirable for the convention to clarify: (1) Should the president have power to instruct the Department of Justice to bring or to end or compromise a federal criminal prosecution or civil action? (2) Should the president be able to order non-enforcement or repeal of a final agency regulation, agency policy, or executive order and, if so, through what process? Should the exercise of power or the process required depend on whether that regulation had been specifically approved by Congress? (3) Should he or she be able to order agency promulgation of a new regulation or enforcement policy and, if so, by what process? Should Congress be able to overturn any such new regulation and, if so, how?

REVITALIZING CONGRESS

In theory, Congress is at the heart of republican government, but in practice, it has become chronically gridlocked, reactive, and unable to meet national challenges with responsive policies. This dysfunction is not due to Congress' lack of legislative authority on paper. Instead, Congress has frequently permitted the president and the courts to assume its rightful place in national affairs. That abdication will only end when the incentives for service in Congress are modified to prevent it from being filled by career politicians with narrow ambitions and little desire to "rock the boat." If Congress is going to become a viable legislative body, serving there cannot continue to consist of a lifetime of secure, well-paid public service with little competition facing incumbents, followed by a lucrative career defending the same special interests which finance elections and lobby Congress. Congressional careers must become competitive, and members of congress need to be people who are ambitious about strengthening the power of their institution, not about using office as a stepping stone to wealth or higher office.

To enable greater competition for congressional seats, the convention should strongly consider imposing constitutionally-mandated term limits, as others have suggested.[525] It might well also be advisable to establish a uniform mandatory retirement age for both members of Congress and the presidency. If the convention does not establish term limits or a retirement age, it is a virtual certainty that Congress and many states will not do so.

Choosing an appropriate term limit for members of Congress should not prove unduly difficult. Two Senate terms and six House terms are currently each twelve-year periods. That is longer than the president's constitutionally mandated two-term limit, and sufficiently long to permit members of Congress to learn their jobs and make any productive contribution they have to make. (In that connection, the convention might do well to consider whether either staff or family members of incumbents should be eligible to succeed term-limited members to avoid evasion of such limits). Nor should it be difficult to agree on a mandatory retirement age, such as 70, given the performance of today's American political gerontocracy.

Term and age limits will open positions to new individuals seeking public service who do not want to make a lifetime commitment. Such limits would undoubtedly mean that some exceptionally gifted political figures would be forced to leave Congress and that voters would be denied complete freedom of choice. But that is equally true of the effects of the Constitution's two-term limit on the presidency, which has widespread public support. The convention may well decide that limits on voters' freedom of choice are a price worth paying for increased competition and significantly weakening the special interest stranglehold on Congress.

The convention should also seriously consider other ways of making congressional seats more competitive. One important way to do this would be to draw congressional district lines so that they cross state and regional boundaries, so that to be an effective representative, a member of Congress would be required to represent a more diverse range of interests. The convention should also seriously consider recommending that a significant number of Senators and congresspeople be elected on a regional or national at-large basis, so that their performance is judged on how well they represent a much broader range of interests than other representatives, not on how well they "bring home the bacon" to their state or district. The size of

Congress could be increased to accommodate these at-large seats.[526] The convention should also consider whether to impose new limits on certain forms of post-congressional employment such as lobbying to avoid conflicts of interest.

LIMITING THE POWER OF THE SUPREME COURT

The Supreme Court is not a representative institution, and it can reasonably be argued that that is as it should be given its constitutional role. But the Supreme Court has moved by default into a power vacuum as representative government institutions have decayed, and its power needs to be limited to protect their proper functioning. There are two primary ways that this can be done straightforwardly.

The first is to limit the terms of Supreme Court justices, perhaps to eighteen years, as most recently recommended by the AAAS report. Limiting the terms of Supreme Court justices will allow for increased diversity of views on the Court over time; increase the odds that each president and new Senators will have the ability to appoint some justices; and decrease support for "packing" the Court to advance particular views of the Constitution. Term limits would increase the Court's representativeness without destroying its strongest basis of legitimacy, its relative independence from politics.[527]

A second means of limiting the Court's power would be to provide either that certain kinds of legal issues are excluded from the Court's jurisdiction or that the Senate can review and overturn Court decisions in those types of disputes, perhaps by a three-fifths vote. Either approach would be considerably narrower than proposals to deprive the courts of any power to review the constitutionality of federal statutes made by leading constitutional scholars such as Mark Tushnet.[528] The United Kingdom used the principle of parliamentary review of court decisions for hundreds of years, and Parliament still retains its authority to reverse any court ruling if it chooses to do so even after recent reforms intended to make the British courts more independent.[529]

The convention will need to decide whether the Supreme Court should continue to have an essentially unlimited roving commission to intervene in—or to decline to intervene in—an exceptionally broad range of legal and constitutional issues, many of which are better viewed as political disputes. For example, was it really better for the country and for the continued vitality of representative government to have the Supreme Court determine the outcome of the 2000 presidential election in *Bush v. Gore* rather than forcing Congress to decide it? I think that it would be strongly preferable to have a contested presidential election decided by Congress, since its members have far more political experience than the Court and because unlike the Court they can be held accountable for the result by voters.

The larger point is that we have increasingly permitted the Supreme Court to become the final political arbiter of what are fundamentally issues of national policy simply because they can be framed as involving one or more constitutional issues based on ambiguous constitutional provisions, some of which were clearly never intended to govern such disputes. The convention needs to decide whether democratic political processes should replace court rulings in specific types of cases in order to protect the vitality of representative government.

DEBATING A BALANCED BUDGET AMENDMENT AND SLAVERY REPARATIONS

Despite the increasingly partisan nature of the debate over a balanced budget amendment ("BBA"), consideration of such an amendment should be a part of any new convention's agenda. There are several reasons. First, twenty-eight states containing nearly half the American population have made requests to Congress that the issue be formally considered, and that alone suggests that it deserves consideration. Second, efforts by BBA opponents to prevent its consideration by a new convention should be seen for what they are—efforts to kill such an amendment permanently. When the nation's debt is steadily increasing and social safety net resource demands and middle-class tax burdens are also going to escalate, a debate over long-term fiscal policy is an important debate for the country to have, and one that may also influence national policies on wealth taxation.

Finally, if a new convention were held, and a BBA amendment were not fully debated, it would severely damage the legitimacy of the convention's work in the eyes of many citizens who support the BBA concept. It would materially strengthen claims that the convention was a "stacked deck" intended to further only the constitutional reform goals of certain special interest or partisan groups, and not those of others, and thus significantly damage ratification prospects for the convention's work. For all of these reasons, a balanced budget amendment should be fully considered by the convention.

Many of the same considerations that support convention consideration of a BBA also argue persuasively for convention consideration of reparations for slavery. Ta-Nehisi Coates and others have presented a case for reparations that is strong enough to justify making the issue part of the convention's agenda, despite intense disagreements over its merits.[530] If the convention is going to reconsider the fiscal system, it should take the question of reparations into account. Debating the issue will also undoubtedly contribute positively to the convention's work on a variety of other issues such as improving the criminal justice system and law enforcement roles as well. And many Americans, including many whites as well as African-Americans, will regard the convention's work as either unfinished or illegitimate if the reparations issue is not given full and fair consideration while other issues such as the BBA are debated.

RENEWING FEDERALISM

The states have had their detractors since the Constitution was written. Some scholars believe that several leading Founders wanted to abolish them.[531] But states have historically had important functions in our federal system. By resisting oppressive federal government policies, they can limit abuses of power. And they can protect dissent against recurrent majority efforts to control freedom of thought and expression, which Thomas Jefferson famously called the "reign of witches" during the bitter controversy over the repressive, partisan Alien and Sedition Acts.[532] States can also usefully serve as laboratories for social experimentation, as Supreme Court Justice Louis D. Brandeis famously argued in a New Deal era dissent, often without risk to the rest of the country.[533]

But in chapter 6 we saw that many states are no longer viable financially. It seems equally apparent that many states are no longer functionally capable of meeting important contemporary national needs, particularly those involving regulating global businesses, or that depend on operating and maintaining very expensive, complex high-level technology or making difficult scientific fact determinations. The convention should take the steps necessary to strengthen the states, because they can serve important roles both in maintaining citizens' sense of attachment to government and in increasing their sense of empowerment as they play a more direct role in shaping government policies at the local level.

As the first step in renewing federalism, a new constitution should include a clear, specific restatement of the respective roles and powers of the federal government and the states. We need to stop controlling the division of responsibility between states and the federal government by employing traditional notions of the "rights" of states. In today's changed conditions, that concept is frequently so vague in practice as to be entirely subjective. Hence it is little more than an invitation to let federal judges without any real experience in governing have the final say in what are essentially political disputes over federalism. The constitution should revise federal and state responsibilities as discussed below and alter states' fiscal resources to match. But to avoid future unproductive, time-consuming disputes, it should also make clear that Congress has power to alter state responsibilities and powers in the future by majority vote. That would mean, for example, that if Congress adopted a law requiring that states should expand Medicaid, they would be compelled to do so.[534]

In order to create a new federalism, the convention will need to decide what capacities states actually have to address contemporary problems. For example, there is little reason to think that most states could effectively address steadily increasing cybersecurity threats, particularly those from foreign governments, or international computer fraud. As another example, states have begun to legalize drugs now classified as dangerous and illegal under federal law. But are states that are legalizing drugs actually capable of regulating what is essentially an international cartel drug business without extensive support by and coordination with federal law enforcement and scientific officials? As the coronavirus pandemic shows, we need to ask whether states are really capable of anticipating or managing serious public health threats that may occur, such as globally spreading viruses, or even lesser but still serious threats such as marijuana-induced vaping lung disease. The convention will need to clearly demarcate the respective boundaries of federal and state authority on such jurisdiction-spanning issues.

Most importantly, the convention needs to decide whether our country should continue to accept the traditional view that states and localities should have primary responsibility for America's system of public education. The results of local control have for decades been both mediocre and often racially discriminatory. Many states clearly lack the extensive resources needed to provide effective education to a large population of English-language learners and children requiring special education. And efforts to integrate increasingly complex workforce training requirements with state-designed education programs have generally been of very poor quality. We have a vital national interest in building and maintaining the world's highest quality education system. That would significantly increase opportunity and social mobility for the poor and middle-class and minority group members, simultaneously strengthening both our economy and our democracy. The convention should decide whether public education needs systematic national reform as part of a new federalism.

After the respective responsibilities of the federal government and the states have been clarified, the second step in renewing federalism will be for the convention to decide whether state revenue sources are adequate to meet the revised demarcation of their responsibilities. Today states are hampered by the fact that their revenue bases are often limited to taxing historically immobile forms of capital such as real property. Their tax systems often result in large inequalities between different local jurisdictions within the same state, particularly where education financing is concerned, which are especially damaging to minority group children. And the states' ability to raise revenue is often limited by the very real possibility of limited property values, capital flight, and efforts at evasion.

The constitution should require that the federal government provide a sufficient level of revenues to states to meet responsibilities they retain that are regarded as tasks they perform on behalf of the nation as a whole. For example, if the United States permits significant immigration from countries where English is not a native language, perhaps the federal government rather than local governments should be required to provide all of the necessary financial resources to ensure effective education for the children of such families. If state and local governments are required to care for the elderly poor, the homeless, and disabled and mentally ill individuals, perhaps the federal government should be required to provide all of the necessary funds to states to carry out such responsibilities.

Another profoundly important priority for creating a new federalism is that the constitutional ideal of equal justice for all must not only be reaffirmed but fully realized in order to regain the allegiance of many citizens to our government. We must strive to make it impossible for any American to claim legitimately that they have been unfairly or discriminatorily treated by any part of the federal, state, or local law enforcement system, criminal or civil. No one should feel as though they can be treated brutally, discriminatorily or oppressed in any other way by law enforcement officials with impunity. Nor should anyone, anywhere legitimately feel as though they are not adequately protected against criminal conduct by others because of their economic or social status. These rights must be fully and effectively enforceable against government officials personally by harmed individuals.

As a country, we already have a theoretical commitment to these goals of fair law enforcement. But many citizens believe that laws are enforced unfairly in either overly harsh or discriminatory ways, often particularly against racial minorities. And in certain areas, particularly highly segregated urban areas, many people do not believe that they receive adequate protection from law enforcement officials. Many of them also believe that the police today are not their allies in maintaining social order, but are instead willing or unwilling tools of enforcement for other potentially oppressive institutions, such as landlord-tenant law. We need to restructure our systems of law enforcement to address these often-legitimate concerns. But the convention will need to consider how that can be done in light of other aspects of rebalancing federal-state relations, including providing necessary funding to states.

INDIVIDUAL RIGHTS REFORMS?

Some constitutional reform supporters who advocate holding a new convention believe that it should avoid any consideration of controversial individual rights issues, such as gun control, abortion, or the intersection between religious freedom and various social duties such as providing medical or pharmaceutical care. There is little question that such issues are among the most politically divisive the country faces. And it is fairly clear in light of those divisions that except through a popular convention, none of the efforts to change the Constitution's current stance on such issues will succeed in the foreseeable future (with the possible exception of the Equal Rights Amendment). That means that supporters of reform on individual rights issues will probably interpret the convention's failure to consider their concerns as a rejection of them. But the convention may be well-advised to avoid most such issues, for several reasons.

First, in the long run, the structural political and institutional reforms discussed above and the creation of a new federalism will have the most influence on the country's ability to make fair and farsighted policy decisions in the national interest. If so, then over time the political process can and probably will significantly lessen the social tension surrounding some of these constitutional issues. For example, if after structural reform of the Senate, Congress adopts clearly constitutional gun control reform legislation, such as making certain that systematic background checks effectively prevent criminals and mentally ill individuals from purchasing firearms, the level of gun violence is likely to diminish over time. If reforms lessen the control of the wealthy over government and that leads to more aggressive enforcement and stronger punishments for white-collar crime, over time we can reasonably expect to see the development of far stronger and wider citizen support for the even-handed administration of justice under the rule of law in other areas than exists today.

Second, the convention clearly cannot afford politically to consider certain major controversies over individual rights, such as gun control, without also considering others that would probably be anathema to many of gun control's supporters, such as abortion. If it were to consider only some controversial individual rights issues, but not others, that would allow reform opponents to argue that the convention is a political stacked deck and threaten ratification of many essential structural reforms. Moreover, if the convention were to consider and debate various individual rights issues in an evenhanded way, but then adopted proposed changes regarding some but not others, the resulting perception of ideological bias could prove just as damaging politically to ratification.

Third, if the convention were to consider a range of controversial individual rights issues, and adopted reforms on several of them, that would significantly increase the amount of political baggage its entire reform proposal would have to carry. There is a delicate balance to be struck between increasing the political appeal of a grand bargain by including in it reforms popular with some groups but opposed by others, and weighting it down with controversy to the point where it sinks under a barrage of objections. For these reasons, I recommend that the convention avoid proposing modifications to the existing Bill of Rights, except as to campaign finance reform and technology company platform public speech regulation. But the convention might decide that Equal Rights Amendment should also be an exception given its very broad public support, and it could nevertheless consider the creation of new rights such as a right of personal data ownership or an expanded right of privacy. The need for such new rights due to technological change should receive serious consideration.[535]

A New Amendment Process

One of the most significant flaws of the Constitution is its strikingly rigid amendment process. Ours is one of the most difficult constitutions to amend in the world.[536] As was discussed in chapter 5, its amendment process was created largely due to political necessity. The wealthy vested interests from different regions whose rights were protected by the Constitution, such as the major slave states and the smaller states, wanted assurance that it would be very difficult at best (and a practical impossibility, in some cases) to attempt to take those rights away from them.

While reasonable constitutional stability is undoubtedly a virtue, firmly tying the hands of future generations in the face of the urgent need for reforms is plainly a vice. The Constitution's excessive rigidity is the ultimate enemy of political resilience, the surest key to our long-term national survival. It is not necessary to agree fully with Thomas Jefferson that no constitution should last for more than twenty years, and that no one generation should have power to bind another, to think that our current method of amending the Constitution is far too restrictive. How can we improve the amendment process?

First, Article V limits the process of initiating constitutional changes to either a supermajority vote of both houses of Congress, or by petitions to Congress made by a supermajority of the states. The inclusion in Article V of the requirement of Congressional action to call a convention was very probably an effort to give Congress an opportunity to manipulate the convention's formation and hence the amendment process itself. That can be said with certainty of Congress' power to decide whether ratification of any amendment should occur through state legislatures or state conventions. Congress has used its Article V power to keep tight control of the constitutional amendment process throughout our history.

A straightforward improvement to Article V would be to remove Congress' power over state-initiated conventions. The amendment process could be modified so that states representing a large enough percentage of the population (say two-thirds) would be able to initiate a convention to discuss either a single subject, or a general convention, and to do so without congressional approval. The resulting convention would also have power to determine the mode of ratification of its proposals. However, as to general conventions at least, the constitution might also provide that such state-initiated conventions could only occur at intervals of at least seven to ten years.

Although a new constitution could not deprive the people of their inalienable right to hold future popular conventions, the convention should consider whether to create an explicit constitutional popular amendment process that would not require the approval of Congress or the states. As an incentive to use that process, meeting its requirements could permit supporters of such popular amendments to make use of state and federal resources such as election machinery.

A popular amendment route might provide that a convention to consider a particular issue could be called with the support of at least fifty percent of registered voters nationwide who vote on a ballot proposal for such a convention. Inclusion of such a single-issue convention proposal on the next general election ballot could be made mandatory in any state where at least ten percent of registered voters petition for such a vote. The convention might decide that such citizen-initiated single-issue conventions that rely on government resources could not occur for some specified time period after any general convention is held.

The Article V ratification process also needs fundamental modification. In general, whatever level of supermajority support is chosen by a new popular convention for ratification of its work should also be the presumptive level of supermajority support required for later amendments at subsequent conventions, other than amendments affecting any aspect of the Bill of Rights. For example, if the popular convention advocated in this book decides that its proposals can be ratified by a two-thirds popular vote nationwide, then most future amendments should be able to be ratified by the same supermajority. But that convention should also consider whether to require a higher, more protective level of supermajority support for any future amendment affecting the Bill of Rights.

Conclusion

> All honor to Jefferson—to the man who, in the concrete
> pressure of a struggle for national independence by a single
> people, had the coolness, forecast, and capacity to introduce
> into a merely revolutionary document, an abstract truth,
> applicable to all men and all times, and so to embalm it there,
> that to-day, and in all coming days, it shall be a rebuke and a
> stumbling-block to the very harbingers of re-appearing
> tyranny and oppression.

> —Abraham Lincoln to Messrs. Henry L.
> Pierce and others, 1859

In this well-known quotation from his letter to Henry Pierce, Abraham Lincoln praised Thomas Jefferson for having proclaimed a universal principle of human equality in the Declaration of Independence. Much less well-known is that in the same letter, Lincoln also described Jefferson as the founder of one of America's two earliest political parties, and that he traced his own political lineage and principles directly back to Jefferson. The party Jefferson founded, he said, was "formed upon its supposed superior devotion to the *personal* rights of men, holding the rights of *property* to be secondary only, and greatly inferior..." Lincoln said that like Jefferson's party, his Republicans were "for both the *man* and the *dollar*; but in cases of conflict, the man *before* the dollar." [537]

Although Lincoln's letter immediately concerned the nation-shattering controversy over slavery, in his view that conflict directly affected the future of free democratic government. The pro-slavery view of politics, he said, rested on and sought to restore earlier aristocratic principles of "classification, caste, and legitimacy. They would delight a convocation of crowned heads, plotting against the people. They are the vanguard—the miners, and sappers—of returning despotism." Lincoln wrote further, "this is a world of compensations; and he who would *be* no slave, must consent to *have* no slave. Those who deny freedom to others, deserve it not for themselves; and, under a just God, can not long retain it."[538] It is tempting for us to gloss over Lincoln's profound insights, thinking that they refer only to a long-dead controversy over a despised institution. But he thought that they were part of a recurring political dispute over the relationship between liberty and property in a democracy.

As we decide whether the United States needs a new constitution, we would do well to heed Lincoln's admonitions. If we accept the continuation of a Constitution under which any one inordinately powerful or wealthy group in society can deny a rightful share of freedom to others, we cannot expect to long retain our own freedom. If we accept the continuation of a Constitution where massive political and economic inequality is not only tolerated but supported, we cannot expect to long remain equals. The very survival of our representative democracy and our ideals of freedom and equality are therefore directly at stake in today's debates over the Constitution. What conclusions can be drawn from this book's examination of the Constitution's flaws, and what action should we take in response to them?

The first conclusion this book reaches is that the increasing corrosion of America's social bonds stemming from our growing economic and political inequality gravely endangers representative government. A wealthy oligarchy now owns much of America's wealth and strongly influences or controls many of its political decisions. Our middle class is collapsing as a result. Its disappearance will ultimately turn America into a country of "haves" and "have nots," a sure recipe for the eventual end of representative government and the rise of an autocracy. The Constitution plays an important role in our broad social malaise in several ways. Above all, it prevents the creation of a badly needed new American social contract that can make us a "single people," as Lincoln knew we must be in order to survive as a democratic nation.

In a politically and socially divided nation, the Constitution unfairly protects our wealthy oligarchy. It worsens the effects of today's long-term partisan divisions by protecting small states whose representatives almost uniformly oppose policies that would increase economic fairness and limit wealth concentration. Supreme Court constitutional rulings have opened the door to an enormous flood of money now being spent by the wealthy to finance elections and lobby government in their selfish interests. The Constitution may also protect major forms of wealth held by the richest Americans against taxation. Middle class households already pay annual wealth taxes on the major source of their wealth—real estate—through regressive property taxes. But it is quite possible that the Supreme Court will decide that the Constitution prevents Congress from imposing wealth taxes on the types of wealth held predominantly by the richest Americans—their capital in forms of property such as stocks and bonds. And the Constitution does little or nothing to prevent the inheritance of great unearned wealth.

Moreover, the Constitution's separation of powers—its mechanism for preventing abuses of government's great powers—does not work as designed. Our major government institutions have become either more or less powerful than was originally intended, and the balance between them has been destroyed. The presidency has become imperial, and increasingly resembles the elective monarchy Jefferson and others rightly feared. Congress, which most of the Founders expected to be a dangerous, aggressively power-seeking institution, has fallen into long-term decay and no longer strongly shapes many national policies. The politically unaccountable Supreme Court has stepped into the vacuum created by Congress' defaults and now exercises unwarranted authority to decide major social and political disputes, including elections.

The Constitution also contains several major provisions that unquestionably violate contemporary principles of representative democracy. Those provisions include equal state voting in the Senate and the Electoral College. They result in chronic large-scale distortions of the popular will on major national policies, elections, and federal court appointments. Among other results, two presidents who lost the popular vote have been elected in this century alone, and the membership of the Supreme Court has been altered by unfortunate appointments made by partisans who represented less than half the country.

The constitutional status quo is a sure recipe for the continued decline of representative government, with autocracy very likely to take its place. To avoid that, it is clear that the Constitution needs fundamental reform, or even full replacement. Yet it also dictates an extremely rigid amendment process. What can be done to cure its defects and restore republican government?

This book shows that the most popular course of action—various proposed remedies for piecemeal incremental repair of the Constitution—will not succeed. Freestanding constitutional amendments such as one to reverse campaign finance rulings including the *Citizens United* decision will not be adopted in the foreseeable future because in a partisan political climate they cannot clear the Constitution's tremendously high bar for amendments. "Informal amendment" of the Constitution or "court packing" plans advocated by some as alternatives to proposals for amendments will be of no use in curing the Constitution's worst defects because they cannot reach its deep structural flaws. Due to that inherent limitation, following these alternatives to amending the Constitution would instead materially contribute to the further decline of representative government. In particular, Congress would be likely to continue to decay because incentives needed to restore it as an effective legislative body would still be entirely lacking. Congress' decline will further diminish government accountability and will inevitably increase presidential power, forming the basis for long-term autocracy.

We cannot expect a divided Congress ruled by partisans of one major party or the other to be a willing participant in constitutional reform. Congress will not adopt proposed constitutional amendments by the necessary two-thirds majority of both Houses. It is exceptionally unlikely to agree to the holding of a constitutional convention for any purpose, even one with a limited scope. Its refusal will extend even to an amendment sought by many states, such as a balanced budget amendment. Because amendments will not be adopted and Congress will not permit a convention, the only realistic alternative for those who seek true constitutional reform is to hold a popular convention organized outside of the Constitution's Article V rules.

Americans have a sovereign right to hold such a popular constitutional convention. It would possess the unquestionable authority to reach a grand bargain to propose a series of reforms that would otherwise be impossible to achieve if any of them were proposed independently. Widespread fears of what such a convention might propose are misguided, because its proposals will inevitably be constrained by political safeguards needed to establish its legitimacy such as supermajority approval to ratify its work. But holding any constitutional convention will nevertheless have many enemies.

There are many powerful forces defending the political status quo and opposing any convention in the United States today. First, there is our wealthy oligarchy, almost all of whose members have little need or desire for social or political reforms. The wealthy would almost uniformly oppose any reform that would limit their wealth or that of the major businesses they control. They have nearly unlimited resources to fund opponents of reform in the media and government. Then there are the elite professional naysayers, many of whom are the well-paid public or private servants of the wealthy. They insist that reform through the only possible effective means, a constitutional convention, would be far too "risky" or "dangerous." They confidently assure us that if needed, the status quo can certainly be mended through a political or legal patch here or there. They seek to control reform that does occur, and to prevent any reform they oppose. There are also many well-intentioned citizens who support piecemeal constitutional reform but who oppose holding a convention due to the steady diet of baseless fears they have been fed by elites. Finally, there are many small states whose voters and representatives are acutely aware that they have a highly privileged position under the Constitution, and loathe the idea of losing it. In sum, the constitutional status quo has many friends. Isn't it just "visionary" or utopian to think that their opposition to fundamental reform can be overcome? Why should we think that major reforms are indeed possible?

Together these supporters of the status quo form what George Washington would have called a "strong phalanx" against constitutional reform. But we can learn important lessons from the way he approached major military and political battles alike. We should be clear-sighted about our adversaries' identities, resources, and plans. But we should not despair of victory, because that would cloud our vision about our own resources and how best to use them in the conflict we anticipate. In particular, we should recognize that the critical battlefield in the war for constitutional reform is a different one than we might at first think, and that the forces favoring reform have a far greater advantage on that field than is commonly understood.

Some leading historians who have written about the Constitution's history disagree about whether it was predictable that the Philadelphia Convention would be able to agree on creating a new national government. Historian John Ferling thinks that the critical battle over the Constitution was the fight over whether to hold the Convention at all, because if one was convened, it was likely to reach agreement.[539] Meanwhile, historian David Hendrickson thinks that even after the Convention convened, it was still uncertain whether people with such opposed views about the nation's future would be able to reach agreement on numerous divisive issues.[540] I believe that the historical evidence reviewed in chapter 6 strongly supports Ferling's view that the decisive battle over the Constitution was the first struggle, over whether to hold a convention at all.

In chapter 6, we saw that opponents of the Philadelphia Convention in major states such as New York and Massachusetts fought relentlessly to block it from ever meeting or, if they could not block it, to make sure that it failed to reach agreement on essential reforms. The fight over holding the convention was actually the surrogate for a fight over whether reform would occur. Had Convention opponents succeeded in their efforts to cripple delegates' authority, it is highly likely that the Constitution as we know it would not have been created, because even if the convention had met, it would have been unable to craft a grand bargain that could achieve national acceptance.

Similarly today, the real battleground on constitutional reform will be over calling a new convention, not one over whether one or more reforms will be possible to achieve once a convention is convened. Once a convention is held, a successful grand bargain for reform can in all likelihood be reached. That is one of the central lessons to be drawn from the history of the successful "runaway" Philadelphia Convention.

We can be confident that when a movement begins to organize a popular convention in the next few years, all of the forces defending the status quo will tirelessly attack the idea that it should be held at all, or will seek to cripple it by various means. For example, we can fully expect that outraged smaller states' representatives will protest in legislatures, Congress, and the courts against any proposal that delegate seats at a convention should be allocated proportionally to state populations. Chapter 7 discussed a number of the other tactics that convention opponents will use, and the reasons why convention organizers should be able to anticipate and defeat them.

Chapter 7 shows that if a popular convention is properly organized and called by a carefully recruited national coordinating committee, it should be able to raise from small private donors the necessary funds for electing delegates, conducting a convention, and holding a ratification vote. And it should be able to tap successfully into a pool of private leadership to elect convention delegates who will be fully capable of resisting special interest pressures in order to deliberate effectively on needed reforms. As a society, we have no dearth of leadership—but many of our most talented leaders are not elected officials. And, unlike elected officials, private leaders do not have an inordinately large stake in preserving their privileges under the existing system of government. A well-structured popular convention movement can successfully encourage these leaders to participate actively in its work.

Once the convention is convened, we can be fairly confident it will be able to reach a grand bargain on reform. The ultimate shape of a grand bargain cannot be predicted before the fight over holding a new convention begins in earnest and perhaps not until delegate elections are underway. As was true in 1787, there may even be some elements of an ultimate agreement that cannot be foreseen until the meeting of the convention itself. But it is possible now to form a general opinion about whether the necessary elements that might form such a bargain are probably present in a group of reform proposals. Following is an example of the considerations involved in making such a judgment.

One basic divide in contemporary American politics is that between the political and economic interests of large and small states. The Constitution's artificial exaggeration of small state powers has adversely influenced almost every aspect of national politics. It has altered who wins the presidency; who sits on the Supreme Court; and what policies Congress agrees to support across a broad range of issues. In many cases, the unfortunate result has been that the nation took a political course different than it would have taken if political power were allocated using republican principles of majority will and relative population. How can a convention cure this serious constitutional defect? Chapter 8 discusses a broad range of social and political reforms which include the necessary elements for a grand bargain between large and small states on various issues including the issue of states' relative political powers. The following example shows how such a bargain could occur.

One fundamentally important reform to strengthen republican government by sharply improving the quality of Congress' legislative actions would be to give larger states greater relative voting strength in the Senate. At least some and perhaps even many smaller states will inevitably oppose that reform, but they are also very likely to benefit from the federalism reforms discussed in chapter 8. Those could include fiscal strengthening of smaller states, and clarified state rights and responsibilities, including larger federal responsibility for the care of vulnerable populations, for example. At a convention, larger states would be able to offer smaller states such federalism reforms in return for the convention's agreement on a shift in the distribution of Senate voting power. Many states, large cities, and businesses seeking more stable, coherent government policies would benefit from such a bargain, as would minorities, younger taxpayers, and many of the elderly. As this example suggests, the reform agenda presented in chapter 8 could form the basis of a still broader convention grand bargain, because it would restructure the federal and state governments in ways that would provide sufficient benefits to a range of potentially conflicting interests.

Many important constitutional reforms will also have broad public benefits that should make them appealing to a large number of citizens of varying political views across the country. All of our citizens should benefit from adopting majority rule in the choice of presidents, because over time as a result we will choose higher-quality leaders whose legitimacy in office will be widely accepted. Citizens generally should also benefit from limits on the powers of the president and the Supreme Court that will protect republican government, together with far more effective and democratic federal decision-making by a revitalized Congress that more accurately represents the will of America's population as a whole. The reforms suggested in chapter 8 will also reinvigorate the separation of powers, limiting future abuses of power.

Moreover, the nation as a whole will benefit from citizens' strengthened allegiance to the country's ideals and to the rule of law that will result from creating a stronger social safety net, bringing private wealth and power under appropriate public control, and making criminal justice reforms to increase fairness and to protect the vulnerable. Such reforms should have broad appeal to people from different economic classes, as well as to minority groups and immigrants. The fact that many of the reforms suggested in this book will have broad public benefits reinforces the conclusion that it will be possible for a popular convention to make reforms that will bring the government of the United States into the twenty-first century.

As this discussion shows, despite the considerable opposition to reform, it will be possible to organize and conduct a successful convention that can reach a grand bargain that will remedy many of the Constitution's main defects. If we fail to cure them, we can expect our republican government to decline further. Instead, partisans will continue to jostle for temporary power in support of short-term goals. As part of their endless struggle, they will seek to empower only those institutions such as an increasingly imperial presidency that they think will favor their interests and that they believe they can control, despite the harm that will cause to the long-term vitality of the republic. There is a well-known historical example that shows the dangers of just such a process of slow, long-term decay.

The Roman republic collapsed and fell as a succession of emperors supported by military force first grasped and then retained political dominance, crushing the Roman Senate into cowed insignificance. There is no reason that the same fate cannot befall us if we continue to accept the status quo. But we have it within our power to prevent that from happening. A new constitution can greatly assist in preparing our country to navigate successfully in today's multipolar world by confronting major challenges such as climate change, while contending successfully with the intense global economic and political competition it certainly faces in the century ahead. We can reform our deeply flawed Constitution if we choose. But we will have to risk bold action, or republican decay will continue inexorably until our republic too exists in name only. You will have to decide the Republic's fate.

ACKNOWLEDGMENTS

The considerable help I've received in writing this book from family, colleagues and friends has made it a much better work. I'm especially grateful for their help because although they sometimes did not agree with the book's arguments, they assisted my work nevertheless.

My wife Mary has been a wonderful companion throughout the book's writing. She read several drafts of every chapter and was an engaged listener as I often "thought out loud." Her comments and support have been invaluable in shaping my efforts to create a dialogue with readers. Her assistance greatly improved the book.

Peter S. Onuf not only provided much needed encouragement but patiently sought to convince me to engage directly with the most difficult issues raised by the book in his comments on it throughout its writing. David S. Tanenhaus was an exceptionally observant and helpful reader of several drafts who went well beyond the call in supporting my work and providing constructive comments on it as it evolved. Jonathan Gienapp provided perceptive comments on a draft; I learned a good deal from his remarkable work *The Second Creation* as well.

I am also fortunate to have received exceptionally thoughtful comments from other distinguished scholars who have been studying and writing about the book's issues for many years. In particular, I'd like to thank Sanford V. Levinson and Mark A. Graber for their comments, which led me to rethink a number of significant points, especially with respect to various issues involved in holding a popular convention. David W. Congdon also provided a number of perceptive comments that caused me to sharpen the book's focus on centrally important issues. John Mikhail provided insightful comments on the book's introduction.

John Tryneski, Christopher A. Bloom, Deborah Sliz, JoAnne Gazarek Bloom, and Jim Rathmann provided helpful comments on the book's introduction and various chapters as well as considerable support for my work over the years. I received thought-provoking comments from several distinguished federal legal officials who wish to remain anonymous. Mimi Goodman provided valuable feedback, particularly on ways I could make the book useful to a broad range of readers. I'd also like to thank members of Professor David Tanenhaus's summer judicial seminar on theory and jurisprudence and the students in his constitutional history course for their comments and questions on various aspects of the book. Frances E. Lee generously provided several chapters of the manuscript of *Can America Govern Itself?* for review prior to its publication.

I offer very warm thanks to Paul Sutter, Chair, Department of History, University of Colorado, Boulder, for facilitating my work through a courtesy appointment that gave me very helpful access to Colorado's libraries. I'd also like to thank John Mikhail and Bill Treanor both for their encouragement and for a generous appointment as Dean's Visiting Scholar at Georgetown University Law Center, which has enabled me to use research tools that have proven very useful while I was finishing the writing of this book. Other teachers, friends, and former colleagues including Joshua Getzler, Michael R.T. Macnair, Perry Gauci, William Pettigrew, Gareth Davies, Paul Holland, Marc D. Freed, John R. Storella, Robert L. Bergman, and Luis M. Acosta, have generously shared their knowledge and have provided important encouragement and support for my work over the years, for which I am very grateful.

Though all of the individuals listed above have provided extraordinarily helpful encouragement and advice, the opinions, errors, and omissions in this book are my sole responsibility.

Appendix A

OLD SENATE VS. NEW SENATE VOTING
ON KEY ISSUES, 1970-1990

Vote	Old Senate Vote	New Senate Vote
Political Institutions Direct Election of President-9/17/70 *Cloture* vote on const. amendment	Y-54 N-36 **Reject**	Y-96 N-42 **Pass cloture**
Foreign Policy		
Deployment of Safeguard ABM System (9/1/70): *Delete* $322.2 million for deployment	Y-47 N-52 **Reject**	Y-81 N-65 **Pass**
Sale of AWACS to Saudi Arabia (10/28/81): *Disapprove* sale	Y-48 N-52 **Reject**	Y-86 N-64 **Pass**
Domestic Policy Federal No Fault Auto Insurance *Motion to table/kill* bill (5/31/76)	Y-49 N-45 **Pass**	Y-68 N-75 **Fail**
Lockheed Bailout (8/2/71) $250 mill. loan guarantee	Y-49 N-48 **Pass**	Y-71 N-76 **Reject**
Waterway User Fees (5/3/78) (Tax barge fuel)	Y-43 N-47 **Reject**	Y-73 N-65 **Pass**
Tobacco Price Support Cuts (*motion to table/kill*)(9/18/81)	Y-41 N-40 **Pass**	Y-53 N-61 **Fail**

Vote	Old Senate Vote	New Senate Vote
Wheat Price Support Cuts 5/24/77	Y-46 N-50 **Reject**	Y-82 N-64 **Pass**
Tellico Dam—Exempt from Endangered Species Act (9/10/79)	Y-48 N-44 **Pass**	Y-69 N-73 **Reject**
Thurmond Antibusing Amendment 9/25/80	Y-49 N-42 **Pass**	Y-64 N-69 **Reject**
Fair Housing Amendments *cloture* vote 2/9/80	Y-43 N-54 **Fail**	Y-90 N-58 **Pass** (cloture)
Labor Law Reform *cloture* vote 6/14/78	Y-58 N-41 **Reject**	Y-97 N-53 **Pass** (cloture)

Notes

Introduction

1. George Van Cleve is Dean's Visiting Scholar, Georgetown University Law Center, and former Research Professor in Law and History, Seattle University School of Law. J.D., Harvard Law School; Ph.D., University of Virginia. The views expressed in this book are the author's sole responsibility.

2. Andrew Ross Sorkin, "Paul Volcker, at 91, Sees 'a Hell of a Mess in Every Direction'," *New York Times*, October 23, 2018.

3. Ibid.

4. Centers for Disease Control Covid-19 website, https://www.cdc.gov/coronavirus/2019-ncov/index.html (accessed 08/31/20); Lena V. Groeger, "What Coronavirus Job Losses Reveal About Racism in America," https://projects.propublica.org/coronavirus-unemployment/ (accessed 08/31/20); *Economist*, August 29, 2020, "Learning and covid."

5. Annette Gordon-Reed, "America's Original Sin: Slavery and the Legacy of White Supremacy," *Foreign Affairs* 97, no. 1 (2018): 2.

Chapter One

6. Frances Lee and Nolan McCarty, eds., *Can America Govern Itself?* (Cambridge: Cambridge Univ. Press, 2019), 1.

7. Yascha Mounk and Roberto Stefan Foa, "This is How Democracies Die," Atlantic, January 29, 2020, https://www.theatlantic.com/ideas/archive/2020/01/confidence-democracy-lowest-point-record/605686/.

8. Tal Axelrod, "More than 4 in 5 Americans angry or dissatisfied with Washington: poll," *The Hill*, November 27, 2018, https://thehill.com/homenews/news/418456-more-than-4-in-5-americans-angry-or-dissatisfied-with-washington-poll.

9. Jeff Clements (American Promise), "Cross-partisan support spurs public hearing to overturn Citizens United," *The Hill*, February 6, 2020, https://thehill.com/blogs/congress-blog/politics/481776-cross-partisan-public-support-spurs-congressional-hearing-to.

10. This is the conclusion reached in a thoughtful book by Ganesh Sitaraman, *The Crisis of the Middle-Class Constitution: Why Economic Inequality*

Threatens our Republic (New York: Alfred A. Knopf, 2017). Sitaraman's views are consistent with those of classic theorists of republican government from Aristotle to James Harrington.

11. Emmanuel Saez and Gabriel Zucman, "Wealth Inequality in the United States Since 1913: Evidence from Capitalized Income Tax Data" (Washington, D.C.: NBER, 2014); Michael Batty et al., *Introducing the Distributional Financial Accounts of the United States* (Washington, D.C.: Board of Governors of the Federal Reserve System, 2019), 2, 25-6 https://doi.org/10.17016/FEDS.2019.017.

12. *Distributional Financial Accounts*, 26. Federal Reserve data also show that there is an enormous difference in the amount of debt owed by different wealth classes. Americans in the lowest fifty percent of the wealth distribution have debts that are roughly double their assets. https://fred.stlouisfed.org/graph/?g=ooZz (accessed 07/25/19).

13. As of 2017, the Gini index for the United States was one of the highest among OECD countries, higher than Lithuania and nearly at the same level as Turkey. OECD iLibrary (2019), Income inequality (indicator). https://www.oecd-ilibrary.org/social-issues-migration-health/income-inequality/indicator/english_459aa7f1-en (accessed 08 July 2019).

14. Dylan Matthews, "You're not imagining it: the rich really are hoarding economic growth," *Vox*, August 8, 2017, https://www.vox.com/policy-and-politics/2017/8/8/16112368/piketty-saez-zucman-income-growth-inequality-stagnation-chart; Isabel V. Sawhill and Eleanor Krause, "Seven Reasons to Worry About the Middle Class," *Brookings Blog* (2018), https://www.brookings.edu/blog/social-mobility-memos/2018/06/05/seven-reasons-to-worry-about-the-american-middle-class/ (accessed 07/10/19).

15. Evidence suggests that intergenerational economic mobility in the United States is lower than in many other developed countries. Juan C. Juan C. Palomino, Gustavo A. Marrero, and Juan Gabriel Rodríguez, "Intergenerational mobility in the U.S.: One size doesn't fit all," https://voxeu.org/article/intergenerational-mobility-us (accessed 07/08/2019). For a different view, see Raj Chetty et al., "Is the United States Still a Land of Opportunity? Recent Trends in Intergenerational Mobility" (Washington, D.C.: NBER, 2014) (U.S. mobility trends have "remained remarkably stable" over the past thirty or forty years, but mobility in some U.S. regions is "persistently less than most other developed countries" : quotes at 10).

16. Isabel V. Sawhill and Eleanor Krause, "Seven Reasons to Worry About the Middle Class," *Brookings Blog*, published electronically June 5, 2018. For details see Raj Chetty et al., "The Fading American Dream: Trends in Absolute Income Mobility Since 1940" (Washington, D.C.: NBER, 2016), particularly Figure 1B. following page 31.

17. The United States poverty rate has not changed substantially since 1970. Ashley Edwards, "Poverty Rate at 12.3 Percent, Down From 14.8 in 2014," September 12, 2018, https://www.census.gov/library/stories/2018/09/poverty-rate-drops-third-consecutive-year-2017.html.

18. Jacob S. Hacker and Paul Pierson, *Winner-Take-All Politics: How Washington Made the Rich Richer—and Turned its Back on the Middle Class* (New York: Simon & Schuster, 2010), 51-72.

19. Lawrence Lessig, *Republic, Lost: The Corruption of Equality and the Steps to End It* (revised ed.) (New York: Twelve: Hachette Book Group, 2016), 49-50.

20. Allan Holmes and Chris Zubak-Skees (Center for Public Integrity), April 1, 2015 (updated May 28, 2015), "U.S. Internet Users Pay More and Have Fewer Choices than Europeans," https://publicintegrity.org/inequality-poverty-opportunity/u-s-internet-users-pay-more-and-have-fewer-choices-than-europeans/.

21. *Economist* Leader (editorial), "Squeezing the rich: In defence of billionaires," *Economist*, November 9, 2019, 12.

22. The original data were presented in Martin Gilens, *Affluence and Influence: Economic Inequality and Political Power in America* (Princeton: Princeton Univ. Press, 2014). Gilens and a colleague analyzed related data in Martin Gilens and Benjamin Page, "Testing Theories of American Politics: Elites, Interest Groups, and Average Citizens," *Perspectives on Politics* 12, no. 3 (2014): 564. They concluded: "economic elites and organized groups representing business interests have substantial independent impacts on U.S. government policy, while mass-based interest groups and average citizens have little or no independent influence." Ibid., 565. For discussion of these and others works that reach similar conclusions, see Lessig, *Republic, Lost*, 137-48.

23. Gilens, *Affluence*, 6.

24. Gilens and Page, "Testing Theories," 577.

25. One account summarized Gilens' data: "…[W]hen the economic élites support a given policy change, it has about a one-in-two chance of being enacted....When the élites oppose a given measure, its chances of becoming law are less than one in five....On many issues, the rich exercise an effective veto…." John Cassidy, "Is America An Oligarchy?," *New Yorker*, April 18, 2014.

26. See chapter 5.

27. Roger H. Davidson et al., *Congress and Its Members* (14th ed.) (Washington, D.C.: CQ Press, 2013), 60. Recent claims of a decline in incumbency advantage may have some support. Gary C. Jacobson, "It's Nothing Personal: The Decline of the Incumbency Advantage in US House Elections," *The Journal of Politics* 77, no. 3 (2015): 861. That change has not yet materially altered the overall situation.

28. Andrew Katz, "Congress is Now Mostly a Millionaires' Club," *Time*, January 9, 2014, https://time.com/373/congress-is-now-mostly-a-millionaires-club/.

29. David Sim and Sam Earle, "50 Richest Members of Congress," *Newsweek*, April 6, 2018. The 2016 Federal Reserve survey found that median household net worth was $97,300; there are large racial disparities. Jesse Bricker et al., "Changes in U.S. Family Finances from 2013 to 2016: Evidence from the Survey of Consumer Finances," *Federal Reserve Bulletin* 103 No. 3 (September, 2017), 12-13.

30. Pew Research Center, *The American Middle Class is Losing Ground* (Washington, D.C.: Pew Charitable Trusts, 2015), December 9, 2015, https://www.pewsocialtrends.org/2015/12/09/the-american-middle-class-is-losing-ground/. The Center reported: "... 'middle-income' Americans are defined as adults whose annual household income is two-thirds to double the national median...Under this definition, the middle class made up 50% of the U.S. adult population in 2015, down from 61% in 1971." Brookings Institution economists Richard Reeves and Katherine Guyot, on the other hand, argue that the middle class is "the middle 60 percent of households on the income distribution." Caitlin Zaloom, "Does the U.S. Still Have a 'Middle Class?," *Atlantic*, November 4, 2018.

31. Pew Research Center, *Middle Class is Losing Ground*.

32. Alissa Quart, *Squeezed: Why Our Families Can't Afford America* (New York: Harper Collins, 2018). Quart interview and quotations: *New York Post*, "America's middle class is slowly being 'wiped out,'" July 23, 2018 (reprinted in https://www.marketwatch.com/story/americas-middle-class-is-slowly-being-wiped-out-2018-07-23).

33. Quart, *Squeezed*, 5.

34. Krause and Sawhill, "Seven Reasons to Worry."

35. Center for American Progress, *Fact Sheet: Child Care* (2012), https://www.americanprogress.org/issues/economy/news/2012/08/16/11978/fact-sheet-child-care/.

36. http://www.oecd.org/els/soc/PF3_4_Childcare_support.pdf (2014 data, updated 2017) (accessed 07/10/19).

37. Gretchen Livingston, "The Changing Profile of Unmarried Parents," Pew Research Center, April 25, 2018, https://www.pewsocialtrends.org/2018/04/25/the-changing-profile-of-unmarried-parents/.

38. National Womens' Law Center, "National Snapshot: Poverty Among Women & Families, 2016," https://nwlc.org/wp-content/uploads/2017/09/Poverty-Snapshot-Factsheet-2017.pdf.

39. National Center for Education Statistics ("NCES"), https://nces.ed.gov/fastfacts/display.asp?id=372 (accessed 07/10/19).

40. Drew Desilver, "U.S. students' academic achievement still lags that of their peers in many other countries," February 15, 2017, https://www.pewresearch.org/fact-tank/2017/02/15/u-s-students-internationally-math-science/.

41. Ibid.

42. Jonathan Rothwell, "The declining productivity of education," *Brookings Blog* (Washington, D.C.: Brookings Institute), December 23, 2016, https://www.brookings.edu/blog/social-mobility-memos/2016/12/23/the-declining-productivity-of-education/.

43. Ibid.

44. Ibid.

45. School Nutrition Association, "School Meal Trends and Stats," https://schoolnutrition.org/aboutschoolmeals/schoolmealtrendsstats/ (accessed 7/12/19).

46. About 19 percent of all California students were ELLs in 2018-19. *CalEdFacts*, "Facts about English Learners in California," https://www.cde.ca.gov/ds/sd/cb/cefelfacts.asp. (accessed 07/15/19).

47. NCES, "English Language Learners in Public Schools," https://nces.ed.gov/programs/coe/indicator_cgf.asp (accessed 07/12/19).

48. ELL numbers were significantly higher in fall 2016 than in fall 2000. Ibid.

49. Claudio Sanchez, "English Language Learners: How Your State is Doing," https://www.npr.org/sections/ed/2017/02/23/512451228/5-million-english-language-learners-a-vast-pool-of-talent-at-risk (accessed 07/16/19).

50. Paul T. Sindelar, Jim Dewey, Elizabeth Bettini, "Explaining the Decline in Special Education Teacher Employment From 2005 to 2012," *Exceptional Children* 83, no. 3 (2017): 315, https://doi.org/10.1177/0014402916684620 (Abstract).

51. Maya Srikrishnan, "Special Education Costs Are Rising," February 8, 2018, https://www.newamerica.org/weekly/edition-193/special-education-costs-are-rising/.

52. Education Commission of the States, *Ednote*, "Do We Spend Too Much on Special Education," https://ednote.ecs.org/do-we-spend-too-much-on-special-education-in-this-country/ (accessed 1/23/20).

53. Rebecca David and Kevin Hesla, National Alliance for Public Charter Schools, "Estimated Public Charter School Enrollment 2017-2018," March, 2018, https://www.publiccharters.org/sites/default/files/documents/2018-03/FINAL%20Estimated%20Public%20Charter%20School%20Enrollment%2C%202017-18.pdf.

54. NCES, *Digest of Education Statistics, 2017*, Table 206.10, https://nces.ed.gov/programs/digest/d17/tables/dt17_206.10.asp.

55. Nick Hanauer, "Education Isn't Enough," *Atlantic*, July, 2019, 20.

56. John R. Logan and Brian Stults, *The Persistence of Segregation in Metropolitan Areas: New Findings from the 2010 Census*. Census Brief prepared for Project US2010, http://www.s4.brown.edu/us2010, 2-3.

57. Ta-Nehisi Coates, "The Case for Reparations," *Atlantic*, June, 2014, 54.

58. https://www.chicagohealthatlas.org/indicators/violent-crime (accessed 06/10/20).

59. Dahleen Glanton, "Growing up with poverty and violence: A North Lawndale Teen's Story," *Chicago Tribune*, March 10, 2017, https://www.chicagotribune.com/columns/dahleen-glanton/ct-poverty-violence-glanton-met-20170309-column.html (accessed 06/10/20).

60. Ibid.

61. https://www.thetrace.org/features/gun-violence-interactive-shootings-map/?place=Chicago-Illinois (accessed 060620). Lee's movie was controversial in respects not relevant here.

62. Quart, *Squeezed*, 137.

63. Alana Semuels, "Segregation Has Gotten Worse, Not Better, and It's Fueling the Wealth Gap Between Black and White Americans," *Time*, June 19, 2020, https://time.com/5855900/segregation-wealth-gap/. One of the reports on which Semuels relies is Richard D. Kahlenberg and Kimberly Quick, *Attacking the Black-White Opportunity Gap that comes from Residential Segregation* (New York: The Century Foundation, 2019).

64. Semuels, "Segregation Has Gotten Worse."

65. Ibid.

66. Heather Long and Andrew Van Dam, "The Black-White Economic Divide is as Large as it was in 1968," *Washington Post,* June 4, 2020. The paper by Moritz Kuhn and others referred to in the cited article can be found at https://www.minneapolisfed.org/research/institute-working-papers/income-and-wealth-inequality-in-america-1949-2016. (accessed 06/09/20).

67. Sergio Pecanha, "These numbers show that black and white people live in two different Americas," *Washington Post*, June 22, 2020.

68. Coates, "The Case for Reparations."

69. Sean F. Reardon and Ann Owens, "60 Years After Brown: Trends and Consequences of School Segregation," *Annual Rev. Sociol.* 40 (2014): 199, 205. See also Richard Fry and Paul Taylor, "The Rise of Residential Segregation by Income," August 1, 2012, Pew Research Center https://www.pewsocialtrends.org/2012/08/01/the-rise-of-residential-segregation-by-income/ (accessed 06/25/20).

70. Technology regulation is discussed in chapter 8.

71. For federal guidelines, see https://aspe.hhs.gov/poverty-guidelines.

72. Stanford Center on Longevity, *Seeing Our Way to Financial Security in the Age of Increased Longevity* (Palo Alto, CA: Stanford University, 2018)

(Sightlines Project Special Report, October 2018), 33, http://longevity.stanford.edu/sightlines-financial-security-special-report-mobile/; Social Security Administration Fact Sheet, https://www.ssa.gov/news/press/factsheets/basicfact-alt.pdf.

73. Stanford Center on Longevity, *Seeing Our Way*, 33.

74. If Social Security's Trust Fund became insolvent, social security benefits would need to be cut by about 20%. The Board of Trustees, Federal Old-Age and Survivors Insurance and Federal Disability Insurance Trust Funds, *The 2019 Annual Report of the board of Trustees of the Federal Old-Age and Survivors Insurance and Federal Disability Insurance Trust Funds* (House Document 116-28, 116th Congress, 1st Sess.).

75. Stanford Center on Longevity, *Seeing Our Way*, 27.

76. Monique Morrissey, "Private-sector pension coverage fell by half over two decades," Economic Policy Institute, *Working Economics Blog*, January 11, 2013, https://www.epi.org/blog/private-sector-pension-coverage-decline/.

77. Stanford Center on Longevity, *Seeing Our Way*, 31, 34.

78. Ibid., 26.

79. Congressional Budget Office, *The Budget and Economic Outlook: 2019 to 2029* (Washington, D.C.: Congress of the United States, Jan. 2019), 85.

80. Emmanuel Saez and Gabriel Zucman, *The Triumph of Injustice: How the Rich Dodge Taxes and How to Make Them Pay* (New York: W.W. Norton, 2019), claims that the overall tax system is regressive, but there is sharp disagreement among economists about that conclusion.

81. Property taxes are wealth taxes because they base taxes on the market value of property, not income. They have been described as "America's regressive middle-class wealth tax." Arik Levinson, "America's Regressive Middle-Class Wealth Tax," *The Hill*, November 20, 2019.

82. https://itep.org/who-pays-taxes-in-america-in-2019/ (accessed 06/09/20).

83. Chuck Marr, Samantha Jacoby, and Kathleen Bryant, *Substantial Income of Wealthy Households Escapes Taxation or Enjoys Special Tax Breaks: Reform is Needed* (Washington, D.C.: Center on Budget and Policy Priorities, November 13, 2019)(unpaginated online text at nn. 8, 13-15), https://www.cbpp.org/research/federal-tax/substantial-income-of-wealthy-households-escapes-annual-taxation-or-enjoys.

84. The three middle income quintiles pay an estimated 30 percent of income taxes. Peter G. Peterson Foundation, "Who Pays Taxes," April 12, 2019 https://www.pgpf.org/budget-basics/who-pays-taxes. At present, this is about $500 billion/year. Their share of a $500 billion tax increase would be $150 billion/year.

85. Isabel V. Sawhill and Christopher Pulliam, "Six Facts about Wealth in the United States," *Brookings* Blog, June 25, 2019, https://www.brookings.edu/blog/up-front/2019/06/25/six-facts-about-wealth-in-the-united-states/.

Chapter Two

86. *Pollock v Farmers' Loan and Trust Co.*, 157 U.S. 429 (1895).

87. For a history, see Ajay K. Mehotra, *Making the Modern American Fiscal State: Law, Politics, and the Rise of Progressive Taxation* (Cambridge: Cambridge Univ. Press, 2013). Thanks to David Tanenhaus for this reference.

88. George William Van Cleve, *We Have Not a Government: The Articles of Confederation and the Road to the Constitution* (Chicago: University of Chicago Press, 2017), esp. chapters 7 and 8. For a history of the debate over economic fairness at the Founding, see Clement Fatovic, *America's Founding and the Struggle over Economic Inequality* (Lawrence: University Press of Kansas, 2015).

89. Alexander Hamilton, *Federalist* No. 78 in J.R. Pole, ed. *The Federalist* (Indianapolis: Hackett Publishing Company, 2005), 411-18, 416 quote. Many Americans then saw poverty and debt as principally a result of human failure and wealth as a reward for virtue. Bruce Mann, *Republic of Debtors: Bankruptcy in the Age of Independence* (Cambridge, MA: Harvard University Press, 2002).

90. Max Farrand, ed. *The Records of the Federal Convention of 1787*, 4 vols., vol. 1 (New Haven: Yale University Press, 1966), 288 (June 18, 1787). For Hamilton's overall thought on economic inequality, see Fatovic, *America's Founding*, 85-125.

91. Richard Hofstadter, *The American Political Tradition & the Men Who Made It* (New York: Vintage Books, 1974), 9-10.

92. Adam Smith, *An Inquiry into the Nature and Causes of the Wealth of Nations*, ed. Edwin Cannan, 2 vols. (1904; Chicago: University of Chicago Press, 1977 repr. ed.), 2: 73-160.

93. For a leading discussion, see Merrill Jensen, *The New Nation: A History of the United States during the Confederation, 1781-1789* (New York: Vintage Books, 1950).

94. U.S. Const., art. 1, sec. 10, cl. 1.

95. Jefferson's Notes of Debates in Julian P. Boyd, Lyman H. Butterfield, and Mina R. Bryan, eds., *The Papers of Thomas Jefferson*, 52 vols., vol. 1 (Princeton: Princeton Univerity Press, 1950), 1: 320-27; Lyman H. Butterfield, ed. *Diary and Autobiography of John Adams*, 4 vols., vol. 2 (Cambridge: Harvard University Press, 1962), II: 229, passim.

96. J.R. Pole, *Political Representation in England and the Origins of the American Republic* (1966; Berkeley: University of California Press, pbk. 1971), 349-50.

97. Michael S. Greve, *The Upside-Down Constitution* (Cambridge: Harvard Univ. Press, 2012) claims that Alexander Hamilton and James Madison wanted to abolish states. Ibid., 45.

98. Van Cleve, *We Have Not a Government*, 281-90.

99. George William Van Cleve, *A Slaveholders' Union: Slavery, Politics, and the Constitution in the Early American Republic* (Chicago: Univ. Chicago Press, 2010), 230 n. 18.

100. The quoted phrase is Sanford Levinson's. Sanford Levinson, *Our Undemocratic Constitution: Where the Constitution Goes Wrong (and How We the People Can Correct It)* (Oxford: Oxford Univ. Press, 2006), 160.

101. Paul Krugman, "Regional Economics: Understanding the Third Great Transition," (2019), https://www.gc.cuny.edu/CUNY_GC/media/LISCenter/pkrugman/REG IONAL-ECONOMICS-3rd-transition.pdf (accessed 02/28/20).

102. There are also important social differences such as those in life expectancy between states and regions. Benjamin Austin, Edward Glaeser, and Lawrence Summers, "Jobs for the Heartland: Place-Based Politics in 21st Century America," *Brookings Papers on Economic Activity* (Spring 2018): 151.

103. Krugman, "Regional Economics: Understanding the Third Great Transition," 9-10 (Brookings Institution data).

104. Ibid.

105. Adam Bonica et al., "Why Hasn't Democracy Slowed Rising Inequality?," *Journal of Economic Perspectives* 27, no. 3 (2013): 103, 107.

106. Ronald Brownstein, "Small States are Getting a Much Bigger Say in Who Gets on the Supreme Court," *CNN,* July 10, 2018, https://www.cnn.com/2018/07/10/politics/small-st ates-supreme-court/index.html.

107. Republicans, who typically oppose government efforts to increase economic fairness, usually advocate policies that they claim will lead to economic "growth" that will benefit everyone. Democrats, who typically support programs for increased economic fairness, claim that they support various forms of social "investment" that will benefit everyone.

108. If the Democratic party instead were the party that controlled the small states, these political advantages would accrue to them.

109. *Economist* Briefing: "America's electoral system gives the Republicans advantages over Democrats," July 14, 2018, 21.

110. Ibid.

111. Ibid.

112. Brownstein, "Small States are Getting a Much Bigger Say."

113. World Population Review, "2016 Election Results By State Population," http://worldpopulationreview.com/states/2016-election-results-by-state/#dataTable (accessed 02/28/20).

114. Lawrence D. Longley and Alan G. Braun, *The Politics of Electoral College Reform* (2d ed.) (New Haven: Yale University Press, 1975), 20. The authors believe that the "unit" (or winner-take-all) rule creates a large-state voting power bias that they regard as more important.

115. *Economist* Briefing, "America's electoral system" (chart).

116. *Bush et al. v. Gore et al.*, 531 U.S. 98 (2000).

117. Breyer, J., dissenting in *Bush v. Gore*, 531 U.S. 144.

118. U.S. Const., art. 2, sec. 1 (as amended by the Twelfth Amendment).

119. *Buckley v. Valeo*, 424 U.S. 1 (1976).

120. Ibid., at 424 U.S. 1, 39-59.

121. *Buckley* upheld federal limits on campaign contributions and disclosures. 424 U.S. 1, 23-38.

122. Bonica et al., "Why Hasn't Democracy Slowed Rising Inequality?," 112 (Figure 5).

123. Scott Bland and Maggie Severns, "Documents reveal massive 'dark-money' group boosted Democrats in 2018," *Politico*, November 19, 2019, https://www.politico.com/news/2019/11/19/dark-money-democrats-midterm-071725 (accessed 11/22/19).

124. Bonica et al., "Why Hasn't Democracy Slowed Rising Inequality?," 113. Emphasis added.

125. Robert G. Kaiser quoted in Lessig, *Republic, Lost*, 36-37.

126. Lessig, *Republic, Lost*, 112, quoting Kaiser, *Act of Congress*.

127. Ibid., 113.

128. *Citizens United v. FEC*, 558 U.S. 310 (2010).

129. *McCutcheon v. FEC*, 572 U.S. 185 (2014). The Federal Election Campaign Act of 1971 (FECA), as amended, imposed two types of contribution limits. Base limits restrict how much money a donor may contribute to a particular candidate or committee; aggregate limits restrict how much total money a donor may contribute. 2 U. S. C. §441a. *McCutcheon* held the aggregate limits unconstitutional.

130. The Court upheld the law's requirements for disclosures and disclaimers by corporate and union groups concerning their spending. *Citizens United*, 558 U.S. 310, 366-72.

131. Quoting *Austin v. Mich. Chamber of Commerce* 494 U.S. 652 (1990), at 659.

132. *Citizens United*, 558 U.S. 310, 350-51 (quote at 350).

133. President Barack Obama, "Address Before a Joint Session of the Congress on the State of the Union," in *Public Papers of the Presidents: Barack Obama* (Washington, DC: Government Printing Office, 2010), 81.

134. Referred to as the "Democracy for All" amendment. See https://www.tomudall.senate.gov/imo/media/doc/Democracy%20For%20All%20Amendment%20Final%20Bill%20Text.pdf (accessed 02/28/20).

135. For discussion, see Kathleen Sullivan, "Two Concepts of Freedom of Speech" *Harv. L. Rev.* 124 (2010): 143.

136. Robert B. Reich, *The System: Who Rigged It, How We Fix It* (New York: Alfred A. Knopf, 2020), 14-16.

137. Asher Stockler, "Nearly Half of All Individual Donations Made to Super PACs were made by 25 mega-wealthy individuals, new report says," Newsweek, January 15, 2020, https://www.newsweek.com/super-pac-donations-citizens-united-report-1482436?utm_source=GoogleNewsstandUS&utm_medium=Feed&utm_campaign=Partnerships.

138. Ibid.

139. Ibid. Top 100: Lessig, *Republic, Lost*, 14-15.

140. Michelle Ye Hee Lee, "Wealthy Donors Now Allowed to Give Over Half a Million Dollars Each to Support Trump's Reelection," *Washington Post*, January 15, 2020.

141. Michael Beckel (Issue One), "Dark Money Illuminated," September, 2018, https://www.issueone.org/dark-money/; Campaign Legal Center, https://campaignlegal.org/update/clc-analysis-fec-rule-kept-much-769-million-political-spending-dark (accessed 11/14/19); Anna Missoglia (OpenSecrets.org), January 27, 2020, "Dark Money in Politics Skyrocketed after Citizens United," https://www.opensecrets.org/news/2020/01/dark-money-10years-citizens-united/.

142. Lessig, *Republic, Lost*, 34-37 (quote 34).

143. Nour Abdul-Razzak, Carlo Prato, and Stephane Wolton, "After Citizens United: How Outside Spending Shapes American Democracy," *SSRN Electronic Journal* (Mar. 2019), doi:10.2139/ssrn.2823778.

144. By 2016, Republican party committees raised significantly less than independent groups — $652.4 million v. $810.4 million. Thomas B. Edsall, "Meet the New Boss. Actually Quite Different From the Old Boss," *New York Times,* April 26, 2018.

145. U.S. Const., art. 1, sec 9.

146. *Pollock v Farmers' Loan and Trust Co.*, 157 U.S. 429 (1895).

147. Ibid., 151 U.S. at 695.

148. For a history, see Mehotra, *Making the Modern American Fiscal State.*

149. The Sixteenth Amendment provides: "The Congress shall have power to lay and collect taxes on incomes, from whatever source derived, without apportionment among the several States, and without regard to any census or enumeration."

150. Urban Institute, "Property Taxes," https://www.urban.org/policy-centers/cross-center-initiatives/state-and-local-finance-initiative/projects/state-and-local-backgrounders/property-taxes (accessed 04/14/20).

151. A rough estimate is that an average of about fifteen to twenty percent of capital gains were realized annually during the period 2010-2014, or about $2.5 trillion out of a market gain of roughly $12 trillion. Tax Policy Center, "Historical Capital Gains and Taxes," https://www.taxpolicycenter.org/statistics/historical-capital-gains-and-taxes (taxable gains data) (accessed 04/13/20).

152. Tax Policy Center, "T18-0231 - Distribution of Long-Term Capital Gains and Qualified Dividends by Expanded Cash Income Percentile, 2018," https://www.taxpolicycenter.org/model-estimates/distribution-individual-income-tax-long-term-capital-gains-and-qualified-30 (accessed 04/13/20).

153. Tax Policy Center, "Historical Capital Gains and Taxes," https://www.taxpolicycenter.org/statistics/historical-capital-gains-and-taxes (accessed 04/13/20).

154. United States Senate, Committee on the Budget, "Tax Expenditures: Compendium of Background Material on Individual Provisions," S. Prt. 112-45, 112th Congress, 2nd session (Washington: GPO, 2012), 429. This estimate apparently does not include estate taxation effects.

155. The following discussion expresses no view on the desirability or practicability of such taxes.

156. Elizabeth Warren for President, "Ultra-Millionaire Tax," https://elizabethwarren.com/ultra-millionaire-tax/ (accessed 08/16/19).

157. Isabel V. Sawhill and Edward Rodrigue, "Wealth, Inheritance, and Social Mobility," *Brookings Blog* (2015), https://www.brookings.edu/blog/social-mobility-memos/2015/01/30/wealth-inheritance-and-social-mobility/ (literature review supports 35 to 45 percent); Facundo Alvaredo, Bertrand Garbinti, and Thomas Piketty, "On the Share of Inheritance in Aggregate Wealth: Europe and the USA, 1900-2010" *Economica* 84 (2017): 239 (estimates 55 to 65 percent).

158. Letter from Bruce Ackerman, et al. to Senator Elizabeth Warren, January 24, 2019, https://www.warren.senate.gov/imo/media/doc/Constitutionality%20Letters.pdf (accessed 02/28/20); Dawn Johnsen and Walter Dellinger, "The Constitutionality of a National Wealth Tax," *Indiana Law Journal* 93 (2018): 111.

159. Noah Feldman, "Wealth Tax's Legality Depends on What 'Direct' Means," *Bloomberg Opinion* (2019), https://www.bloomberg.com/opinion/articles/2019-01-30/elizabeth-warren-s-wealth-tax-is-probably-constitutional (accessed 08/23/19). Feldman thinks that the tax is probably constitutional.

160. Ibid.

161. *Hylton v. U.S.*, 3 Dallas 171 (1796).

162. What is often referred to as Hamilton's "brief" was actually Hamilton's argument notes. Maeva Marcus, ed. *The Documentary History of the Supreme Court of the United States*, vol. 7 (New York: Columbia University Press, 2004): 456, 467.

163. *Pollock v Farmers Loan*, 157 U.S. 429, 568-70.

164. Holmes, J. dissenting in *Eisner v. Macomber*, 232 U.S. 189, 220 (1920).

165. Erik M. Jensen, "The Taxing Power, the Sixteenth Amendment, and the Meaning of 'Incomes,'" *Arizona State Law Journal* 33, no. 4 (2001): 1057, 1061.

166. Ibid. at 1116 n. 296 (1909 Senate debate).

167. Feldman, "Wealth Tax's Legality."

168. See his opinion in *Rucho et al. v Common Cause et al.*, 139 S. Ct. 2484 (2019) as an example (see chapter 4).

169. Some reform advocates claim they can achieve the same results without amending the Constitution through "court packing" (discussed in chapter 5).

Chapter Three

170. James Madison, "Notes of Debates," June 30, 1787, in Farrand, *Records*, 1: 483 (abbreviation expanded).

171. Richard Beeman, *Plain, Honest Men: The Making of the American Constitution* (New York: Random House 2009), 128-29, passim. In a parliamentary government, the executive is typically chosen from the parliament (its legislative branch). Parliament typically has strong powers over the executive, including removal by a majority vote.

172. Political scientist Robert Dahl famously argued that the goals of democracy can be met just as well by parliamentary systems that permit proportional voting as they can be by our current Constitution. Robert Dahl, *How Democratic is the American Constitution?* (2nd ed.) (New Haven: Yale University Press, 2003).

173. This chapter is not intended to contribute to debates over what powers the Founders actually intended to give each major branch, such as disputes over the "unitary executive" theory. See, e.g., Julien Davis Mortenson, "Article II Vests the Executive Power, Not the Royal Prerogative," *Columbia Law Review* 119, no. 5 (2019): 1169.

174. For an authoritative account, see Beeman, *Plain, Honest Men*.

175. James Madison, Nos. 47 & 48 in Pole ed., *The Federalist*.

176. James Madison, No. 51 in Pole ed., *The Federalist*. For modern criticisms of Madison's view, see David Fontana and Aziz Z. Huq, "Institutional Loyalties in Constitutional Law," *Univ. Chicago Law Rev.* 85, no. 1 (2018): 1.

177. Beeman, *Plain, Honest Men*, 141-42.

178. Stephen Skowronek, "Shall We Cast Our Lot with the Constitution? Thinking about Presidential Power in the Twenty-first Century," in *The Presidency in the Twenty-First Century*, ed. Charles W. Dunn (Lexington: University Press of Kentucky, 2011), 28.

179. Arthur M. Schlesinger Jr., *The Imperial Presidency* (New York: Houghton Mifflin, 1973).

180. Michael A. Genovese and Iwan W. Morgan, eds., *Watergate Remembered: The Legacy for American Politics* (New York: Palgrave Macmillan, 2012).

181. Andrew Rudalevige, *The New Imperial Presidency: Renewing Presidential Power after Watergate* (Ann Arbor: Univ. Michigan Press, 2005); William G. Howell, "The Future of the War Presidency: The Case of the War Powers Consultation Act," in *The Presidency in the Twenty-First Century*, ed. Charles W. Dunn (Lexington: Univ. Press of Kentucky, 2011), 83.

182. Andrew Rudalevige, ""The Contemporary Presidency": The Decline and Resurgence and Decline (and Resurgence?) of Congress" *Presidential Studies Quarterly* 36, no. 3 (2006): 506.

183. Howell, "The Future of the War Presidency."

184. Rudalevige, *The New Imperial Presidency*.

185. "Pelosi: US arms sales, troop deployments to Saudi Arabia and UAE 'outrageous,'" *CNN,* September 21, 2019, https://www.cnn.com/2019/09/21/politics/pelosi-saudi-uae-arms-sales-troops-outrageous/index.html.

186. Council on Foreign Relations, "Trends in Military Spending," July 25, 2014, https://www.cfr.org/report/trends-us-military-spending.

187. Claudia Goldin and Frank D. Lewis, "The Economic Cost of the American Civil War: Estimates and Implications," *Journal of Economic History* 35, no. 2 (1975): 299; Neta C. Crawford, *United States Budgetary Costs of the Post-9/11 Wars Through FY 2019: $5.9 Trillion Spent and Obligated* (Providence: Watson Institute, Brown University, 2018).

188. Rebecca U. Thorpe, *The American Warfare State: The Domestic Politics of Military Spending* (Chicago: University of Chicago Press, 2014).

189. Paul Kennedy, *The Rise and Fall of Great Powers: Economic Change and Military Power from 1500 to 2000* (New York: Penguin Random House LLC, 1987).

190. Howell, "The Future of the War Presidency."

191. Congress has adopted a one-house legislative veto procedure in various statutes. One instance of such a procedure was struck down by the Supreme Court in *INS v. Chadha*, 462 U.S. 919 (1983). Such Congressional control efforts do not materially alter the conclusion that Congress has made numerous vague authority delegations. The Supreme Court also struck down Congress' effort to delegate dramatically increased authority to the president by creating a line-item veto for budget and some tax bills. *Clinton v. City of New York*, 524 U.S. 417 (1998).

192. Kagan, J. plurality opinion, *Gundy v. United States*, 139 S. Ct. 2116, 2129-30. (2019).

193. The Court has developed various devices for "saving" delegations. In *Gundy v. United States*, for example, Justice Kagan's plurality opinion offered a construction of the challenged statute that she contended preserved it against the charge that it was a standardless delegation; an equally large number of Justices in dissent contended that the statutory language could not support Justice Kagan's construction.

194. Norman J. Ornstein and Thomas E. Mann, *The Broken Branch: How Congress is Failing America and How to Get it Back on Track* (Oxford: Oxford Univ. Press, 2006).

195. Quoted in Lessig, *Republic, Lost*, 127-28.

196. Examples include Thomas E. Mann and Norman J. Ornstein, *It's Even Worse than it Looks: How the American Constitutional System Collided with the New Politics of Extremism* (New York: Basic Books, 2012); Mark A. Graber, "Belling the Partisan Cats: Preliminary Thoughts on Identifying and Mending a Dysfunctional Constitutional Order," *Boston University Law Review* 94 (2014): 611; and Nolan McCarty, "Polarization and the Changing American Constitutional System," in *Can America Govern Itself?*, ed. Frances Lee and Nolan McCarty (Cambridge: Cambridge Univ. Press, 2019), 301.

197. Yuval Levin, "Congress Is Weak Because Its Members Want It to Be Weak," *Commentary*, July/August 2018, 15-20, https://www.commentarymagazine.com/articles/yuval-levin/congress-weak-members-want-weak/.

198. Ornstein and Mann, *The Broken Branch*.

199. Levin, "Congress Is Weak," 17-18.

200. As Maya MacGuineas has said, the underlying reason for Congress' inaction is that both parties are increasingly engaged in "free lunchism" economics (in Richard Cowan, "As U.S. debt, deficits mount, presidential candidates sweep them under the rug," *Reuters*, July 12, 2019).

201. Congress delegated enormous power to the presidency during periods when it was under control of one party for extended periods. Levin, "Congress Is Weak," 17-18.

202. Nicholas Carnes, *The Cash Ceiling: Why Only the Rich Run for Office— and What We Can Do About it* (Princeton: Princeton Univ. Press, 2018).

203. For an astute analysis of congressional dysfunction, see Tim Alberta, "When Impeachment Meets a Broken Congress," *Politico Magazine*, https://www.politico.com/magazine/story/2019/09/27/impeachment-trump-congress-house-228346.

204. Katelin P. Isaacs, "Retirement Benefits for Members of Congress," CRS Report RL30631, updated August 8, 2019; Tom Campbell,

"Americans' Average Social Security in 2019: How Do you Compare?" *The Motley Fool*, October 28, 2018 https://www.fool.com/retirement/2018/10/28/americans-average-social-security-in-2019-how-do-y.aspx#: (accessed 07/11/20).

205. Lessig, *Republic, Lost,* 226-28.

206. Brookings Institution, "Vital Statistics on Congress," http://www.brookings.edu/VitalStats, Table 5-1.

207. Alberta, "When Impeachment Meets a Broken Congress."

208. *U.S. Term Limits, Inc. v. Thornton*, 514 U.S. 779 (1995).

209. Over a longer timeframe, the percentages are even higher. Carrie Eaves, "Running in Someone Else's Shoes: The Electoral Consequences of Running as an Appointed Senator" *Soc. Sci. 2018* 7, 75 (2018).

210. John N. Friedman and Richard T. Holden, "The Rising Incumbent Reelection Rate: What's Gerrymandering Got to Do With It?" *Journal of Politics* 71, no. 2 (2009): 593, Fig. 1 (594); Open Secrets.org, "Reelection Rates Over the Years," https://www.opensecrets.org/overview/reelect.php (accessed 02/28/20).

211. Tim Groseclose and Jeff Milyo, "Buying the Bums Out: What's the Dollar Value of a Seat in Congress?" (Stanford, CA: Stanford University, Graduate School of Business, 1999)(Research Paper No. 1601, July 8, 1999): $5 million (2019 dollars) based on retirement patterns. A later study using a more general economic model arrives at lower estimates: about $1-1.3 million for a House seat, and $2.8 million for a Senate seat (2019 dollars). Daniel Diermeier, Michael Keane, and Antonio Merlo, "A Political Economy Model of Congressional Careers," *American Economic Review* 95, no. 1 (2005): 347, 368-69.

212. Lessig, *Republic, Lost,* 225.

213. Ibid., 106.

214. Carnes, *The Cash Ceiling.* Ornstein and Mann, *The Broken Branch,* at 19/196 (unpaginated online version): "a few dozen" competitive House seats. Tim Alberta agrees that "...There can be no understanding Congress's existential plight without recognizing, at a foundational level, a basic structural problem: There are 435 districts...in the House of Representatives—and only a few dozen of them are contested in November." Alberta, "When Impeachment Meets a Broken Congress."

215. Gallup historical data, https://news.gallup.com/poll/15370/party-affiliation.aspx (accessed 02/28/20).

216. Howell, "The Future of the War Presidency."

217. Stephen M. Griffin, *Broken Trust: Dysfunctional Government and Constitutional Reform* (Lawrence: University Press of Kansas, 2015), 10.

218. Ibid., 46-51, 58-65, 73-75.

219. The Supreme Court has consistently interpreted the Constitution to permit Congress to make delegations of authority so broad as to leave federal agencies with almost complete discretion about how to resolve a problem. See Kagan plurality opinion, *Gundy v. United States*, 139 S. Ct. 2116, 2129-30 (2019).

220. For an extensive discussion, see Levinson, *Our Undemocratic Constitution,* 29-38.

221. See Ronald Brownstein, "This is Why Congress Remains Deadlocked on Climate and Guns," *CNN*, https://www.cnn.com/2019/09/03/politics/guns-climate-senate-standoff-smaller-states/index.html, for underlying data.

222. For a challenge to the idea of judicial supremacy based on popular constitutionalism in Britain and America, see Larry D. Kramer, *The People Themselves: Popular Constitutionalism and Judicial Review* (Oxford: Oxford Univ. Press, 2004).

223. There may be cases in which the Supreme Court should be able to exercise judicial review; the question here is what the limits of that power should be in a republic.

224. *Bush v. Gore,* 531 U.S. 98 (2000).

225. Ibid., 153-54. The law provided for various contingencies: "If, for example, a State submits a single slate of electors, Congress must count those votes unless both Houses agree that the votes 'have not been ... regularly given.'" Ibid., 155 (Breyer, J. dissenting).

226. Republicans controlled a majority of state House delegations, so in all likelihood Bush would have received the necessary majority. But the Senate might have refused to permit the House to decide the 2000 election by insisting on a recount or even a new Florida election. By one estimate, if the 2016 election had gone to the House, and members had voted by party, Donald Trump would have received 35 out of 50 votes, though he had received 46 percent of the popular vote and Republicans held only 55 percent of the House seats. Lawrence Lessig, *They Don't Represent Us: Reclaiming Our Democracy* (New York: Dey Street Books, 2019), 164 n. 36.

227. A leading account is John Ferling, *Adams vs. Jefferson: The Tumultuous Election of 1800* (Oxford: Oxford Univ. Press, 2004).

228. *Bush v. Gore,* 531 U.S. 98, at 128-29 (Stevens, J., dissenting), quoted in Erwin Chemerinsky, "*Bush v. Gore* Was Not Justiciable," *Notre Dame Law Rev.* 76, no. 4 (2001): 1093, 1112.

229. Gallup News, July 17, 2001, "Seven Out of Ten Americans Accept Bush As Legitimate President," https://news.gallup.com/poll/4687/seven-americans-accept-bush-legitimate-president.aspx.

230. *National Federation of Independent Business et al. v. Sebelius, Secretary of Health and Human Services, et al.,* 132 S. Ct. 2566 (2012) (hereafter *NFIB v. Sebelius*).

231. For an analysis of the decision focused on its broadest effects on the law, particularly the "New Deal settlement," see Lawrence B. Solum,

"How *NFIB v. Sebelius* Affects the Constitutional Gestalt" *Washington Univ. Law Rev.* 91, no. 1 (2013): 1.

232. Chief Justice Roberts in particular sought to reconcile the Court's stark conflict over Congress' powers by limiting its authority to a power of persuasion using incentives. But the Chief Justice's position left open what line distinguished persuasion from command.

233. *Sebelius,* 567 U.S. 533-38 (opinion of Chief Justice Roberts).

234. Solum, "How *NFIB* Affects...Gestalt," 49.

235. *Helvering v. Davis,* 301 U.S. 619 (1937).

236. These justices essentially accepted the post-New Deal view that federalism concerns are best addressed not as rights conflicts but instead as safeguarded through the political process. Under that view, if Congress debates the boundaries of state versus federal power on a particular topic, and decides to act against the wishes of individual states, the Court should accept Congress' choice unless it offends some non-majoritarian principle such as individual rights. See Cornell Clayton and J. Mitchell Pickerill, "Guess What Happened on the Way to Revolution? Precursors to the Supreme Court's Federalism Revolution" *Publius: The Journal of Federalism* 34, no. 3 (2004): 85, 88.

Chapter Four

237. A leading account is Sean Wilentz, *The Rise of American Democracy: Jefferson to Lincoln* (New York: Norton, 2005).

238. Levinson, *Our Undemocratic Constitution,* 49-62, 81-101, 123-40; Sabato, *A More Perfect Constitution,* 139-48, 24-26, 110-14.

239. *Rucho et al. v Common Cause et al.* (No. 18-422), 139 S. Ct. 2484 (June 27, 2019), decided together with No. 18-726, *Lamone et al. v. Benisek et al.*

240. Levinson, *Our Undemocratic Constitution,* 38-49, 63-64; Mark Tushnet, *Taking the Constitution Away from the Courts* (Princeton: Princeton University Press, 1999).

241. *Hugh Stuart v. John Laird,* 5 U.S. (1 Cranch) 299 (1803); *Marbury v. Madison,* 5 U.S. (1 Cranch) 137 (1803).

242. Albert J. Beveridge, *The Life of John Marshall,* 4 vols. (Cambridge: Houghton Mifflin Company, 1919), 3: 175-79 (quote 178).

243. Both Senators from nineteen states voted for Kavanaugh. Senators from 11 divided states also voted for confirmation. The full populations of the unanimous states, and one-half the population of the divided states, together represent approximately 44 percent of the 2019 U.S. population.

244. At the time, the average white American life expectancy at birth was as low as forty-four years. J. David Hacker, "Decennial Life Tables for the White Population of the United States, 1790-1900," *Historical Methods* 43, no.

2 (2010), 74. Eighteenth century life expectancy varied significantly by region and social class, among other differences.

245. Louise Kantrow, "Life Expectancy of the Gentry in Eighteenth and Nineteenth-Century Philadelphia," *Proceedings of the American Philosophical Society* 133, no. 2 (Jun. 1989), 318 (Table 2). Estimates of American white male life expectancy at age 10 in the 1790s range from about 50-57 years. Dora L. Costa, "Health and Economy in the United States from 1750 to the Present," *Journal of Economic Literature* 53, no. 3 (Sep. 2015), 504 (Figure 1); Kantrow, "Life Expectancy of the Gentry," 318 (Table 2). I have used an average life expectancy of fifty years at age 10 for gentry to take various factors into account.

246. https://www.cdc.gov/nchs/products/databriefs/db244.htm (accessed 03/10/20).

247. Stephen Calabresi and James Lindgren, "Term Limits for the Supreme Court: Life Tenure Reconsidered," *Harv. Jnl. Law & Pub. Policy* 29 (2006): 769 provides a comprehensive analysis of lifetime Supreme Court tenure and possible reforms.

248. https://www.cdc.gov/nchs/fastats/life-expectancy.htm (accessed 03/10/20) (average life expectancy as of 2017 was more than 78 years).

249. Calabresi and Lindgren, "Term Limits," 771.

250. Levinson, *Our Undemocratic Constitution*, 128, discussing the views of the exceptionally distinguished appellate judge Richard Posner.

251. Calabresi and Lindgren, "Term Limits," 789.

252. Ibid, 773-74. And see Levinson, *Our Undemocratic Constitution*, 135-36.

253. The majority view appears to be that a constitutional amendment would be required, but a variety of statutory proposals have been made as well. Calabresi and Lindgren, "Term Limits," 770, 824-868.

254. Frances E. Lee and Bruce I. Oppenheim, *Sizing Up the Senate: The Unequal Consequences of Equal Representation* (Chicago: Univ. of Chicago Press, 1999), 14-15.

255. The New Senate would be expanded to 150 total votes. Each state would receive one vote based on statehood. An additional 100 votes are distributed essentially in proportion to population, excluding the smallest states from additional votes. For example, under this method, using the 1980 census, in the New Senate New York would have 9 votes, Ohio 6 votes, and Idaho 2 votes. Senators in the New Senate are counted as voting the same way they did in the old Senate.

256. Details on these votes: see Appendix A.

257. The Senate would have approved cloture on the amendment, then understood to mean willingness to send the amendment to the states. The New Senate would not have approved the 1979 Electoral College abolition proposal.

258. May 31, 1976, vote on motion to recommit (kill) bill to establish federal standards for no-fault motor vehicle insurance.

259. Justice Clarence Thomas was confirmed by Senators representing forty-eight percent of the population, according to one study. Another scholar concluded that if the Senate voted based on population, Thomas would have lost narrowly. See Levinson, *Our Undemocratic Constitution*, 58.

260. According to the Supreme Court, all fifty state legislatures could choose the Presidential electors themselves, and negate the results of a popular vote. Alexander Keyssar, *The Right to Vote: The Contested History of Democracy in the United States* (rev. ed.; New York: Basic Books, 2009), 262. A good Electoral College overview is Lawrence D. Longley and Neal R. Pierce, *The Electoral College Primer* (New Haven: Yale Univ. Press, 1996). Also informative is Longley and Braun, *The Politics of Electoral College Reform*. For analyses of the Electoral College see Akhil Reed Amar, "An Accident Waiting to Happen," in *Constitutional Stupidities, Constitutional Tragedies*, ed. William N. Eskridge Jr. and Sanford Levinson (New York: New York University Press, 1998), 15 and George C. Edwards III, *Why the Electoral College is Bad for America* (New Haven: Yale University Press, 2004).

261. Beeman, *Plain, Honest Men*, 135, 232, 299-303, 349.

262. Amar, "A Constitutional Accident," 15-17.

263. Beeman, *Plain, Honest Men*, 231-32.

264. Delegate Hugh Williamson feared that an official elected as President could become an "elective King, and feel the spirit of one." Beeman, *PHM*, 248.

265. Amar, "A Constitutional Accident," 15-17.

266. Various systems have been employed by partisan-dominated legislatures to choose favorable electors. The method most commonly used is election by plurality statewide vote in a "winner-take-all" system.

267. Amar, "A Constitutional Accident," 15.

268. The Supreme Court decided in 2020 that a state's electors can be punished for failing to cast their votes as required by state law. *Chiafolo et al. v. Washington*, No. 19-465, decided July 6, 2020.

269. Longley and Pierce, *The Electoral College Primer*, 135; Edwards III, *Why the Electoral College is Bad for America*, 45.

270. Michael Geruso, Dean Spears, and Ishaana Talesara, "Inversions in U.S. Presidential Elections: 1836-2016" (Washington, DC: NBER, 2019)(Working Paper No. 26247).

271. A very close result is much more likely to elect the Republican candidate. For example, if a Republican receives 49.5 percent of the vote, he has a 46 percent chance of winning, while a Democrat has 21 percent chance. Ibid. The current advantage for Republicans is a result of partisan and geographic factors. Ibid., 13. At times in the past, such as the Reconstruction Era, the Electoral College would have similarly advantaged Democrats. Ibid.

272. Edwards III, *Why the Electoral College is Bad for America*, xvi.

273. Robert S. Mueller III et al., REPORT ON THE INVESTIGATION INTO RUSSIAN INTERFERENCE IN THE 2016 PRESIDENTIAL ELECTION (2 vols.)(Washington, D.C., GPO, Mar. 2019); REPORT OF THE SELECT COMMITTEE ON INTELLIGENCE, UNITED STATES SENATE, ON RUSSIAN ACTIVE MEASURES CAMPAIGNS AND INTERFERENCE IN THE 2016 ELECTION, VOLUME 4: *Review of the Intelligence Community Assessment with Additional Views* (released 04/21/20).

274. http://www.census.gov/popest/states/NST-ann-est.html (accessed 03/03/20).

275. Levinson, *Our Undemocratic Constitution*, 90.

276. Some political scientists think that another bias stems from the widely used "winner-take-all" system, which awards all of a state's Electoral College votes to the candidate who wins a plurality. According to one analysis, citizens of forty-five out of the fifty-one voting jurisdictions had less than average voting power per voter, while residents of the six largest states had more than average voting power per voter. See Longley and Pierce, *The Electoral College Primer*, 141-46. Some argue that winner-take-all is a problem for which the College is not to blame. Suzanna Sherry, "Democracy Uncaged," *Constitutional Commentary* 25 (2008): 141 (review of Levinson, *Our Undemocratic Constitution*).

277. *The Electoral College Primer*, Table 21, 148.

278. Lessig, *They Don't Represent Us*, 40-41. For Lessig's critique of the Electoral College, see ibid., 33-43.

279. Edwards III, *Why the Electoral College is Bad for America*, xvi (Gallup poll data). 500 proposals: Longley and Braun, *The Politics of Electoral College Reform*, 43.

280. Longley and Braun, *Politics of Reform*, 150. Direct election was supported by a range of groups from the U.S. Chamber of Commerce to the AFL-CIO and President Nixon.

281. Longley and Braun, The Politics of Electoral College Reform, 172-75.

282. Edwards III, *Electoral College is Bad*, xi (foreword by Neal R. Pierce).

283. Sabato, *A More Perfect Constitution*, 138-39.

284. Longley and Braun, *Politics of Reform*, 9.

285. Longley and Braun, *Politics of Reform*, 8-17; Edwards, *Electoral College is Bad*, 67-71.

286. Joseph A. Pika and John Anthony Maltese, *The Politics of the Presidency* (6th ed.; Washington, D.C.: CQ Press, 2004), 68.

287. Van Cleve, *We Have Not a Government*, 31-32, 241-42, 266-67.

288. Concerns that the Electoral College changes the geographic shape of presidential campaigns are far less significant given the Internet.

289. *Rucho et al. v. Common Cause et al.*, 139 S. Ct. 2484 (2019).

290. Lessig, *Republic, Lost*, 27.

291. http://www.ncsl.org/research/about-state-legislatures/partisan-composition.aspx (accessed 04/21/20).

292. https://www.americanprogress.org/issues/democracy/news/2019/10/01/475166/impact-partisan-gerrymandering/ (accessed 04/21/20).

293. *Rucho*, Kagan, Justice, dissent (joined by all minority Justices), 139 S. Ct. 2484, 2509-11.

294. *Rucho*, Roberts majority opinion, 139 S. Ct. 2484, 2494.

295. The majority opinion suggests that the Founders' omission was intentional.

296. Roberts majority opinion, 139 S. Ct. 2484, 2506.

297. Ibid., 139 S. Ct. 2495.

298. Ibid., 139 S. Ct. 2507-08.

299. Roberts majority opinion, 139 S. Ct. 2484, 2499.

300. Roberts majority opinion, 139 S. Ct. 2484, 2499-2500.

301. Sabato, *A More Perfect Constitution*, 35.

302. National Conference of State Legislatures, http://www.ncsl.org/research/about-state-legislatures/partisan-composition.aspx (accessed 04/24/20).

303. Pippa Norris, "Choosing Electoral Systems: Proportional, Majoritarian, and Mixed Systems," *International Political Science Review* 18, no. 3 (1997): 297; Bonica et al., "Why Hasn't Democracy Slowed Rising Inequality?," 118.

Chapter Five

304. Lessig, *Republic, Lost*, 265.

305. For Jefferson's and Madison's conflicting views, see Levinson, *Our Undemocratic Constitution*, 16-19.

306. Ibid., 160.

307. The "iron cage" phrase is Levinson's, ibid. 165. On Article V, see ibid., 159-66.

308. Sarah Kleiner, "Democrats Say Citizens United Should Die. Here's Why That Won't Happen," *Time*, August 31, 2017, https://time.com/4922542/democrats-citizen-united/.

309. Scott Bomboy (National Constitution Center), July 7, 2016, "A Short List of Constitutional Amendments Proposed in the Current Congress," https://constitutioncenter.org/blog/a-short-list-of-constitutional-amendments-proposed-in-the-current-congress (accessed 07/13/20).

310. Levinson, *Undemocratic Constitution*, 21 (citing Donald Lutz).

311. Lee and McCarty, *Can America Govern Itself?*, 3.

312. Graber, "Belling the Partisan Cats."

313. Geoffrey Skelley, "Abolishing The Electoral College Used To Be A Bipartisan Position. Not Anymore," April 2, 2019, https://fivethirtyeight.com/features/abolishing-the-electoral-college-used-to-be-bipartisan-position-not-anymore/.

314. Edwards III, Electoral College is Bad, xi.

315. Skelley, "Abolishing the Electoral College."

316. Ibid.; Miles Parks, "Abolishing The Electoral College Would Be More Complicated Than It May Seem," *NPR* March 22, 2019, https://www.npr.org/2019/03/22/705627996/abolishing-the-electoral-college-would-be-more-complicated-than-it-may-seem.

317. Jessica Corbett, "Over 120 Groups Call on Congress to Back Constitutional Amendment Overturning Citizens United," https://www.commondreams.org/news/2019/09/05/over-120-groups-call-congress-back-constitutional-amendment-overturning-citizens; https://www.congress.gov/bill/116th-congress/house-joint-resolution/2/cosponsors (accessed 11/14/19); Jeff Clements (American Promise), February 6, 2020, *The Hill*, "Cross-partisan public support spurs Congressional hearing to overturn Citizens United," https://thehill.com/blogs/congress-blog/politics/481776-cross-partisan-public-support-spurs-congressional-hearing-to.

318. Ashley Balcerzak, "Study: Most Americans Want to Kill 'Citizens United' with Constitutional Amendment," https://publicintegrity.org/federal-politics/study-most-americans-want-to-kill-citizens-united-with-constitutional-amendment/ (May 10-15, 2018, published and updated).

319. Ibid.

320. http://reclaimtheamericandream.org/progress-amend/ (accessed 11/13/19).

321. Lessig, *Republic, Lost*, 268 (emphasis omitted).

322. http://reclaimtheamericandream.org/progress-amend/ (accessed 11/13/19). In at least three and perhaps as many as five listed supportive states, there was no formal legislature action. Ibid.

323. Patrick M. Condray and Timothy J. Conlan, "Article V Conventions and American Federalism: Contemporary Politics in Historical Perspective," *Publius: The Journal of Federalism* 49, no. 3 (2019): 515.

324. Issue One, *Dark Money Illuminated*, September, 2018, https://www.issueone.org/dark-money/; https://campaignlegal.org/update/clc-analysis-fec-rule-kept-much-769-million-political-spending-dark (accessed 11/14/19).

325. Center for Responsive Politics, *2016 Outside Spending by Group* (Washington, D.C.: Center for Responsive Politics), https://www.opensecrets.org/outsidespending/summ.php?cycle=2016&disp=O&type=U&chrt=D (accessed 11/13/19).

326. Kleiner, "Democrats Say 'Citizens United' Should Die."

327. Ibid.; Scott Bland and Maggie Severns, "Documents reveal massive 'dark-money' group boosted Democrats in 2018," *Politico Magazine*, https://www.politico.com/news/2019/11/19/dark-money-democrats-midterm-071725.

328. Rachel Treisman, "Poll: Number Of Americans Who Favor Stricter Gun Laws Continues To Grow," *NPR* October 20, 2019, https://www.npr.org/2019/10/20/771278167/poll-number-of-americans-who-favor-stricter-gun-laws-continues-to-grow.

329. H. J. Res 2, House Roll call No. 138, Cong. Rec. April 12, 2018, Vol. 164, No. 59, at H3193.

330. The possible state targets remaining are quite limited, because Democratic-controlled states will not approve such resolutions.

331. Michael Biesecker, "Scott Walker, other budget hawks hatch plan to force constitutional convention," Associated Press, July 31, 2020, in https://www.startribune.com/budget-hawks-hatch-plan-to-force-constitutional-convention/571967802/. Thanks to Marc Freed for this reference.

332. Estimates of the total number of states differ slightly; this is the most common number.

333. Lessig, *Republic, Lost*, 271.

334. Ibid., 283.

335. For historical background, see Condray and Conlan, "Article V Conventions."

336. H.J. Res. 208, March 22, 1972, 92nd Cong., 2d. sess.

337. Thomas H. Neale, *The Proposed Equal Rights Amendment: Contemporary Ratification Issues* (Washington, D.C.: Library of Congress (Congressional Research Service), 2018), July 28, 2018. Some ERA supporters claim that the preamble does not set a valid deadline. Ibid, 5.

338. Ibid.

339. Nevada ratified in 2017, Illinois in 2018.

340. Russell Berman, "Justice Ginsburg versus the Equal Rights Amendment," *Atlantic*, February 15, 2020.

341. NARAL, "Campaign ERA Y-E-S," https://www.prochoiceamerica.org/campaign/era_yes/ (accessed 11/25/19); NRLC, "Equal Rights Amendment," https://www.nrlc.org/federal/era/ (accessed 11/25/19). For a leading account of the earlier debate over the ERA, see Reva B. Siegel, "Constitutional Culture, Social Movement Conflict, and Constitutional Change: The Case of the de facto ERA," *California Law Review* 94, no. 5 (2006): 1323.

342. https://www.prnewswire.com/news-releases/breaking-americansby-94---overwhelmingly-support-the-equal-rights-amendment-era-300286472.html (accessed 11/15/19); https://www.equalrightsamendment.org/faq (question 17)(accessed 11/15/19).

343. For a leading example, see Jack M. Balkin, *Living Originalism* (Cambridge: Harvard University Press, 2011). A variant emphasizing the relationship between social movements and contested changes in constitutional understanding is found in Siegel, "Constitutional Culture."

344. See generally, Solum, "How *NFIB v. Sebelius* Affects the Constitutional Gestalt."

345. Levinson, *Our Undemocratic Constitution*, 163-65.

346. Stephen Skowronek and Karen Orren, "The Adapability Paradox: Constitutional Resilience and Principles of Good Government in Twenty-First Century America," *Perspectives on Politics* 18, no. 2 (2020): 354, quote 356. The authors also sharply criticize originalism.

347. *Dred Scott v. Sandford*, 60 U.S. (19 How.) 393 (1857).

348. For additional background, see Thomas H. Neale and Andrew Nolan, *The National Popular Vote (NPV) Initiative: Direct Election of the President by Interstate Compact*, Rept. No. 43823 (Washington, DC: Congressional Research Service, 2018, updated 2019). States have power to sanction electors who do not follow state laws instructing them to cast their votes for the popular vote winner. *Chiafolo et al. v. Washington*. (No. 19-465, decided July 6, 2020).

349. The bill has passed at least one chamber in 9 additional states with 88 more electoral votes. https://www.nationalpopularvote.com/written-explanation (accessed 7/13/20).

350. National Conference of State Legislatures, http://www.ncsl.org/research/about-state-legislatures/partisan-composition.aspx (accessed 11/15/19).

351. Thomas H. Neale, *NPV—The National Popular Vote Initiative: Proposing Direct Election of the President Through an Interstate Compact* (Washington, DC: Congressional Research Service, 2019), 2; Neale and Nolan, The National Popular Vote (NPV) Initiative.

352. Neale and Nolan, *The National Popular Vote (NPV) Initiative*.

353. Ibid., 24.

354. Dr. John Koza, "Myths about Interstate Compacts and Congressional Consent," (2019), https://www.nationalpopularvote.com/ (video) (accessed 11/18/19).

355. Neale and Nolan, *The National Popular Vote (NPV) Initiative*. Sanford Levinson's view appears to be that the compact would require Congressional approval. Levinson, *Our Undemocratic Constitution*, 97.

356. Marian C. Mckenna, *Franklin Roosevelt and the Great Constitutional War: The Court-Packing Crisis of 1937* (New York: Fordham Univ. Press, 2002) is a revisionist account. For a brief overview more sympathetic to Roosevelt, see David M. Kennedy, *Freedom from Fear: The American People in Depression and War, 1929-1945* (Oxford: Oxford Univ. Press, 1999), 330-37.

357. Kennedy, *Freedom from Fear*, 333.

358. Ibid.

359. United States Senate (Committee on the Judiciary), *Reorganization of the Federal Judiciary*, S. Rept. 711, 75th Cong., 1st Sess. (1937), 8-23.

360. United States Senate, July 22, 1937, Cong. Rec. 75th Cong., 1st. sess., S7381; Mckenna, *Franklin Roosevelt and the Great Constitutional War*, 517-21.

361. That narrative has been sharply challenged. See Barry Cushman, "Court-Packing and Compromise," 29 *Constitutional Commentary* (2013): 1, 28 n. 145.

362. Akhil Reed Amar, *America's Unwritten Constitution: The Precedents and Principles We Live By* (New York: Basic Books, 2012), 354-55, defends the constitutionality of a proposal such as FDR's. For a skeptical perspective on Amar's position, see Curtis A. Bradley and Neil S. Siegel, "Historical Gloss, Constitutional Conventions, and the Judicial Separation of Powers " *Georgetown Law Journal* 105 (2017): 255 at 276-78.

363. Stephen Breyer, *Making Democracy Work: A Judge's View* (New York: Knopf, 2010).

364. Erin Delaney, "Searching for constitutional meaning in institutional design: The debate over judicial appointments in the United Kingdom" *International Journal of Constitutional Law* 14, no. 3 (2016): 752; United Kingdom Supreme Court, "The Supreme Court: Significance to the UK," https://www.supremecourt.uk/about/significance-to-the-uk.html (accessed 03/02/20).

365. Sheldon Whitehouse, Mazie Hirono, Richard Blumenthal, et al., "Brief of Senators Sheldon Whitehouse, Mazie Hirono, et al. as Amici Curiae in Support of Respondents," in *New York State Rifle & Pistol Association, Inc. et al. v. City of New York , New York et al.* (S. Ct. Dkt. No. 18-280), August 12, 2019.

366. Kennedy, *Freedom from Fear*, 330.

Chapter Six

367. Kramer, *The People Themselves: Popular Constitutionalism and Judicial Review*, 8, 25-34.

368. Paul Leicester Ford, "The Adoption of the Pennsylvania Constitution of 1776" *Political Science Quarterly* X, no. 3 (1895), 448-49.

369. Thomas Paine, *The rights of man : in two parts : being an answer to Mr. Burke's attack on the French Revolution* (1877; New York: D.M. Bennett, 1877 (orig. pub. 1791)), 133-34.

370. Quoted in Akhil Reed Amar, "Popular Sovereignty and Constitutional Amendment," in *Responding to Imperfection: The Theory and Practice of Constitutional Amendment*, ed. Sanford Levinson (Princeton: Princeton Univ. Press, 1995): 89, 115. Amar wrote elsewhere: "We the People of the United States have a legal right to alter our government—to change our Constitution—via a majoritarian and populist mechanism akin to a national referendum, even though that mechanism is not explicitly specified in Article V." Amar, "The Consent of the Governed: Constitutional Amendment Outside Article V," *Columbia Law Review* 94 (1994): 457. Sanford Levinson apparently agrees with Amar's view. Levinson, *Our Undemocratic Constitution*, 177.

371. Amar, "Popular Sovereignty," at 98.

372. Hofstadter, *The American Political Tradition & the Men Who Made It*, 7.

373. For an argument that the Philadelphia Convention was not a runaway convention, see Paul J. Weber and Barbara A. Perry, *Unfounded Fears: Myths and Realities of a Constitutional Convention* (New York: Greenwood Press, 1989), 13-29.

374. Some contend that Article V's amendment routes were intended to be exhaustive. David R. Dow, "The Plain Meaning of Article V," in *Responding to Imperfection: The Theory and Practice of Constitutional Amendment*, ed. Sanford Levinson (Princeton: Princeton Univ. Press, 1995): 117. But Article V cannot displace popular sovereignty. Popular sovereignty does not mean that the Constitution imposes no legitimate obligations on Americans today. For that contention, see Louis Michael Seidman, *On Constitutional Disobedience* (Oxford: Oxford University Press, 2012), 11-28. For criticisms of popular constitutional action in various countries, see William Partlett, "The Dangers of Popular Constitution-Making," *Brooklyn Journal of International Law* 38, no. 1 (2012): 1; Thomas Fleiner, "Participation of citizens in constitution-making: Assets and challenges – the Swiss experience," in *Participatory Constitutional Change: The People As Amenders of the Constitution,* ed. Xenophon Contiades and Alkmene Fotiadou (Taylor & Francis Group, 2016), 67; Claudia Josi, "Direct democracy vs fundamental rights? A comparative analysis of the mechanisms that limit the 'will of the people' in Switzerland and California," in Contiades and Fotioadou, *Participatory Constitutional Change*, 82. Criticisms of popular action are commonly based on the critic's dislike of its substantive outcomes or claimed process flaws.

375. Article XIII of the Articles of Confederation provided: "nor shall any alteration at any time hereafter be made in any of them; unless such alteration be agreed to in a Congress of the United States, and be afterwards confirmed by the legislatures of every State." Articles of Confederation, March 1, 1781, https://avalon.law.yale.edu/18th_century/artconf.asp.

376. For the events leading to the Convention, see Van Cleve, *We Have Not a Government*, 245-78.

377. In late 1786 and early 1787, Congress went for seventy-two days without achieving a quorum. Beeman, *Plain, Honest Men*, 20.

378. *The Statutes at Large: Being a Collection of All the Laws of Virginia, from the First Session of the Legislature in the Year 1619*, ed. William Walter Hening (Richmond: George Cochran, 1823), 12: 256 (1786 Laws, Ch. VIII).

379. Van Cleve, *We Have Not a Government*, 262.

380. Ibid., 263.

381. Ibid., 267.

382. Delaware's delegates were the only ones with restricted negotiating authority. Jon Elster, "Constitutional Bootstrapping in Philadelphia and Paris," *Cardozo Law Review* 14, nos. 3 & 4 (1992): 549, 563-64.

383. For an overview of ratification, see Pauline Maier, *Ratification: The People Debate the Constitution, 1787-88* (New York: Simon & Schuster, 2010).

384. Levinson, *Our Undemocratic Constitution*, 15-16, quote at 15.

385. Seidman, *On Constitutional Disobedience*, 27.

386. Maier, *Ratification*.

387. Cass Sunstein, "It Could Be Worse," *New Republic*, October 15, 2006 (review of Levinson, *Our Undemocratic Constitution*).

388. Ibid.

389. Suzanna Sherry, "Democracy Uncaged," 152.

390. Sabato, *A More Perfect Constitution*, 198.

391. Jay Riestenberg, Common Cause, "U.S. Constitution Threatened as Article V Convention Movement Nears Success," March 21, 2018, https://www.commoncause.org/resource/u-s-constitution-threatened-as-article-v-convention-movement-nears-success/.

392. Sabato, *A More Perfect* Constitution, 206. Lawrence Lessig believes that Congress has power to limit a convention's scope, but concedes that no court will "second-guess Congress, and neither do I believe that any court is going to regulate a convention." Lessig, *Republic, Lost*, 285.

393. Lawrence Lessig takes a similar view of Article V conventions. His analysis would apply to popular conventions as well. *Republic, Lost*, 283-84.

394. A similar argument about the extensive political safeguards inherent in the convention process under Article V is made in Weber and Perry, *Unfounded Fears: Myths and Realities of a Constitutional Convention*, 105-125.

395. Beeman, *Plain, Honest Men*, 255-56.

396. After an Article V convention, no amendment perceived as partisan has any reasonable chance of being ratified. Lessig, *Republic, Lost*, 285-87. The

same basic political logic applies to popular convention proposals followed by supermajority ratification.

397. Graber, "Belling the Partisan Cats." There are political scientists who think that polarization has contributed to constitutional dysfunction. See, for example, McCarty, "Polarization and the Changing American Constitutional System," 301.

398. Griffin, *Broken Trust*, 21, 46-51, 58-65.

399. Ibid., 130.

400. Griffin thinks such reforms are unlikely as a result. Ibid., 132.

401. Ibid., 101-22.

402. Ryan D. Edwards, "U.S. War Costs: Two Parts Temporary, One Part Permanent," *Journal of Public Economics* 113 (May 2014): 54.

403. McKay Cunningham, "There is No Road Map for Rewriting the Constitution," *The Hill*, August 20, 2019, https://thehill.com/opinion/civil-rights/457985-there-is-no-road-map-for-rewriting-the-constitution.

404. Tom Wells, *The War Within: America's Battle over Vietnam* (1994 Univ. Calif. Press; repr. New York: Open Road Distribution, 2016), 348-354 (quote 354), 368-70.

405. Mark Tushnet, "Abolishing Judicial Review," *Constitutional Commentary* 27 (2011): 581, 588.

406. Sabato, *A More Perfect Constitution*, 211-20; Levinson, *Our Undemocratic Constitution*, 173-77. Lawrence Lessig agrees that a convention should be called under Article V. Lessig, *Republic, Lost*, 275-76, 294-99.

407. Karen Desoto, "Is it time for a U.S. Article V Constitutional convention? A brief discussion about American constitutional reform procedure," *Revista de Investigações Constitucionais* 5, no. 1 (2018), 252.

408. For views on this, see Vincent Pulignano, "A Known Unknown: The Call for an Article V Convention," *Florida Law Review Forum* 67 (2016): 151; Desoto, "Is it time for a U.S. Article V Constitutional convention?"; Thomas H. Neale, *The Article V Convention for Proposing Constitutional Amendments: Historical Perspectives for Congress* (Washington, DC: Congressional Research Service, 2012), 7; Michael B. Rappaport, "The Constitutionality of a Limited Convention: An Originalist Analysis," *Constitutional Commentary* 28, no. 1 (2012): 59.

409. Paul G. Kauper, "The Alternative Amendment Process: Some Observations," *Michigan Law Review* 66, no. 5 (1968): 903, 905-906.

410. Desoto, "Is it time for a U.S. Article V Constitutional convention?," 254.

411. Charles L. Black, Jr. argued that Congress had no power to set convention rules, and that Article V itself prohibited limited conventions. Charles L. Black Jr., "Amending the Constitution: A Letter to a Congressman," *Yale Law Journal* 82, no. 2 (1972): 189; for further support, see Walter E. Dellinger, "The Recurring Question of a 'Limited' Constitutional Convention," *Yale Law Journal* 88, no. 8 (1979): 1623. A debate summary is found in Rappaport, "The Constitutionality of a Limited Convention."

412. North Carolina Senator Samuel J. Ervin and others long ago proposed unsuccessfully that Congress establish convention rules. Sabato, *A More Perfect Constitution,* 206-07.

413. Sabato, *A More Perfect Constitution,* 230; Neale, *The Article V Convention,* 9.

414. Neale, *The Article V Convention.*

415. Pole, *Political Representation in England,* 349-50.

416. For the large state vs. small state debate, see Beeman, *Plain, Honest Men,* 144-225.

417. John S. Kiernan, "Most and Least Federally Dependent States," *WalletHub,* Mar. 19, 2019, https://wallethub.com/edu/states-most-least-dependent-on-the-federal-government/2700/.

418. Tracy Gordon, Richard Auxier, and John Iselin, *Assessing Fiscal Capacities of States: A Representative Revenue System—Representative Expenditure System Approach, Fiscal Year 2012* (Washington, D.C.: Urban Institute, 2016), 7-8.

419. Kentucky and the other four states receive about $225 billion in net federal assistance, and have 2019 state budgets totaling about $120 billion. See Samuel Stebbins, "How much money does your state receive from the federal government? Check out this list," *USA Today,* https://www.usatoday.com/story/money/economy/2019/03/20/how-much-federal-funding-each-state-receives-government/39202299/.

420. A Safra Center on Ethics report defines legal corruption as an official's "political gains in the form of campaign contributions or endorsements…in exchange for providing specific benefits to private individuals or groups…" Oguzhan Dincer and Michael Johnston, *Measuring Illegal and Legal Corruption in American States: Some Results from the Corruption in America Survey* (Safra Center on Ethics, Harvard University, 2014) (accessed 06/16/20).

421. Ibid., unpaginated text preceding n. 1.

422. *Caperton et al. v. A.T. Massey Coal Co. Inc. et al.* , 556 U.S. 868 (2009)

423. Ibid., 873.

424. Ibid., 876.

425. Ibid., 874.

426. 556 US. 868 at 886-87.

427. "Mining Case shows sooty side of big-money judicial elections," *USA Today*, March 2, 2009, usatoday30.usatoday.com/printedition/news/20090303/editorial03_st.art.htm (accessed 06/17/20).

428. Justin Worland, "As clean energy rises, West Virginia looks past Trump's embrace of coal to what comes next," *Time* (2020), https://time.com/coals-last-kick/ (accessed 06/17/20).

429. Ibid.; Charles D. Kolstad, *What is Killing the U.S. Coal Industry?* (Palo Alto: Stanford Institute for Energy Policy Research, 2017), https://siepr.stanford.edu/research/publications/what-killing-us-coal-industry (accessed 06/17/20); Adele C. Morris, *Build a Better Future for Coal Industry Workers and their Communities* (Washington, DC: Brookings Institution, 2016).

430. Worland, "As clean energy rises."

Chapter Seven

431. Jon Elster, "Arguing and Bargaining in Two Constituent Assemblies," *Journal of Constitutional Law* 2, no. 2 (2000): 345; Elster, "Constitutional Bootstrapping in Philadelphia and Paris."

432. William D. Nelson, "The Freedom of Business Association," *Columbia Law Review* 115, no. 2 (2015): 462, 464.

433. Ibid.

434. Ibid.

435. Sabato, *A More Perfect Constitution*, 206-08.

436. In particular, it shifted tax, commerce, and military powers to the national government.

437. Van Cleve, *We Have Not a Government*, 246-86.

438. Lessig, *Republic, Lost*, 271.

439. For a discussion of these techniques, see Lessig, *They Don't Represent Us*, 176-85.

440. Sabato, *A More Perfect Constitution*, 212; Levinson, *Our Undemocratic Constitution*, 213-14 (Afterword, pbk. ed.).

441. Eaves, "Running in Someone Else's Shoes," at 3.

442. The larger House of Representatives committees (e.g., Committee on Agriculture) have in the range of forty members.

443. Sabato, *A More Perfect Constitution*, 211-12.

444. Democratic National Committee, "Delegate Selection Rules for the 2020 Democratic National Convention," https://democrats.org/wp-content/uploads/2019/01/2020-Delegate-Selection-Rules-12.17.18-FINAL.pdf (accessed 06/23/20).

445. Levinson, *Our Undemocratic Constitution*, 213.

446. Griffin, *Broken Trust*, 139.

447. Stuart White, "Parliaments, Constitutional Conventions, and Popular Sovereignty," *British Journal of Politics and International Relations* 19, no. 2 (2017): 320. For historical lottery uses, see Lessig, *They Don't Represent Us*, 187.

448. Ibid.

449. Sabato, *A More Perfect Constitution*, 212-13.

450. After a dispute, the elected members were then formally appointed by Iceland's parliament.

451. Anne Meuwese, "Popular Constitution Making: The Case of Iceland," in *Social and Political Foundations of Constitutions*, ed. Denis J. Galligan and Mila Versteeg (Cambridge: Cambridge University Press, 2013), 479. Some critics have suggested that reform's failure reflected the view that the Constitutional Council was perceived as an illegitimate "end run" of Iceland's constitutional democracy. Bjorg Thorarensen, "Why the Making of a Crowd-sourced Constitution in Iceland Failed," *The Constitution-Making and Constitutional Change Blog* (2014). Others suggest that reform's failure proves that Iceland is a corrupt oligarchy. Thorvaldur Gylfason, "Iceland's Ongoing Constitutional Fight," *verfassungsblog.de on matters constitutional* (2018). See also, Alexander Hudson, "Will Iceland Get a New Constitution? A New Revision Process Is Taking Shape," *Int'l J. Const. L. Blog*, http://www.iconnectblog.com/2018/10/will-iceland-get-a-new-constitution-a-new-revision-process-is-taking-shape/(accessed 06/29/2020).

452. See Sabato, *A More Perfect Constitution*, 212-13.

453. Edmund Burke, "Speech to the Electors of Bristol, 3 November, 1774, in Philip B. Kurland and Ralph Lerner, eds., *The Founders' Constitution* (Chicago: University of Chicago Press, 2000),Volume 1, Chapter 13, Document 7, http://press-pubs.uchicago.edu/founders/documents/v1ch13s7.html.

454. See, for example, American Legislative Exchange Council ("ALEC"), "Compact for America: Balanced Budget Amendment," https://www.alec.org/model-policy/resolution-to-effectuate-the-compact-for-america/ (accessed 06/26/20)(Article VI, Section 3, "Replacement or Recall of Delegates). Indiana has a statute authorizing recall for any state delegate who violates scope limits in an article V convention. https://www.prnewswire.com/news-releases/indiana-act-ensures-faithful-us-amendment-convention-delegates-says-balanced-budget-amendment-task-force-207294321.html (accessed 06/26/20). Georgia law permits recall of any delegate who votes for an "unauthorized" amendment at an Article V convention. Georgia Code (General Assembly), § 28-6-8.

455. For example, this estimate assumes that it would cost at most about $1 million/day to hold the convention by providing transport, hotels, food, delegate compensation, and a secure convention site for 435 delegates and staff; over six months, this would be about $150-$180 million.

456. https://www.gofundme.com/c/about-us (accessed 06/26/20).

457. Griffin, *Broken Trust*, 139.

458. League of Conservation Voters: https://www.opensecrets.org/news/2019/12/environmental-grps-saw-revenue-spikes/ (accessed 06/08/20); Sierra Club, Environmental Defense Fund, Natural Resources Defense Council: 2019 annual reports online (accessed 06/22/20).

459. https://blog.actblue.com/2020/06/15/may-20-recap/ (accessed 06/22/20).

460. Registered voters data: https://www.statista.com/statistics/273743/number-of-registered-voters-in-the-united-states/ (accessed 06/08/20).

461. https://www.pewresearch.org/fact-tank/2017/05/17/5-facts-about-u-s-political-donations/ (accessed 06/08/20).

462. https://www.opensecrets.org/overview/donordemographics.php (accessed 1/9/2020).

463. Lessig, *They Don't Represent Us*, 231-36.

464. Levinson, *Our Undemocratic Constitution*, 214.

465. This is the same right any private organization would have to protect its "brand" against tortious interference.

466. Griffin, *Broken Trust*, 118-122.

467. *NAACP v. Alabama ex rel. Patterson*, 357 U.S. 449 (1958) (freedom of expressive association); *New York State Bd. of Elections v. Lopez Torres* 128 S. Ct. 791 (2008), 797-98 (2008) (state role needed as basis for regulating party action under state action doctrine); *Williams v. Rhodes,* 393 U.S. 23 (1968); *California Democratic Party v. Jones* 530 U.S. 567 (2000); Nelson, "The Freedom of Business Association," 462-64.

468. Some people attribute this saying to the economist Herbert Simon.

469. Condray and Conlan, "Article V Conventions," 525-27.

470. Rhode Island's governing party feared that the Constitution was likely to explicitly strip states of important economic powers, including the ability to modify debts and to create paper money. George William Van Cleve, "The Anti-Federalists' Toughest Challenge: Paper Money, Debt Relief, and the Ratification of the Constitution," *Journal of the Early Republic* 34, no. 4 (2014): 547-48.

471. Ibid.

472. For example, a generous $400/day allowance for hotels and food for six months for 435 delegates and 100 staff would cost a total of about $39 million; providing $150/day compensation for them would add an additional $15 million.

473. Beeman, *Plain, Honest Men*, 82.

474. Sabato, *A More Perfect Constitution*, 215.

475. Beeman, *Plain, Honest Men*, 83.

476. Ibid.

477. Elster, "Arguing and Bargaining," 411-13 (quote at 411); ——, "Constitutional Bootstrapping," 569-72.

478. Mark Tushnet, "Comparative Constitutional Law," in *Oxford Handbook of Comparative Law*, ed. Mathias Reimann and Reinhard Zimmerman (Oxford: Oxford University Press, 2012), 1236.

479. Meuwese, "Popular Constitution Making: The Case of Iceland," 470.

480. Ibid., 483.

481. As Meuwese notes, one important failure of the Council's process was that the decision to seek a referendum on its work was made at its end. Ibid., 493.

482. Ibid., 486.

483. Ibid., 487.

484. Congressional committees involved in national security, intelligence and foreign policy matters routinely close their deliberations. For example, during 2019 impeachment proceedings against President Trump, the House Intelligence committee took testimony from numerous witnesses in secret and refused to share the testimony with or admit even other members of Congress to their proceedings. Russell Berman and Elaine Godfrey, "The Closed-Door Impeachment," *Atlantic*, October 19, 2019, https://www.theatlantic.com/politics/archive/2019/10/closed-door-impeachment/600355/ (accessed 06/22/20).

485. John F. Manning and Matthew C. Stephenson, *Legislation and Regulation: Cases and Materials* (3rd: Foundation Press, 2017), 179-232.

486. Sabato, *A More Perfect Constitution*, 216.

487. For competing considerations in creating a particular supermajority rule, see Stephan Michael and Ignacio N. Cofone, "Majority Rules in Constitutional Referendums," *Kyklos: International Review for Social Scientists* 70, no. 3 (2017).

488. Ibid.

489. For the ratification strategies of the Federalists and Anti-Federalists, see Maier, *Ratification*. For Madison's view as applied to Virginia's ratification, see JM to Thomas Jefferson, December 9, 1787, Founders Online, http://founders.archives.gov.

Chapter Eight

490. Van Cleve, *We Have Not a Government*, 245-90. The political transformation is traced in the leading work by Wilentz, *The Rise of American Democracy*.

491. Van Cleve, *We Have Not A Government*, 295 (Henry and Lee quotes).

492. TJ to JM, December 20, 1787, in National Archives and Records Administration, Founders Online, http://founders.archives.gov (hereafter "FO").

493. See the thoughtful proposals in Levinson, *Our Undemocratic Constitution*; Sabato, *A More Perfect Constitution*; American Academy of Arts and Sciences, *Our Common Purpose: Reinventing American Democracy for the 21st Century* (Cambridge, Mass.: American Academy of Arts and Sciences, 2020); and Griffin, *Broken Trust*, for example.

494. Lawrence Lessig advocates a modest form of grand bargain, which he refers to as "bundling" of reform topics. Under his proposal, states would seek fiscal reform, campaign finance reform, and federalism reform as topics Congress would approve for consideration at an Article V convention. He appears to think that if the states request such a convention, Congress must call it. Lessig, *Republic, Lost*, 275-76, 294-99.

495. Lessig, *They Don't Represent Us*, 247-48.

496. Madison's views were expressed in *Federalist* No. 48. His similar analysis of the problem of religious freedom is found in James Madison to Thomas Jefferson, October 24, 1787, FO.

497. Emily Zackin, *Looking for Rights in all the Wrong Places: Why State Constitutions Contain America's Positive Rights* (Princeton: Princeton University Press, 2013).

498. As of 2015, for example, in five U.S. cities consumers paid as much as 3 1/2 times more for internet service as in five French cities. Allan Holmes and Chris Zubak-Skees (Center for Public Integrity), April 1, 2015 (updated May 28, 2015), "U.S. Internet Users Pay More and Have Fewer Choices than Europeans," https://publicintegrity.org/inequality-poverty-opportunity/u-s-internet-users-pay-more-and-have-fewer-choices-than-europeans/.

499. For a "neo-Brandeisian" critique of some current antitrust policies, see Tim Wu, *The Curse of Bigness: Antitrust in the New Gilded Age* (New York: Columbia Global Reports, 2018).

500. For the complex free speech issues raised by digital technology, see Jack M. Balkin, "Free Speech is a Triangle," *Columbia Law Review* 118, no. 7 (2018): 2011. For a discussion of some of the other significant issues raised by digital platforms, see Jack M. Balkin and Jonathan Zittrain, "A Grand Bargain to Make Tech Companies Trustworthy," *Atlantic*, October 3, 2016.

501. Other writers have different concerns about Congress' structure, or in some cases even doubt that it can be reformed successfully. See Levinson,

Our Undemocratic Constitution, 29-38 (bicameralism problems); and particularly William G. Howell and Terry M. Moe, *Relic: How Our Constitution Undermines Effective Government, and Why We Need a More Powerful Presidency* (New York: Basic Books, 2016), arguing that Congress is broken beyond repair and the president should be given added power over legislation.

502. Article V provides in part that "no State, without its consent, shall be deprived of its equal Suffrage in the Senate."

503. Larry Sabato proposes a more modest but substantial restructuring of the Senate. Sabato, *A More Perfect Constitution,* 225.

504. American Academy of Arts and Sciences, *Our Common Purpose: Reinventing American Democracy for the 21st Century* , Recommendation 1.1.

505. Larry Sabato advocates 3 year House terms. Sabato, *A More Perfect Constitution,* 93-97.

506. A review of past failed campaign reform efforts is Fred Wertheimer, "The Legacy of 'Citizens United' Has Been Destructive. We Need Campaign Finance Reform," Washington Post, January 20, 2020, https://www.washingtonpost.com/opinions/the-legacy-of-citizens-united-has-been-destructive-we-need-campaign-finance-reform/2020/01/20/1fc3a570-3973-11ea-bf30-ad313e4ec754_story.html.

507. https://www.politico.com/news/2020/06/26/fec-caroline-hunter-resigns-341396 (accessed 07/02/20).

508. American Academy of Arts and Sciences, *Our Common Purpose: Reinventing American Democracy for the 21st Century*, recommendations 1.2-1.3, at 25-28.

509. For background see Arend Lijphart, *Patterns of Democracy: Government Forms and Performance in Thirty-Six Countries* (2nd; New Haven: Yale University Press, 2012); and Norris, "Choosing Electoral Systems."

510. Graber, "Belling the Partisan Cats," 611-16, passim.

511. AAAS, *Our Common Purpose,* recommendation 1.4, at 28-29 (advocates state-by-state reform).

512. Sabato, *A More Perfect Constitution,* 33-35.

513. Ibid., 35. Justice Kagan dissenting in *Rucho,* slip opn. at 139 S. Ct. 2484, 2523-25.

514. Lessig, *They Don't Represent Us,* 13.

515. AAAS, *Our Common Purpose,* recommendation 2.7, at 41-42.

516. Larry Diamond, "Will America Remain a Democracy in 2020?," *The American Interest* 15 No. 6, April 24, 2020.

517. For the history of these devices, see Griffin, *Broken Trust,* 101-122. On redistricting reform, ibid. 103-04, 138.

518. Ibid., 138. Griffin recommends deliberative polling and referendum mechanisms with limited powers. Ibid., 149-56.

519. Kaare Strom, Wolfgang Muller, and Torbjo Bergman, *Delegation and Accountability in Parliamentary Democracies* (Oxford: Oxford University Press, 2004), 4.

520. Ibid., 13-18 provides a helpful literature review.

521. Lijphart, *Patterns of Democracy* is the most prominent proponent of "consensus" governments based primarily on parliamentary systems using proportional representation, as opposed to "majoritarian" presidential governments. A recent contribution to the debate is Amal Ahmed, *Democracy and the Politics of Electoral System Choice: Engineering Electoral Dominance* (Cambridge, UK: Cambridge University Press, 2012).

522. For discussion, see James Pfiffner, "White House Staff Versus the Cabinet: Centripetal and Centrifugal Roles" *Presidential Studies Quarterly* 16, no. 4 (1986): 666; and ———, "Cabinet Secretaries vs. the White House Staff," *Fixgov* (Brookings blog), March 24, 2015 https://www.brookings.edu/blog/fixgov/2015/03/24/cabinet-secretaries-versus-the-white-house-staff/. For a review of the cabinet role, see Elizabeth D. Brown and John D. Graham, *Leading the Executive Branch: Strategies and Options for Achieving Success*, Occasional Paper (Santa Monica: Rand Corporation, 2007).

523. Rob Salmond, "Parliamentary Question Times: How Legislative Accountability Mechanisms Affect Mass Political Engagement," *The Journal of Legislative Studies* 20, no. 3 (2014): 321 analyzes parliamentary question time and popular mobilization.

524. Administrative Procedure Act, 5 U.S.C. §§551 et. seq.

525. Term limits: Sabato, *A More Perfect Constitution,* 40-53.

526. Sabato proposes increasing the size of both the House and Senate. Ibid., 23-32, 37-40.

527. See Levinson, *Our Undemocratic Constitution*, 123-39; *Our Common Purpose*, Recommendation 1.8, 33; Calabresi and Lindgren, "Term Limits."

528. Tushnet, "Abolishing Judicial Review," 581. For a searching examination of the pros and cons of different methods of Supreme Court reform, see Ryan D. Doerfler and Samuel Moyn, "Democratizing the Supreme Court," July 29, 2020, https://papers.ssrn.com/sol3/papers.cfm?abstract_id=3665032 (*California Law Review*, forthcoming).

529. Delaney, "Searching for constitutional meaning."

530. Coates, "The Case for Reparations"; Rashawn Ray and Andre M. Perry, *Why we need reparations for Black Americans* (Washington, DC: Brookings Institution, 2020).

531. Greve, *The Upside-Down Constitution*, 45.

532. Thomas Jefferson to John Taylor, June 4, 1798, FO.

533. *New State Ice Co. v. Liebmann*, 285 U.S. 262 (1932), 280 (Brandeis, J., dissenting).

534. This would effectively reverse part of the decision in *NFIB v. Sebelius*, 567 U.S. 519 (2012).

535. It would be appropriate to consider European countries' experiences in thinking about possible new rights.

536. Levinson, *Our Undemocratic Constitution*, 21.

Conclusion

537. Roy P. Basler, Marion Dolores Pratt, and Lloyd A. Dunlap, eds., *The Collected Works of Abraham Lincoln* (New Brunswick, N.J.: Rutgers University Press, 1953), 3: 375-76.

538. Ibid.

539. John Ferling, *A Leap in the Dark: The Struggle to Create the American Republic* (Oxford: Oxford University Press, 2003).

540. David C. Hendrickson, *Peace Pact: The Lost World of the American Founding* (Lawrence: University Press of Kansas, 2003).

Bibliography

Abdul-Razzak, Nour, Carlo Prato, and Stephane Wolton. "After Citizens United: How Outside Spending Shapes American Democracy." *SSRN Electronic Journal* (Mar. 2019). doi:10.2139/ssrn.2823778.

Ahmed, Amal. *Democracy and the Politics of Electoral System Choice: Engineering Electoral Dominance.* Cambridge, UK: Cambridge University Press, 2012.

Alberta, Tim "When Impeachment Meets a Broken Congress." *Politico Magazine.* Published electronically September 27, 2019. https://www.politico.com/magazine/story/2019/09/27/impeachment-trump-congress-house-228346.

Alvaredo, Facundo, Bertrand Garbinti, and Thomas Piketty. "On the Share of Inheritance in Aggregate Wealth: Europe and the USA, 1900-2010." *Economica* 84 (2017): 239-60.

Amar, Akhil Reed. "An Accident Waiting to Happen." In *Constitutional Stupidities, Constitutional Tragedies*, edited by William N. Eskridge Jr. and Sanford Levinson, 15-17. New York: New York University Press, 1998.

———. *America's Unwritten Constitution: The Precedents and Principles We Live By.* New York: Basic Books, 2012.

———. "The Consent of the Governed: Constitutional Amendment Outside Article V." *Columbia Law Review* 94 (1994): 457-508.

———. "Popular Sovereignty and Constitutional Amendment." In *Responding to Imperfection: The Theory and Practice of Constitutional Amendment*, edited by Sanford Levinson, 89-115. Princeton: Princeton Univ. Press, 1995.

American Academy of Arts and Sciences. *Our Common Purpose: Reinventing American Democracy for the 21st Century.* Cambridge, MA: American Academy of Arts and Sciences, 2020.

Austin, Benjamin, Edward Glaeser, and Lawrence Summers. "Jobs for the Heartland: Place-Based Politics in 21st Century America." *Brookings Papers on Economic Activity* (Spring 2018): 151-232.

Austin v. Mich. Chamber of Commerce, 494 U.S. 652 (1990).

Balkin, Jack M. "Free Speech Is a Triangle." *Columbia Law Review* 118, no. 7 (November, 2018) : 2011-56.

———. *Living Originalism.* Cambridge, MA: Harvard University Press, 2011.

Balkin, Jack M., and Jonathan Zittrain. "A Grand Bargain to Make Tech Companies Trustworthy." *Atlantic*, October 3, 2016.

Basler, Roy P., Marion Dolores Pratt, and Lloyd A. Dunlap, eds. *The Collected Works of Abraham Lincoln.* New Brunswick: Rutgers University Press, 1953.

Batty, Michael, Jesse Bricker, Joseph Briggs, Elizabeth Holmquist, and Susan McIntosh. *Introducing the Distributional Financial Accounts of the United States*. Washington, DC: Board of Governors of the Federal Reserve System, 2019.

Beeman, Richard. *Plain, Honest Men: The Making of the American Constitution*. New York: Random House 2009.

Berman, Russell. "Justice Ginsburg Versus the Equal Rights Amendment." *Atlantic*, February 15, 2020.

Beveridge, Albert J. *The Life of John Marshall*. 4 vols. Cambridge, MA: Houghton Mifflin Company, 1919.

Black Jr., Charles L. "Amending the Constitution: A Letter to a Congressman." *Yale Law Journal* 82, no. 2 (1972): 189-215.

Bland, Scott, and Maggie Severns. "Documents Reveal Massive 'Dark-Money' Group Boosted Democrats in 2018." *Politico Magazine*. Published electronically November 19, 2019. https://www.politico.com/news/2019/11/19/dark-money-democrats-midterm-071725.

Bonica, Adam, Nolan McCarty, Keith T. Poole, and Howard Rosenthal. "Why Hasn't Democracy Slowed Rising Inequality?" *Journal of Economic Perspectives* 27, no. 3 (2013): 103-24.

Boyd, Julian P., Lyman H. Butterfield, and Mina R. Bryan, eds. *The Papers of Thomas Jefferson*. 52 vols. Vol. 1. Princeton: Princeton Univerity Press, 1950.

Bradley, Curtis A., and Neil S. Siegel. "Historical Gloss, Constitutional Conventions, and the Judicial Separation of Powers." *Georgetown Law Journal* 105 (2017): 255-322.

Breyer, Stephen. *Making Democracy Work: A Judge's View*. New York: Knopf, 2010.

Bricker, Jesse et al., "Changes in U.S. Family Finances from 2013 to 2016: Evidence from the Survey of Consumer Finances," *Federal Reserve Bulletin*, September, 2017.

Brown, Elizabeth D., and John D. Graham. *Leading the Executive Branch: Strategies and Options for Achieving Success*. Santa Monica: Rand Corporation, 2007.

Brownstein, Ronald. "Small States are Getting a Much Bigger Say in Who Gets on the Supreme Court," *CNN*, July 10, 2018.

Brownstein, Ronald. "This Is Why Congress Remains Deadlocked on Climate and Guns." *CNN*. Published electronically September 3, 2019. https://www.cnn.com/2019/09/03/politics/guns-climate-senate-standoff-smaller-states/index.html.

Buckley v. Valeo, 424 U.S. 1 (1976).

Burke, Edmund. "Speech to the Electors of Bristol, 3 November, 1774. In Philip B. Kurland and Ralph Lerner, eds., *The Founders' Constitution* (Chicago: University of Chicago Press, 2000), vol. 1.

Bush et al. v. Gore et al., 531 U.S. 98 (2000).

Butterfield, Lyman H., ed. *Diary and Autobiography of John Adams*. 4 vols. Vol. 2. Cambridge: Harvard University Press, 1962.

Calabresi, Stephen, and James Lindgren. "Term Limits for the Supreme Court: Life Tenure Reconsidered." *Harv. Jnl. Law & Pub. Policy* 29 (2006): 769-877.

California Democratic Party v. Jones, 530 U.S. 567 (2000).

Caperton et al. v. A.T. Massey Coal Co. Inc. et al., 556 U.S. 868 (2009).

Carnes, Nicholas. *The Cash Ceiling: Why Only the Rich Run for Office—and What We Can Do About It*. Princeton: Princeton Univ. Press, 2018.

Cassidy, John. "Is America an Oligarchy?" *New Yorker*, April 18, 2014.

Center for Responsive Politics. "2016 Outside Spending by Group." Washington, DC: Center for Responsive Politics.

Chemerinsky, Erwin. "*Bush v. Gore* Was Not Justiciable." *Notre Dame Law Review* 76, no. 4 (2001): 1-21.

Chetty, Raj, David Grusky, Maximilian Hell Hell, Nathaniel Hendren, Robert Manduca, and Jimmy Narang. "The Fading American Dream: Trends in Absolute Income Mobility since 1940." Washington, DC: NBER, 2016.

Chetty, Raj, Nathaniel Hendren, Patrick Kline, Emmanuel Saez, and Nicholas Turner. "Is the United States Still a Land of Opportunity? Recent Trends in Intergenerational Mobility." Washington, DC: NBER, 2014.

Chiafolo et al. v. Washington, U.S. Supreme Court, No. 19-465 (July 6, 2020).

Citizens United v. FEC, 558 U.S. 310 (2010).

Clayton, Cornell, and J. Mitchell Pickerill. "Guess What Happened on the Way to Revolution? Precursors to the Supreme Court's Federalism Revolution." *Publius: The Journal of Federalism* 34, no. 3 (Summer 2004): 85-114.

Clinton v. City of New York, 524 U.S. 417 (1998).

Coates, Ta-Nehisi. "The Case for Reparations." *Atlantic* (June 2014): 54-71.

Condray, Patrick M., and Timothy J. Conlan. "Article V Conventions and American Federalism: Contemporary Politics in Historical Perspective." *Publius: The Journal of Federalism* 49, no. 3 (2019): 515-39.

Corbett, Jessica. "Over 120 Groups Call on Congress to Back Constitutional Amendment Overturning Citizens United." Published electronically September 5, 2019. https://www.commondreams.org/news/2019/09/05/over-120-groups-call-congress-back-constitutional-amendment-overturning-citizens.

Costa, Dora L. "Health and Economy in the United States from 1750 to the Present." *Journal of Economic Literature* 53, no. 3 (Sep. 2015): 503-70.

Crawford, Neta C. "United States Budgetary Costs of the Post-9/11 Wars through Fy 2019: $5.9 Trillion Spent and Obligated." Providence: Watson Institute, Brown University, 2018.

Cushman, Barry. "Court-Packing and Compromise," 29 *Constitutional Commentary* (2013): 1-30.

Dahl, Robert. *How Democratic Is the American Constitution?* 2nd ed. ed. New Haven: Yale University Press, 2003.

Davidson, Roger H., Walter J. Oleszek, Frances E. Lee, and Eric Schickler. *Congress and Its Members.* 14th ed. Washington, DC: CQ Press, 2013.

Delaney, Erin. "Searching for Constitutional Meaning in Institutional Design: The Debate over Judicial Appointments in the United Kingdom." *International Journal of Constitutional Law* 14, no. 3 (2016): 752-68.

Dellinger, Walter E. "The Recurring Question of a 'Limited' Constitutional Convention." *Yale Law Journal* 88, no. 8 (1979): 1623-40.

Desoto, Karen. "Is It Time for a U.S. Article V Constitutional Convention? A Brief Discussion About American Constitutional Reform Procedure." *Revista de Investigações Constitucionais*, 5 no. 1 (2018): 249-60.

Diamond, Larry. "Will America Remain a Democracy in 2020?" *The American Interest*, April 24, 2020.

Diermeier, Daniel, Michael Keane, and Antonio Merlo. "A Political Economy Model of Congressional Careers." *American Economic Review* 95, no. 1 (2005): 347-73.

Dincer, Oguzhan, and Michael Johnston. "Measuring Illegal and Legal Corruption in American States: Some Results from the Corruption in America Survey." Safra Center on Ethics Blog, Harvard University, December 1, 2014, https://ethics.harvard.edu/blog/measuring-illegal-and-legal-corruption-american-states-some-results-safra (accessed 07/22/20).

Doerfler, Ryan and Moyn, Samuel. "Democratizing the Supreme Court." (July 29, 2020). *California Law Review*, Forthcoming, Available at SSRN: https://ssrn.com/abstract=3665032.

Dow, David R. "The Plain Meaning of Article V." In *Responding to Imperfection: The Theory and Practice of Constitutional Amendment*, edited by Sanford Levinson, 117-44. Princeton: Princeton Univ. Press, 1995.

Dred Scott v. Sandford, 60 U.S. (19 How.) 393 (1857).

Eaves, Carrie. "Running in Someone Else's Shoes: The Electoral Consequences of Running as an Appointed Senator." *Soc. Sci. 2018* 7 (May 3, 2018): 75.

Economist Briefing. "America's electoral system gives the Republicans advantages over Democrats," July 14, 2018, 21-25.

Economist Leader (editorial). "Squeezing the rich: In defence of billionaires." *Economist*, November 9, 2019, 10-12.

Economist, "The lives of the 0.0001%." November 9, 2019, 64-68.

Edwards III, George C. *Why the Electoral College Is Bad for America.* New Haven: Yale University Press, 2004.

Edwards, Ryan D. "U.S. War Costs: Two Parts Temporary, One Part Permanent." *Journal of Public Economics* 113 (May 2014): 54-66.

Eisner v. Macomber, 232 U.S. 189 (1920).

Elster, Jon. "Arguing and Bargaining in Two Constituent Assemblies." *Journal of Constitutional Law* 2, no. 2 (Mar. 2000): 345-421.

———. "Constitutional Bootstrapping in Philadelphia and Paris." *Cardozo Law Review* 14, no. 3 & 4 (1992/Jan. 1993): 549-75.

Farrand, Max, ed. *The Records of the Federal Convention of 1787*. 4 vols. Vol. 1. New Haven: Yale University Press, 1966.

Fatovic, Clement. *America's Founding and the Struggle over Economic Inequality*. Lawrence: University Press of Kansas, 2015.

Feldman, Noah. "Wealth Tax's Legality Depends on What 'Direct' Means." *Bloomberg Opinion* (2019). Published electronically January 30, 2019. https://www.bloomberg.com/opinion/articles/2019-01-30/elizabeth-warren-s-wealth-tax-is-probably-constitutional.

Ferling, John. *Adams vs. Jefferson: The Tumultuous Election of 1800*. Oxford: Oxford University Press, 2004.

———. *A Leap in the Dark: The Struggle to Create the American Republic*. Oxford: Oxford University Press, 2003.

Fleiner, Thomas. "Participation of Citizens in Constitution-Making: Assets and Challenges – the Swiss Experience." Chap. 4 In *Participatory Constitutional Change : The People as Amenders of the Constitution,*, edited by Xenophon Contiades and Alkmene Fotiadou, 67-81. Milton Park, UK: Taylor & Francis Group, 2016.

Fontana, David, and Aziz Z. Huq. "Institutional Loyalties in Constitutional Law." *The University of Chicago Law Review* 85, no. 1 (2018): 1-84.

Ford, Paul Leicester. "The Adoption of the Pennsylvania Constitution of 1776." *Political Science Quarterly* X, no. 3 (1895): 426-59.

Friedman, John N., and Richard T. Holden. "The Rising Incumbent Reelection Rate: What's Gerrymandering Got to Do with It?" *Journal of Politics* 71, no. 2 (2009): 593-611.

Genovese, Michael A., and Iwan W. Morgan, eds. *Watergate Remembered: The Legacy for American Politics*. New York: Palgrave Macmillan, 2012.

Geruso, Michael, Dean Spears, and Ishaana Talesara. "Inversions in U.S. Presidential Elections: 1836-2016." Washington, DC: NBER, 2019.

Gilens, Martin. *Affluence and Influence: Economic Inequality and Political Power in America*. Princeton: Princeton Univ. Press, 2014.

Gilens, Martin, and Benjamin Page. "Testing Theories of American Politics: Elites, Interest Groups, and Average Citizens." *Perspectives on Politics* 12, no. 3 (2014): 564-81.

Glanton, Dahleen. "Growing up with Poverty and Violence: A North Lawndale Teen's Story." *Chicago Tribune*, March 10, 2017.

Goldin, Claudia, and Frank D. Lewis. "The Economic Cost of the American Civil War: Estimates and Implications." *Journal of Economic History* 35, no. 2 (1975): 299-326.

Gordon-Reed, Annette. "America's Original Sin: Slavery and the Legacy of White Supremacy." *Foreign Affairs* 97, no. 1 (January/February 2018): 2-7.

Gordon, Tracy, Richard Auxier, and John Iselin. *Assessing Fiscal Capacities of States: A Representative Revenue System—Representative Expenditure System Approach, Fiscal Year 2012*. Washington, DC: Urban Institute, 2016.

Graber, Mark A. "Belling the Partisan Cats: Preliminary Thoughts on Identifying and Mending a Dysfunctional Constitutional Order." *Boston University Law Review* 94 (2014): 611-47.

Greve, Michael S. *The Upside-Down Constitution*. Cambridge: Harvard Univ. Press, 2012.

Griffin, Stephen M. *Broken Trust: Dysfunctional Government and Constitutional Reform*. Lawrence: University Press of Kansas, 2015.

Groseclose, Tim, and Jeff Milyo. "Buying the Bums Out: What's the Dollar Value of a Seat in Congress?" Research Paper No. 1601. Stanford, CA: Stanford University, Graduate School of Business, 1999.

Gundy v. United States, 139 S. Ct. 2116 (2019).

Gylfason, Thorvaldur. "Iceland's Ongoing Constitutional Fight." *verfassungsblog.de on matters constitutional* (2018). Published electronically November 29, 2018. https://verfassungsblog.de/icelands-ongoing-constitutional-fight/

Hacker, J. David. "Decennial Life Tables for the White Population of the United States, 1790-1900." *Historical Methods* 43, no. 2 (2010): 45-79.

Hacker, Jacob S., and Paul Pierson. *Winner-Take-All Politics: How Washington Made the Rich Richer—and Turned Its Back on the Middle Class*. New York: Simon & Schuster, 2010.

Hanauer, Nick. "Education Isn't Enough." *Atlantic* (July, 2019), 19-22.

Helvering v. Davis, 301 U.S. 619 (1937).

Hendrickson, David C. *Peace Pact: The Lost World of the American Founding*. Lawrence: University Press of Kansas, 2003.

Hofstadter, Richard. *The American Political Tradition & the Men Who Made It*. New York: Vintage Books, 1974.

Howell, William G. "The Future of the War Presidency: The Case of the War Powers Consultation Act." In *The Presidency in the Twenty-First Century*, edited by Charles W. Dunn, 83-100. Lexington: Univ. Press of Kentucky, 2011.

Howell, William G., and Terry M. Moe. *Relic: How Our Constitution Undermines Effective Government, and Why We Need a More Powerful Presidency*. New York: Basic Books, 2016.

Hudson, Alexander. "Will Iceland Get a New Constitution? A New Revision Process Is Taking Shape." *Int'l J. Const. L. Blog* (2018). Published electronically October 23, 2018. http://www.iconnectblog.com/2018/10/will-iceland-get-a-new-constitution-a-new-revision-process-is-taking-shape/.

Hylton v. U.S., 3 Dallas 171 (1796).

INS v. Chadha, 462 U.S. 919 (1983).

Jacobson, Gary C. "It's Nothing Personal: The Decline of the Incumbency Advantage in Us House Elections." *The Journal of Politics* 77, no. 3 (2015): 861-73.

Jensen, Erik M. "The Taxing Power, the Sixteenth Amendment, and the Meaning of 'Incomes'." *Arizona State Law Journal* 33, no. 4 (2001): 1057-1158.

Jensen, Merrill. *The New Nation: A History of the United States During the Confederation, 1781-1789*. New York: Vintage Books, 1950.

Johnsen, Dawn, and Walter Dellinger. "The Constitutionality of a National Wealth Tax." *Indiana Law Journal* 93 (2018): 111-37.

Josi, Claudia. "Direct Democracy vs Fundamental Rights? A Comparative Analysis of the Mechanisms That Limit the 'Will of the People' in Switzerland and California." Chap. 5 in *Participatory Constitutional Change : The People as Amenders of the Constitution,* edited by Xenophon Contiades and Alkmene Fotiadou, 82-99. Milton Park, UK: Taylor & Francis Group, 2016.

Juan C. Palomino, Juan C., Gustavo A. Marrero, and Juan Gabriel Rodríguez. "Intergenerational Mobility in the U.S.: One Size Doesn't Fit All." Published electronically January 3, 2019. https://voxeu.org/article/intergenerational-mobility-us.

Kahlenberg, Richard D., and Kimberly Quick. *Attacking the Black-White Opportunity Gap That Comes from Residential Segregation.* New York: The Century Foundation, 2019.

Kantrow, Louise. "Life Expectancy of the Gentry in Eighteenth and Nineteenth-Century Philadelphia." *Proceedings of the American Philosophical Society* 133, no. 2 (Jun. 1989): 312-27.

Katz, Andrew. "Congress Is Now Mostly a Millionaires' Club." *Time,* January 9, 2014.

Kauper, Paul G. "The Alternative Amendment Process: Some Observations." *Michigan Law Review* 66, no. 5 (1968): 905-20.

Kennedy, David M. . *Freedom from Fear: The American People in Depression and War, 1929-1945.* Oxford: Oxford Univ. Press, 1999.

Kennedy, Paul. *The Rise and Fall of Great Powers: Economic Change and Military Power from 1500 to 2000.* New York: Penguin Random House LLC, 1987.

Keyssar, Alexander. *The Right to Vote: The Contested History of Democracy in the United States.* rev. ed. New York: Basic Books, 2009.

Kleiner, Sarah. "Democrats Say 'Citizens United' Should Die. Here's Why That Won't Happen." *Public Integrity Blog.* Published electronically August 31, 2017 (rev. September 5). https://publicintegrity.org/politics/democrats-say-citizens-united-should-die-heres-why-that-wont-happen/.

Kolstad, Charles D. *What Is Killing the U.S. Coal Industry?.* Palo Alto: Stanford Institute for Energy Policy Research, 2017.

Koza, Dr. John. "Myths About Interstate Compacts and Congressional Consent." (2019). https://www.nationalpopularvote.com/.

Kramer, Larry D. *The People Themselves: Popular Constitutionalism and Judicial Review.* Oxford: Oxford University Press, 2004.

Krugman, Paul. "Regional Economics: Understanding the Third Great Transition." (2019). https://www.gc.cuny.edu/CUNY_GC/media/LISCenter/pkrugman/REGIONAL-ECONOMICS-3rd-transition.pdf.

Kurland, Philip B. and Ralph Lerner, eds. *The Founders' Constitution* (Chicago: University of Chicago Press, 2000). http://press-pubs.uchicago.edu/founders/.

Lee, Frances E., and Bruce I. Oppenheim. *Sizing up the Senate: The Unequal Consequences of Equal Representation.* Chicago: University of Chicago Press, 1999.

Lee, Frances, and Nolan McCarty, eds. *Can America Govern Itself?* Cambridge: Cambridge Univ. Press, 2019.

Lee, Michelle Ye Hee. "Wealthy Donors Now Allowed to Give over Half a Million Dollars Each to Support Trump's Reelection." *Washington Post*, January 15, 2020.

Lessig, Lawrence. *Republic, Lost: The Corruption of Equality and the Steps to End It.* Revised ed. New York: Twelve: Hachette Book Group, 2016. 2011.

———. *They Don't Represent Us: Reclaiming Our Democracy.* New York: Dey Street Books, 2019.

Levin, Yuval. "Congress Is Weak Because Its Members Want It to Be Weak." *Commentary* (July/August 2018), 15-20.

Levinson, Arik. "America's Regressive Middle-Class Wealth Tax." *The Hill.* Published electronically November 20, 2019. https://thehill.com/opinion/finance/471313-americas-regressive-middle-class-wealth-tax.

Levinson, Sanford. *Our Undemocratic Constitution: Where the Constitution Goes Wrong (and How We the People Can Correct It).* Oxford: Oxford Univ. Press, 2006.

Lijphart, Arend. *Patterns of Democracy: Government Forms and Performance in Thirty-Six Countries.* 2nd ed. New Haven: Yale University Press, 2012.

Livingston, Gretchen. "The Changing Profile of Unmarried Parents." Pew Research Center, April 25, 2018, https://www.pewsocialtrends.org/2018/04/25/the-changing-profile-of-unmarried-parents/.

Logan, John R., and Brian Stults. *The Persistence of Segregation in Metropolitan Areas: New Findings from the 2010 Census.* Census Brief prepared for Project US2010. http://www.s4.brown.edu/us2010.

Longley, Lawrence D., and Alan G. Braun. *The Politics of Electoral College Reform.* 2d ed. New Haven: Yale University Press, 1975.

Longley, Lawrence D., and Neal R. Pierce. *The Electoral College Primer.* New Haven: Yale Univ. Press, 1996.

Maier, Pauline. *Ratification: The People Debate the Constitution, 1787-88.* New York: Simon & Schuster, 2010.

Mann, Bruce. *Republic of Debtors: Bankruptcy in the Age of Independence.* Cambridge, MA: Harvard Univ. Press, 2002.

Mann, Thomas E., and Norman J. Ornstein. *It's Even Worse Than It Looks: How the American Constitutional System Collided with the New Politics of Extremism.* New York: Basic Books, 2012.

Manning, John F., and Matthew C. Stephenson. *Legislation and Regulation: Cases and Materials.* 3rd ed. New York: Foundation Press, 2017.

Marcus, Maeva, ed. *The Documentary History of the Supreme Court of the United States* Vol. 7. New York: Columbia University Press, 2004.

Marr, Chuck, Samantha Jacoby, and Kathleen Bryant. *Substantial Income of Wealthy Households Escapes Taxation or Enjoys Special Tax Breaks: Reform Is Needed.* Washington, DC: Center on Budget and Policy Priorities, 2019.

McCarty, Nolan. "Polarization and the Changing American Constitutional System." In *Can America Govern Itself?*, edited by Frances Lee and Nolan McCarty, 301-28. Cambridge, UK: Cambridge Univ. Press, 2019.

McCutcheon v. FEC, 572 U.S. 185 (2014).

Mckenna, Marian C. *Franklin Roosevelt and the Great Constitutional War: The Court-Packing Crisis of 1937.* New York: Fordham Univ. Press, 2002.

Mehotra, Ajay K. *Making the Modern American Fiscal State: Law, Politics, and the Rise of Progressive Taxation.* Cambridge, UK: Cambridge Univ. Press, 2013.

Meuwese, Anne. "Popular Constitution Making: The Case of Iceland." Chap. 17 in *Social and Political Foundations of Constitutions*, edited by Denis J. Galligan and Mila Versteeg, 469-96. Cambridge, UK: Cambridge University Press, 2013.

Michael, Stephan, and Ignacio N. Cofone. "Majority Rules in Constitutional Referendums." *Kyklos: International Review for Social Scientists* 70, no. 3 (2017): 402-24.

Morris, Adele C. *Build a Better Future for Coal Industry Workers and Their Communities.* Washington, DC: Brookings Institution, 2016.

Morrissey, Monique. "Private-sector pension coverage fell by half over two decades." Economic Policy Institute, *Working Economics Blog*, January 11, 2013.

Mortenson, Julien Davis. "Article II Vests the Executive Power, Not the Royal Prerogative." *Columbia Law Review* 119, no. 5 (2019): 1169-1272.

Mueller III, Robert S. et al., *Report on the Investigation Into Russian Interference in the 2016 Presidential Election* (2 vols.)(Washington, DC, GPO, Mar. 2019).

NAACP v. Alabama ex rel. Patterson, 357 U.S. 449 (1958).

National Organization for Women, Inc. et al. v. Idaho et al.; and *Carmen, Administrator of General Services v. Idaho et al.*, 459 U.S. 809 (1982).

National Womens' Law Center. "National Snapshot: Poverty Among Women & Families, 2016." https://nwlc.org/wp-content/uploads/2017/09/Poverty-Snapshot-Factsheet-2017.pdf.

Neale, Thomas H. *The Article V Convention for Proposing Constitutional Amendments: Historical Perspectives for Congress.* Rept. 42592. Washington, DC: Library of Congress (Congressional Research Service), 2012.

———. *The Article V Convention for Proposing Constitutional Amendments: Contemporary Issues for Congress.* Rept. 42589. Washington, DC: Library of Congress (Congressional Research Service), 2016.

———. *NPV—The National Popular Vote Initiative: Proposing Direct Election of the President through an Interstate Compact.* IF 11191. Washington, DC: Library of Congress (Congressional Research Service), 2019.

————. *The Proposed Equal Rights Amendment: Contemporary Ratification Issues.* Rept. 42979. Washington, DC: Library of Congress (Congressional Research Service), 2018.

Neale, Thomas H., and Andrew Nolan. *The National Popular Vote (Npv) Initiative: Direct Election of the President by Interstate Compact.* Rept. 43823. Washington, DC: Library of Congress (Congressional Research Service), 2018 (updated May 9, 2019).

Nelson, William D. "The Freedom of Business Association." *Columbia Law Review* 115, no. 2 (2015): 461-513.

New State Ice Co. v. Liebmann, 285 U.S. 262 (1932).

New York State Bd. Of Elections v. Lopez Torres 128 S. Ct. 791 (2008).

NFIB v. Sebelius, 567 U.S. 519 (2012).

Norris, Pippa. "Choosing Electoral Systems: Proportional, Majoritarian, and Mixed Systems." *International Political Science Review* 18, no. 3 (1997): 297-312.

Obama, President Barack. "Address before a Joint Session of the Congress on the State of the Union." In *Public Papers of the Presidents: Barack Obama,* 1: 75-85. Washington, DC: Government Printing Office, 2010.

Ornstein, Norman J., and Thomas E. Mann. *The Broken Branch: How Congress Is Failing America and How to Get It Back on Track.* Oxford: Oxford Univ. Press, 2006.

Paine, Thomas. *The Rights of Man: In Two Parts: Being an Answer to Mr. Burke's Attack on the French Revolution* 1877 ed. New York: D.M. Bennett, 1877 (orig. 1791).

Parks, Miles. "Abolishing the Electoral College Would Be More Complicated Than It May Seem." *NPR* (2019). Published electronically March 22, 2019. https://www.npr.org/2019/03/22/705627996/abolishing-the-electoral-college-would-be-more-complicated-than-it-may-seem.

Partlett, William. "The Dangers of Popular Constitution-Making." *Brooklyn Journal of International Law* 38, no. 1 (2012): 1-47.

Pecanha, Sergio. "These Numbers Show That Black and White People Live in Two Different Americas." *Washington Post,* June 22, 2020.

Pew Research Center. "The American Middle Class Is Losing Ground." Washington, DC: Pew Charitable Trusts, 2015.

Pfiffner, James. "White House Staff Versus the Cabinet: Centripetal and Centrifugal Roles." *Presidential Studies Quarterly* 16, no. 4 (Fall 1986): 666-90.

Pika, Joseph A., and John Anthony Maltese. *The Politics of the Presidency.* 6th ed. Washington, DC: CQ Press, 2004.

Pole, J.R., ed. *The Federalist.* Indianapolis: Hackett Publishing Company, 2005.

Pole, J.R. *Political Representation in England and the Origins of the American Republic.* 1966 ed. Berkeley: University of California Press, pbk 1971.

Pollock v. Farmers' Loan and Trust Co., 157 U.S. 429 (1895).

Pulignano, Vincent. "A Known Unknown: The Call for an Article V Convention." *Florida Law Review Forum* 67 (2016): 151-60. http://www.floridalawreview.com/wp-content/uploads/Pulignano.pdf.

Quart, Alissa. *Squeezed: Why Our Families Can't Afford America.* New York: Harper Collins, 2018.

Rappaport, Michael B. "The Constitutionality of a Limited Convention: An Originalist Analysis." *Constitutional Commentary* 28, no. 1 (Spring 2012): 53-109.

Ray, Rashawn, and Andre M. Perry. "Why We Need Reparations for Black Americans." Washington, DC: Brookings Institution, 2020.

Reardon, Sean F. and Ann Owens, "60 Years After Brown: Trends and Consequences of School Segregation," *Annual Review Sociol.* 40 (2014): 199–218.

Reich, Robert B. *The System: Who Rigged It, How We Fix It.* New York: Alfred A. Knopf, 2020.

Rothwell, Jonathan. "The Declining Productivity of Education." *Brookings Blog.* Washington, DC: Brookings Institute (December 23, 2016).

Rucho et al. v. Common Cause et al., 139 S. Ct. 2484 (2019).

Rudalevige, Andrew. "The Contemporary Presidency: The Decline and Resurgence and Decline (and Resurgence?) of Congress." *Presidential Studies Quarterly* 36, no. 3 (2006): 506-24.

———. *The New Imperial Presidency: Renewing Presidential Power after Watergate.* Ann Arbor: Univ. Michigan Press, 2005.

Sabato, Larry J. *A More Perfect Constitution: Why the Constitution Must Be Revised.* New York: Walker Publishing, 2007.

Saez, Emmanuel, and Gabriel Zucman. "Wealth Inequality in the United States since 1913: Evidence from Capitalized Income Tax Data." Washington, DC: NBER, 2014.

Saez, Emmanuel, and Gabriel Zucman. *The Triumph of Injustice: How the Rich Dodge Taxes and How to Make Them Pay.* New York: W.W. Norton, 2019.

Salmond, Rob. "Parliamentary Question Times: How Legislative Accountability Mechanisms Affect Mass Political Engagement." *The Journal of Legislative Studies* 20, no. 3 (2014): 321-41.

Sanchez, Claudio. "English Language Learners: How Your State Is Doing." Published electronically February 23, 2017. https://www.npr.org/sections/ed/2017/02/23/512451228/5-million-english-language-learners-a-vast-pool-of-talent-at-risk.

Sawhill, Isabel V., and Eleanor Krause. "Seven Reasons to Worry About the Middle Class." *Brookings Blog* (2018). Published electronically June 5, 2018. https://www.brookings.edu/blog/social-mobility-memos/2018/06/05/seven-reasons-to-worry-about-the-american-middle-class/.

Sawhill, Isabel V., and Christopher Pulliam. "Six Facts About Wealth in the United States." *Brookings Blog,* June 25, 2019. https://www.brookings.edu/blog/up-front/2019/06/25/six-facts-about-wealth-in-the-united-states/.

Sawhill, Isabel V., and Edward Rodrigue. "Wealth, Inheritance, and Social Mobility." *Brookings Blog* (2015). Published electronically January 30, 2015. https://www.brookings.edu/blog/social-mobility-memos/2015/01/30/wealth-inheritance-and-social-mobility/.

Schlesinger Jr., Arthur M. *The Imperial Presidency*. New York: Houghton Mifflin, 1973.

Seidman, Louis Michael. *On Constitutional Disobedience*. Oxford: Oxford Univ. Press, 2012.

Semuels, Alana. "Segregation Has Gotten Worse, Not Better, and It's Fueling the Wealth Gap between Black and White Americans." *Time*, June 19, 2020.

Sherry, Suzanna. "Democracy Uncaged." *Constitutional Commentary* 25, no. 1 (Spring 2008): 141-55.

Siegel, Reva B. "Constitutional Culture, Social Movement Conflict, and Constitutional Change: The Case of the de facto ERA." *California Law Review* 94, no. 5 (2006): 1323-1420.

Sim, David, and Sam Earle. "50 Richest Members of Congress." *Newsweek*, April 6, 2018.

Sindelar, Paul T., Jim Dewey, Elizabeth Bettini, et al., "Explaining the Decline in Special Education Teacher Employment From 2005 to 2012," *Exceptional Children* 83, no. 3 (2017): 315-329.

Sitaraman, Ganesh. *The Crisis of the Middle-Class Constitution: Why Economic Inequality Threatens Our Republic*. New York: Alfred A. Knopf, 2017.

Skelley, Geoffrey. "Abolishing the Electoral College Used to Be a Bipartisan Position. Not Anymore." Published electronically April 2, 2019. https://fivethirtyeight.com/features/abolishing-the-electoral-college-used-to-be-bipartisan-position-not-anymore/.

Skowronek, Stephen. "Shall We Cast Our Lot with the Constitution? Thinking About Presidential Power in the Twenty-First Century." In *The Presidency in the Twenty-First Century*, edited by Charles W. Dunn, 28-54. Lexington: University Press of Kentucky, 2011.

Skowronek, Stephen, and Karen Orren. "The Adapability Paradox: Constitutional Resilience and Principles of Good Government in Twenty-First Century America." *Perspectives on Politics* 18, no. 2 (June, 2020): 354-69.

Smith, Adam. *An Inquiry into the Nature and Causes of the Wealth of Nations*. Edwin Cannan ed. 1904. 2 vols. Chicago: University of Chicago Press, 1977 repr. ed.

Solum, Lawrence B. "How *NFIB v. Sebelius* Affects the Constitutional Gestalt." *Washington Univ. Law Rev.* 91, no. 1 (2013): 1-58.

Sorkin, Andrew Ross. "Paul Volcker, at 91, Sees 'a Hell of a Mess in Every Direction'." *New York Times*, October 23, 2018.

Stanford Center on Longevity. *Seeing Our Way to Financial Security in the Age of Increased Longevity*. Palo Alto, CA: Stanford University, 2018.

Stebbins, Samuel. "How Much Money Does Your State Receive from the Federal Government? Check out This List." *USA Today*. Published

electronically March 20, 2019.
https://www.usatoday.com/story/money/economy/2019/03/20/how-much-federal-funding-each-state-receives-government/39202299/.

Stockler, Asher. "Nearly Half of All Individual Donations Made to Super Pacs Were Made by 25 Mega-Wealthy Individuals, New Report Says." *Newsweek*, January 15, 2020.

Strom, Kaare, Wolfgang Muller, and Torbjo Bergman. *Delegation and Accountability in Parliamentary Democracies.* Oxford: Oxford University Press, 2004.

Sullivan, Kathleen. "Two Concepts of Freedom of Speech." *Harv. L. Rev.* 124 (2010): 143-77.

Sunstein, Cass. "It Could Be Worse." *New Republic*, October 15, 2006. (Review of Levinson, *Our Undemocratic Constitution*).

Tax Policy Center. "Historical Capital Gains and Taxes." https://www.taxpolicycenter.org/statistics/historical-capital-gains-and-taxes.

———. "T18-0231 - Distribution of Long-Term Capital Gains and Qualified Dividends by Expanded Cash Income Percentile, 2018." https://www.taxpolicycenter.org/model-estimates/distribution-individual-income-tax-long-term-capital-gains-and-qualified-30.

Thorarensen, Bjorg. "Why the Making of a Crowd-Sourced Constitution in Iceland Failed." *The Constitution-Making and Constitutional Change Blog* (2014). Published electronically 2/26/2014. https://constitutional-change.com/why-the-making-of-a-crowd-sourced-constitution-in-iceland-failed/.

Thorpe, Rebecca U. *The American Warfare State: The Domestic Politics of Military Spending.* Chicago: University of Chicago Press, 2014.

Treisman, Rachel "Poll: Number of Americans Who Favor Stricter Gun Laws Continues to Grow." *NPR* (2019). Published electronically October 20, 2019. https://www.npr.org/2019/10/20/771278167/poll-number-of-americans-who-favor-stricter-gun-laws-continues-to-grow.

Tushnet, Mark. "Abolishing Judicial Review." *Constitutional Commentary* 27 (2011): 581-89.

———. "Comparative Constitutional Law." In *Oxford Handbook of Comparative Law*, edited by Mathias Reimann and Reinhard Zimmerman, 1226-57. Oxford: Oxford Univ. Press, 2012.

———. *Taking the Constitution Away from the Courts.* Princeton: Princeton University Press, 1999.

United States Congress, Congressional Budget Office, *The Budget and Economic Outlook: 2019 to 2029* (Washington, DC: Congress of the United States, Jan. 2019).

United States Senate, REPORT OF THE SELECT COMMITTEE ON INTELLIGENCE, UNITED STATES SENATE, ON RUSSIAN ACTIVE MEASURES CAMPAIGNS AND INTERFERENCE IN THE 2016 ELECTION. Volume 4: *Review of the Intelligence Community Assessment with Additional Views* (released 04/21/20).

U.S. Term Limits, Inc. v. Thornton, 514 U.S. 779 (1995).

Van Cleve, George William. "The Anti-Federalists' Toughest Challenge: Paper Money, Debt Relief, and the Ratification of the Constitution." *Journal of the Early Republic* 34, no. 4 (2014): 529-60.

———. *A Slaveholders' Union: Slavery, Politics, and the Constitution in the Early American Republic.* Chicago: Univ. Chicago Press, 2010.

———. *We Have Not a Government: The Articles of Confederation and the Road to the Constitution.* Chicago: University of Chicago Press, 2017.

Weber, Paul J., and Barbara A. Perry. *Unfounded Fears: Myths and Realities of a Constitutional Convention.* New York: Greenwood Press, 1989.

Wells, Tom. *The War Within: America's Battle over Vietnam.* 1st ed. 1994. New York: Open Road Distribution, repr. ed. 2016.

White, Stuart. "Parliaments, Constitutional Conventions, and Popular Sovereignty." *British Journal of Politics and International Relations* 19, no. 2 (2017): 320-35.

Whitehouse, Senator Sheldon, Senator Mazie Hirono, et al., "Brief of Senators Sheldon Whitehouse, Mazie Hirono, Richard Blumenthal, Richard Durbin and Kirsten Gillibrand as Amici Curiae in Support of Respondents." In *New York State Rifle & Pistol Association, Inc.* et al. *v. City of New York , New York et al.* (United States Supreme Court, No. 18-280)." (2019).

Wilentz, Sean. *The Rise of American Democracy: Jefferson to Lincoln.* New York: Norton, 2005.

Worland, Justin. "As Clean Energy Rises, West Virginia Looks Past Trump's Embrace of Coal to What Comes Next." *Time*, 2020, https://time.com/coals-last-kick/.

Wu, Tim. *The Curse of Bigness: Antitrust in the New Gilded Age.* New York: Columbia Global Reports, 2018.

Zackin, Emily. *Looking for Rights in All the Wrong Places: Why State Constitutions Contain America's Positive Rights.* Princeton: Princeton University Press, 2013.

Zaloom, Caitlin. "Does the U.S. Still Have a 'Middle Class'?" *Atlantic*, November 4, 2018.

INDEX